THE
EMPEROR'S CLOTHES

THE
EMPEROR'S CLOTHES

THE NAKED TRUTH ABOUT WESTERN SAHARA

There once was an Emperor so foolish that swindlers were able to convince him that he was wearing garments of the finest silk, whereas in truth he was wearing nothing at all....

KATLYN THOMAS

GLOBAL DIRECTIVES LLC
NEW YORK, 2021

Global Directives LLC
New York

This book is dedicated to Boukhari Ahmed

CONTENTS

INTRODUCTION

FEW DISPUTES HAVE given the international community as clear cut a chance to put into practice the principles of international law and policy that its political members so consistently embrace in their speeches than the dispute over Western Sahara, yet few disputes have been as monumentally mishandled by the international community as the Western Sahara issue.

Western Sahara, known as Spanish Sahara when it was a colony of Spain, is a small place: a territory no larger than the state of Colorado, situated between Morocco to the north, Mauritania to the south, and Algeria to the east. It is mostly desert which, until the very recent past, was the ancestral home of nomadic tribes. Yet for more than forty years this small, remote part of the planet has occupied center stage in the politics of northwest Africa, and the process of its decolonization has raised implications for the application of principles of international law and policy—and the role of the United Nations and the United States in applying such principles—that have given it an importance far beyond its importance as a territory.

Ever since Spain decided to withdraw from the territory in 1974, its future has been in limbo due to conflicting claims of the indigenous tribes of the territory, the Saharawis, and Morocco, who claims sovereignty over it on the basis of alleged historic allegiances between members of certain of these tribes and the Moroccan Sultans in the pre-colonial Alawite dynasty. These conflicting claims set off a war in the mid 1970s that not only ignited the entire African continent, but also engulfed the major superpowers, the African Union, the European Union and the United Nations in decades of dissent and years of costly peacekeeping activities. The fact that more than forty years after the departure of Spain the conflict has still not been resolved, is a monument to the failure of present day international institutions and international law to create a proper mechanism to enforce commonly espoused principles of decolonization, dispute settlement among states, and the right to self-determination under international law, and raises serious questions about United States policy with respect to those issues and the future role of the United Nations in peacekeeping efforts. Why these facts are not common knowledge is a tribute to the skill of diplomats, well-paid lobbyists and others in obfuscating the facts. Indeed, one is reminded of the fable of the Emperor's new clothes, for most of what has emanated from the United Nations and other "official" sources on the subject of Western Sahara—not to mention Morocco and its apologists—has been an elaborately concocted smokescreen to hide the naked truth.

This book will attempt to lift this smokescreen to examine the history of the dispute over sovereignty in Western Sahara, the role of the United Nations and the major players in the dispute, and the legal issues that have been raised, and will offer possible solutions to the crisis.

PART I

The History of the Dispute[1]

(1) The Period of Spanish Colonization

(a) Geography

SPANISH TIES TO the shores of present day Western Sahara can be traced as far back as June of 1492, when Portugal, the first European power to claim territory in North Africa, ceded to Spain, then Europe's leading maritime power, the territory from present day Morocco to Cape Bojador along the Atlantic coast to the south, a distance of 400 miles. Spain built a fortress on the coast of this territory at Santa Cruz, opposite its already existing outposts on the Canary Islands. Its presence on those shores, however, was short-lived. When attackers sacked the fort in 1524, the Spanish abandoned it, and with it any attempt to establish permanent links with the African coast for the next three hundred years.

By the time the Western powers gobbled up slices of Africa in the 19th century, Spain's position as a leading maritime power had declined significantly from what it had been in the mid 15th century. Nevertheless, it attempted to gain at least a foothold on the continent by once again turning to the territory in North Africa it had acquired from Portugal centuries earlier. In 1884, spurred into action by a number of businessmen who hoped to reap commercial rewards from the expansion of Spanish influence in Africa,[2] a Spanish trader landed on the coast of

---

[1]   The following history of the territory in pre-colonial and colonial times is primarily taken from the research on the subject of Tony Hodges and contained in his book WESTERN SAHARA: THE ROOTS OF A DESERT WAR (Lawrence Hill & Co. 1983)("Hodges"), which in turn is based upon the research contained in earlier works such as the major Spanish treatise on the subject of Western Sahara written in 1955 by Julio Caro Baroja, entitled *Estudios Saharianos* (Instituto de Estudios Africanos, Madrid, 1955).

[2]   The Sociedad Espanola de Africanistas y Colonistas, founded in 1884, amassed the financial backing to establish trading establishments along the Rio de Oro, and to finance trade with the inhabitants of the area using schooners

1

Western Sahara, and in the name of Spain declared sovereignty over an enormous expanse of territory extending 150 miles inland. His establishment of a trading center at Rio de Oro, with the permission of the local tribesmen,[3] permitted Spain to claim the territory at the 1884-5 Conference of Berlin.

Fifteen years later Spain and France delineated the southern border of this colony and the contours of the present day Western Sahara began to emerge.[4] Four years afterwards, in the Franco-Spanish Convention of 1904[5]—and the secret accords published in 1911 under which Spain recognized French influence in most of Morocco—Spanish rule over Western Sahara and a few of its already established fishing villages to the north was solidified. The borders of the Spanish territory were further confirmed in 1912 by a convention demarcating the French-Spanish zones,[6] and the Treaty of Fez of 1912 under which Sultan Moulay Hafid of Morocco handed over his country to French "protection."

However, the final borders of Western Sahara as we know it today were not established until 1958, after Morocco had won its independence from France. The Spanish at that time controlled both the regions of Rio de Oro and Saguia el Hamra, which together comprised the territory of present day Western Sahara, and a swath of land in the north extending from Saguia el Hamra to shortly beyond Tarfaya, in present day Morocco. Whereas the former lands were considered in the various treaties between Spain and the other Western powers to be outside the lands belonging to Morocco, the later region was deemed to be included in a Morocco "protectorate" which was to be administered by Spain. In January of 1958 Spain converted the former area and Ifni, an enclave on the coast of Northern Morocco, into fully fledged Spanish provinces. However, it excluded its "protectorate" region, dubbed Spanish Southern Morocco, and after Morocco gained its independence, in return for aid in quelling Saharawi resistance movements, Spain ceded back to Morocco this territory—including the enclaves of Tan Tan, Goulimene and Tarfaya.

---

from the Canaries.

[3] Three representatives of the local tribe, the Oulad Bou Sbaa, signed a treaty with the representative of Spain, Don Emilio Bonelli, on November 28, 1884, granting the Spanish government rights over the coastal area of Western Sahara near the Rio de Oro.

[4] This convention, signed on June 27, 1900, defined the borders of Western Sahara and present day Mauritania by defining the southeastern frontiers of the Spanish colony as far as the intersection of the Tropic of Cancer with the meridian 14 degrees 20' west of Paris.

[5] Convention Respecting Morocco, Oct. 3, 1904, Fr-Spain, 196 Consol. T.S. 353.

[6] Convention Respecting Relations in Morocco, Nov. 27, 1912, Fr.-Spain, 217 Consol. T.S. 288. This convention ratified Article Six of the 1904 convention, thus confirming that Saguia el-Hamra (the northern part of Western Sahara) was "outside Moroccan territory" and could become a Spanish colony rather than part of Spain's protectorate zone in Morocco. As was noted by the US State Department, the Treaty "recognized the Sultan of Morocco as having civil and religious authority north of the parallel of 27 degrees 40' North, but south of the parallel the area was outside of Morocco and under Spanish jurisdiction." US Department of State, Office of Geographer, Bureau of Intelligence and Research, "International Boundary Study No. 9" (Sept. 14, 1961) at 3.

By the 1970s, therefore, the boundaries of Spanish Sahara included the regions of Rio de Oro in the south and Saguia el Hamra to the north,[7] within which were the small enclaves of El Aiun and Boujdour along the coast, Smara in the interior, and Villa Cisneros on the southern shores.

(b) People

The region of Spanish Sahara was largely an inhospitable expanse of arid land comprised of undulating sand dunes and rocky plateaus, dominated by searing winds called *irifi* and scorching sun, where seasonal river beds and the occasional oasis provided the only source of water. A land in which only the hardiest animals and men could survive.

But men did survive in this land. Long before the Western powers seized control of Africa, at a time before there were modern day "states" in the continent, across a huge largely barren expanse of desert in North Africa[8] extending from the Atlantic ocean in the West to the Nile river and beyond to the gardens of Babylon, small groups of sheep, camel and goat herders wandered in nomadic or semi-nomadic tribal caravans within loosely defined and often overlapping grazing areas. As Hodges noted, the political structure of these units was based on allegiance to family, fraction, subfraction, and tribe,[9] in that order, and on a stratified political and social system[10] which classified tribes in terms of military power. The goal of each tribe was to achieve dominance in the region and the history of the region for as far back as modern history goes is strife with intertribal warfare to establish such dominance.[11]

Within each tribe political and legal affairs were usually conducted by elders, called *sheikhs*, in councils called *djemmas*.

The tribes which exercised dominion over 19th century Western Sahara, according to historians, included the Oulad Delim, the Oulad Tidrarin, the

---

[7] Both of these regions were named after the river beds, or *wadis* that they contained.

[8] The history of the coastal populations is in stark contrast to the history of the population that lived in the interior regions. The coastal population of Africa was for the most part sedentary and relied on commerce, and was invaded many times during its history by people who intermingled, resulting in a cultural, religious and ethnic mix and permitting the establishment of centers of learning and civilization. This was not the history of the Berber or mixed Berber-Arab nomads who inhabited the desert regions of North Africa.

[9] The members of any tribe or *qabila* could trace their decent, patrilineally, from a common ancestor at the apex of the tribal genealogical tree. The *qabila* was divided into a series of fractions (*akhad*, singular *fakhd*) with their own common ancestors, and in turn into smaller sub-fractions or "extended families." Hodges, *supra* at 10.

[10] Politically, each Western Saharan tribe and fraction regulated its affairs through an assembly (*djemma*) of the heads of its most distinguished families—men who, by virtue of their valor, age, wisdom, piety or wealth, enjoyed the greatest respect. The *djemma* selected the group's sheikh, established its own body of laws, the *orf*, to complement the basic Islamic judicial code, the *sharia*, and appointed a *qadi*, or judge, to administer justice. *Id.* at 14

[11] *Id.* at 1–16.

Reguibat, the Arosien, the Ait Larsen, Izarguien, Oulad Bou Abba, and a number of other smaller tribes.[12] The members of each of these tribes migrated, according to the season and availability of water, over roughly delineated territories in present day Western Sahara, northern Mauritania, western Algeria and southern Morocco.

By the fifteenth century, according to Hodges and other scholars, these tribes had adopted their own language, Hassaniya, a dialect of Arabic that had been introduced a century earlier by the Beni Hassan, a group of tribes originating in the Arab peninsula that began migrating southward from the Draa Valley into the Sahara from about the end of the thirteenth century. The Beni Hassan[13] had intermarried with the native Berber peoples, called the Sanhaja,[14] to give rise to a people colloquially referred to as the "Moors." The Moors, according to historical accounts, migrated with their goats, sheep and camels seasonally over an expanse of the Sahara from the Draa River in the north to the banks of the Senegal and the bend of the Niger in the south, and from the Atlantic seaboard to a series of sand dune zones, the Erg Iguidi, the Erg Cheh and the Majabat al-Kubra, in what is now eastern Mauritania.

When the Spanish established their first settlements on the coast of Spanish Sahara in the late 1880s they found it populated by members of those indigenous tribes that were descendants of the Moors, living their nomadic existence in much the same way as they had for centuries. They were later named the Saharawi.

(c) History of Colonization

By the time of the Treaty of Fez, France had consolidated an empire that at its peak in the 1950s included Algeria, Mauritanian, and the Morocco "protectorate," all firmly under the direction of French administration and controlled by the French military.

Spain, on the other hand, struggled during most of the early 20th century to solidify its relations with the inhabitants of three of its tiny "protectorate"

---

[12] According to documents submitted by Spain to the International Court of Justice, by the 17th century almost all of these tribes of the Sahara had been formed. *See, International Court of Justice: Documents Submitted In the Case of Western Sahara* ["ICJ Documents"], Vol. I, p. 229–230. According to Morocco, by the end of the 19th century three types of tribes, including two subfractions of Tekna (Izarguien and Yaggout), the Arosien, Oulad Tidrarin, Reguibat, and Ouled Delim, lived in the Sahara, all of whom allegedly paid tribute to the Tekna. *Id.*, Vol. III, at 182.

[13] The Beni Hassan were a group of tribes of Arab Bedouins, called Maqil, thought to be originally from Yemen, who migrated to the Western Sahara region in the eleventh century bringing with them their own form of Arabic, Hassanyia, considered today to be one of the dialects closest to classical Arabic. Hodges, *supra* at 8.

[14] During the 8th and 9th centuries Arab expeditions to the "far Maghreb" resulted in the conversion of the local tribes to Islam, but a form of Islam that was to incorporate many of the local customs and traditions. The tribes that were living at the time in the western belt of the Sahara were offshoots of two main Berber peoples of northwest Africa, the Zenata, who occupied the major oases of the north, and the Sanhaja, who were tribes of camel herding nomads in the southern desert, in present day Western Sahara, Mali and Mauritania. *Id.* at 3–4.

settlements in Morocco: Ceuta, Melilla and Larache, and it did little more than maintain trading posts in present day Western Sahara at Villa Cisneros (present day Dakhla) and two other locations along the coast. It paid virtually no attention to the interior of the Sahara—or the tribes which inhabited it, who were able to retain their ancient ways.

The French method of colonization was vastly different from the *laissez-faire* attitude of the Spanish. Rather than being content to leave the inhabitants of their colonies to their own devices, the French attempted to impose strict rules upon the population. This policy did not go over well with the proud and independent inhabitants of the region. From the dawn of the 20th century, as France gradually extended its presence in Mauritania, and established firm control over Morocco and Algeria, there emerged resistance among the tribes of the region to French rule. The center of this resistance shifted across the borders to the un-policed desert of Spanish Sahara, from which long range raiding parties, called *ghazzi* by the natives, would swoop upon the French settlements. One of the foremost leaders of this resistance was the son of the most respected religious leader of the Saguia el-Hamra, Sheikh Ma el-Ainin, a holy man who, through his teachings, inspired rebellion, both in Mauritania and Morocco, until his death in 1910.

After the death of Ma el-Ainin's son, and as a result of considerable efforts on the part of the French to route out his supporters in the territories they controlled, the resistance to French rule was limited to bases in what was nominally Spanish territory. From deep within the desert Saharawi tribes were to continue to harass the French in Mauritania until the 1930s. However, despite their mastery of guerilla tactics and the desert terrain they were ultimately no match for the better armed French, who eventually were able to coordinate pincer like attacks from their colonies to the north, the south and the east. But it was the completion of the French conquest of southern Morocco in early 1934, and the military campaign of the French that year to wipe out the remaining centers of dissidence in the Anti-Atlas—that was to pave the way for their final pacification.

For most of this period Spain was content to sit on the sidelines, content with the revenue it was receiving from its small coastal enclaves. This was to change in the mid 1930s. After the fall of the Spanish monarchy in 1931 the newly proclaimed head of state, Generalissimo Franco, began to take more of an interest in the Saharan colony. As a result of pressure from the French who wanted to curb attacks on French outposts by anti-French nomads originating in the Spanish territory,[15] Franco finally installed troops in locations within the interior of what

---

[15]   During this period there were numerous clashes between Oulad Delim and Reguibat freedom fighters and French forces in Mauritania and Algeria. On many of these occasions the nomads, after staging lightning raids (*ghazzi*), on

is present day Western Sahara. On May 15, 1934 a camel corps unit from Tarfaya reached Smara, Ma el-Ainin's old capital, and set up permanent residence. This was followed by the establishment of a Spanish military presence in other enclaves in the interior of the colony.

However, even after the Spanish established a presence in the interior of the Sahara, the Saharawis continued their largely nomadic lifestyle and customs. Neither the civil war in Spain in 1937–39 nor the Second World War changed the lifestyle that had dominated the region for centuries. Only one major additional settlement was established during this period: El Aiun—"the source"—a small village along the coast which became the territory's capital. But neither this nor any of the other small settlements established by the Spanish attracted much of the Saharawi population.[16] The vast majority remained nomads who continued to administer their own affairs through their *djemmas*.

This was all to change with the discovery in the 1950s of significant deposits of phosphates in Western Sahara, leading to increased Spanish interest in the territory and the establishment of a state run mining compound *Fosboucraa* ("Boucraa"), in 1972. Jobs in the mining industry gradually lured the Saharawis to the small towns. The population of the three major towns—Smara, Villa Cisneros and El-Aiun—more than tripled to 40,000 between 1967 and 1974.

However, the 1950s also brought an awakening sense of nationalism and desire for independence to the peoples of Africa and the dawn of the period of African de-colonization. Calls for independence from colonial domination—initially emanating from 'freedom fighters' in colonial capitals—began to be embraced by both the United Nations and the newly created Organization for African Unity (OAU).

Morocco, which had been a "protectorate" of France since the Treaty of Fez in 1912, was the first state in northwest Africa to benefit from this development. Following the Second World War France had sent Sultan Mohammed V into exile and had replaced him on the throne of Morocco with his uncle. However, a nationalist popular movement—led in large measure by a group of revolutionaries in Morocco who had formed the *Istiqlal* party—forced his return to the throne in 1955. One year after his return Morocco won its independence from France, inspiring similar independence movements in Algeria and Mauritania—and Spanish Sahara—as well as continued resistance within Morocco itself.

For although Morocco had gained its independence from France in theory, in

---

French outposts, would retreat into the relative safety of Western Sahara. Ma el-Anin's strategic alliance with the Sultan of Morocco for the purpose of expelling the French from North Africa was later to be cited by Morocco as a basis for its claim to the territory of Western Sahara.

[16] Besides Dakhla, Smara, La Guera and El Aiun there existed only small military outposts in Tichla, Bir Gandous, Guelta Zemmour and Zug by 1946.

practice the French continued to dominate the economy of its former protectorate, as well as exert a heavy political influence. The continued influence of France within Morocco, as well as its continued presence elsewhere in the region, inflamed segments of the population to rise in what was euphemistically called the "Army of Liberation." From hideouts within the Atlas regions as well as deep within the Sahara, troops of mostly Berber and Saharawi origin swooped on Moroccan and Mauritanian settlements, causing havoc and disrupting commerce during the mid 1950s. Soon the disruption spread into the Spanish colony. Finally, in 1958 the combined efforts of the Moroccan Sultan, now calling himself "King," the French Foreign Legion, and the Spanish government, put down the rebellion. By 1969 many of the members of the Army of Liberation who had resided in Spanish Sahara had fled to southern Morocco, Mauritania or western Algeria.

But the victories of the colonial powers on the battlefield did not translate into victories on the political front. One year after Morocco's independence Spain, in order to forestall a similar move for independence on the part of its African colonies, announced the incorporation of Spanish Sahara into metropolitan Spain, declaring it an integral part of the Spanish state. This move, however, could not stem the tide of decolonization that was rapidly spreading throughout the world or stifle the calls for such decolonization from the inhabitants of the region, who had been inspired by Morocco's gain of independence from the French, which many of them had fought to achieve.[17]

By 1960 colonialism in Africa was clearly on the decline. In that year Mauritania gained its independence, with Algeria gaining it two years later. France and Spain were left with mere remnants of influence in the region. At the same time, fueled by rhetoric at the UN and OAU, freedom movements by the indigenous peoples of African colonies had gained in strength and political influence and, one by one, over the next fifteen years would force the release of all African colonies from the shackles of colonial rule. All but one. Unfortunately for the Saharawis their struggle for independence ran quickly into another political roadblock: the competing territorial claims of their neighbors to the north and south, Morocco and Mauritania. The 1960s and 70s would pit the competing claims of Saharawi nationalists—fueled by the emerging doctrine of "self determination" for colonial peoples—against sovereignty claims of their neighbors based on the principle of territorial integrity and the argument that the territory once belonged to them—a conflict which in the case of Morocco has persisted to this day.

---

[17] A number of Saharawis joined with Moroccan freedom fighters in the so-called "Army of Liberation"—an unofficial guerilla movement of freedom fighters dedicated to ousting both the French and the Spanish from their remaining colonies in North Africa—whose efforts were only halted by the combined military efforts of the French and Spanish armies at the close of 1959.

(2) Rise of the Principle of Self-Determination

The Second World War loosened the chains that had bound the peoples of the third world to colonial overseers and paved the way for a new organization—the United Nations—to be established, founded on principles of emancipation and equality. The *ancient regime* had collapsed, and with it the assumption that the peoples of Europe were destined to rule the peoples of the Third World.[18]

The idea that people should generally be considered entitled to determine their own future free from colonization or coerced annexation by others—what we now refer to as the "principle of self-determination"—was recognized implicitly in at least three Articles of the United Nations Charter,[19] and swept through the colonies of Northeast Africa like a tsunami underpinning the independence of Morocco, Mauritania and Algeria in the late 50s and early 60s.

However, it was not until a decade after the Second World War, when third world populations began to disengage themselves *en masse* from their colonial rulers, that a consensus began to emerge that this principle should be considered a "right" under international law,[20] and then, according to some of them, only when applied to "non-self-governing-territories," i.,e. *colonies.*

The fact that this "right" existed was finally acknowledged in 1960 when the UN General Assembly proclaimed that "all peoples have a right to self-determination" in a Declaration on the Granting of Independence to Colonial Countries and Peoples, better known as Resolution 1514.[21] A year later, the General Assembly created a special committee, the Special Committee on the Situation with Regard to the Implementation of the Declaration on the Granting of Independence to Colonial

---

[18]   Actually the genesis of this idea was earlier, when, after WWI, the League of Nations was created. Woodrow Wilson had arrived at the Versailles peace conference with the notion that "all peoples had the right to self-determination," and the victorious nations were forced to create a system to manage colonial territories, the Mandate System, that allowed, to a degree, the exercise of this newly articulated right. *See,* Hanauer, *supra,* at 133–138. However, the idea wasn't recognized as important until the creation of the United Nations after WWII.

[19]   Article 1 describes "[t]he principle of equal rights and self-determination of peoples," as a measure that "strengthens universal peace." Article 55 recognizes that respect for the principle of self-determination is necessary for the "creation of conditions of stability and well-being which are necessary for peaceful and friendly relations among nations." Article 73(b) obliges member states with colonies "to develop self-government, to take account of the political aspirations of the peoples, and to assist them in the progressive development of their free political institutions." Hanauer, L. The Irrelevance of Self-Determination Law To Ethno-National Conflict: A New Look at the Western Sahara Case [in italics], 9 Emory Int'l L. Rev. 133 to 138 (1995).

[20]   As Professor Ian Brownlie of Oxford once said: "Until recently the majority of Western jurists assumed or asserted that the principle [of self-determination] had no legal content, being an ill-defined concept of policy and morality. Since 1945 developments in the United Nations have changed this position, and Western jurists generally admit that self-determination is a legal principle." BROWNLIE'S PRINCIPLES OF PUBLIC INTERNATIONAL LAW, 8th ed., James Crawford (ed.) 2012, ("Brownlie") at 553.

[21]   Resolution 1514 also went on to say that "Immediate steps shall be taken, in Trust and Non-Self-Governing Territories or all other territories which have not yet attained independence, to transfer all powers to the peoples of those territories, without any conditions or reservations, in accordance with their freely expressed will and desire, without any distinctions as to race, creed or colour, in order to enable them to enjoy complete independence and freedom."

Countries and Peoples, dubbed the Committee of 24, to oversee the struggle of colonial populations to enforce this right. Throughout the years Resolution 1514 supported the liberation of a number of third world peoples in non-self-governing-territories—the latest being the inhabitants of East Timor in 1999.

In 1963 Spanish Sahara was included on the UN's list of non self governing territories to which Resolution 1514 applied, with Spain being designated its "administering power." From that date forward demands that the inhabitants of Spanish Sahara be liberated from colonial status resounded with increasing forcefulness in meetings of the United Nations General Assembly. Within a year of its inclusion on the list the Committee of 24 passed was to be the first of a number of resolutions calling on Spain to implement the Saharawis right to self-determination.[22] The General Assembly quickly followed suit[23] and went further, reaffirming in 1965 the 'inalienable right' of colonial peoples to self-determination in accordance with the principles embodied in Resolution 1514(XV), and requesting Spain "...to take immediately all necessary measures for the liberation of...Spanish Sahara from colonial domination..."[24]

In 1966 the General Assembly went a step further, outlining in Resolution 2229(XXI) the process by which such self-determination was to be exercised—a referendum.[25]

The provisions of Resolution 2229(XXI) formed the basis of all resolutions of the General Assembly on the subject until 1974.[26] It affirmed the right of the Saharawi people to self-determination, and stipulated that this was a legal right inextricably linked with the decolonization process. It further mandated that such self-determination be carried out through a referendum conducted under the auspices of the United Nations. The privilege of voting in the referendum would be extended only to indigenous Saharawis, with exiles permitted to freely return to the territory in order to vote. It invited Spain to determine the procedures for this referendum "at the earliest possible date"[27]

Resolution 2229(XXI) also requested the Secretary General to appoint a special mission to be sent to Western Sahara for the purpose of recommending practical steps for the full implementation of the relevant resolutions of the General Assembly

---

[22]   19 GAOR, Annexes, Annex No. 8 (Part I), at 290–91, UN Doc. A/5800/Rev.1 (1964).

[23]   G.A. Res. 2072(XX), 20 GAOR Supp. 14, at 59–60, UN Doc. A/6014 (1965).

[24]   G.A. Res. 2072(XX), *supra*, at para. 2.

[25]   G.A. Res. 2229(XXI), 21 GAOR Supp. 16, at 72, UN Doc. A/6316 (1966).

[26]   Between 1967 and 1973, as skirmishes increased between the Spanish and the Saharawis, the General Assembly adopted six more resolutions, all of which repeated the proposal of a referendum and which became progressively harsher in tone. *See*, G.A. Res. 2354, 2428, 2591, 2711, 2983.

[27]   G.A. Res. 2229(XXI), *supra*, at 72–73. Although the claims to the territory asserted by Morocco and Mauritania were not recognized, it granted these two countries standing to negotiate with Spain and "other interested parties" the procedures for conducting the referendum.

and in particular for determining the extent of United Nations participation in the preparation and supervision of the referendum.

The essence of Resolution 2229(XXI) was repeated in six additional resolutions adopted by the General Assembly between 1967 and 1973.[28]

The General Assembly avoided discussing the future status of Western Sahara in its resolutions during this period. However, by 1972 it was clear to most observers that if the indigenous population were to vote freely the result would most likely be the creation of an independent state.[29] The General Assembly acknowledged this by reaffirming in Resolution 2983(XXVII) not only the right of the Saharawi people to self-determination, but also to independence.[30]

Although the theoretical principle of "self-determination" may have emanated from the United Nations, its application to the colonies of Africa was primarily the result of intense lobbying by the African nations themselves. In the late 1960s a number of African countries banded together to form the Organization of African Unity (OAU), which later was to become the African Union. From its inception its main focus was on the liberation of the countries of Africa from colonial rule. Almost immediately after it was formed it began to urge Spain to withdraw from its African colonies and initiated the idea of a referendum for the inhabitants of Spanish Sahara. At its nineteenth ordinary session, held in Rabat on June 5–19, 1972, the OAU Council of Ministers called on Spain "to create a free and democratic atmosphere in which the people of that territory can exercise their right to self-determination and independence" and requested African states "to intensify their efforts vis-à-vis the Spanish Government to induce it to implement Resolution 2711 of the UN General Assembly and, in particular, its provisions relating to the holding, as soon as possible, of a referendum designed to enable the population of the Sahara under Spanish domination to freely exercise their right to self-determination, in accordance with the principles of the United Nations Charter, under the auspices and with the full guarantees of that international organization." A similar resolution was adopted a year later by a session of the OAU Council of Ministers in Addis Ababa. The UN resolutions were endorsed at

---

[28] G.A. Res. 2428, 23 GAOR Supp. 18, at 63–64, UN Doc. A/7218 (1968); G.A. Res. 2591, 24 UN GAOR Supp. 30, at 73–74, UN Doc. A/7630 (1969); G.A. Res. 2711, 25 UN GAOR Supp. 28, at 100–101, UN Doc. A/8228 (1970); G.A. Res. 2983, 27 UN GAOR Supp. 30, at 84–85, UN Doc. A/8730 (1972); G.A. Res. 3162, 28 UN GAOR Supp. 30, at 110–111, UN Doc. A/9030 (1973).

[29] As one commentator put it: " By 1972, the intensity with which the question of self-determination for the Saharawi people was discussed in the international community and the heightened political awareness of the Saharawi people combined to produce the near certainty that a referendum would lead to independence for Western Sahara." Robert T. Vance, Jr., *Recognition as an Affirmative Step in the Decolonization Process: The Case of Western Sahara*, 7 Yale J. Wold Pub. Ord. 45, 50 (1980).

[30] G.A. Res. 2983, 27 UN GAOR, Supp. 30, at 84, UN Doc. A/8955 (1972).

the same time by both the nonaligned movement, at the nonaligned states' fourth summit, held in Algiers on September 5–9, 1973, and the world's Muslim states, at the fifth Islamic summit, held in Kuala Lumpur, Malaysia, on June 21–25, 1974.

Spain at first ignored all these resolutions, reasserting the position that its African territories—which it had recently converted to "provinces" of Spain—were not subject to self-determination.[31] When this argument failed to be accepted, and wary of the territorial ambitions of Morocco and Mauritania, Franco acquiesced in the calls for self-determination, but sought to buy time to cultivate a political group in the territory that would be friendly to Spain, arguing that because of the nomadic nature of the population it required time to prepare the Saharawi people to participate in an act of self-determination.[32]

Morocco, for its part, had by 1966 pronounced a claim to the territory that was in direct conflict with the call for self-determination through a referendum. Nevertheless, perhaps under the impression that the inhabitants of the territory would welcome rejoining the "motherland" if such a referendum were held,[33] it proposed in 1966 that both the Sahara and the other Spanish colonies in North Africa as soon as possible be granted their independence from Spain.[34] Mauritania, which by 1966 had also expressed claims to the territory, advanced the same position, but added that "independence" meant independence not only from Spain, but also from Morocco.[35]

However, despite their decade long public support for the idea of a referendum, by the mid-1970s neither Morocco nor Mauritania had ever pushed for its implementation. Instead, as one observer commented, "what occurred…was the acceleration of efforts by all parties to arrange their preferred outcome behind a façade of support for self-determination."[36]

---

[31] 13 UN GAOR, Annexes, Agenda Item 36 at 37, UN Doc. A/C.4/L385/Rev. 1 (1958).

[32] Letter dated Sept. 8, 1966 from the Permanent Representative of Spain to the United Nations addressed to the Chairman of the Special Committee, 21 UN GAOR, 1 Annexes (Addendum to Agenda Item 23) 621, UN Doc. A/6300/Rev.1 (1966).

[33] *See* Hodges at 119. A writer in *Maroc-Soir*, had observed in an article on July 23, 1973 that "although the Moroccan character of this part of the Sahara is historically and geographically obvious" Morocco had accepted the idea of a referendum "certain that the population will vote in favor of returning to the motherland."

[34] Report of the Special Committee on the Situation with Regard to the Implementation of the Declaration on the Granting of Independence to Colonial Countries and Peoples, 21 GAOR, Annexes, Addendum to Agenda Item No. 23 at 603, UN Doc. A/6300/Rev.1 (1966). At the special session of the UN Committee of 24 held in Addis Ababa in June 1966, both the Moroccan and the Mauritanian delegations upheld their countries' claims to the territory but accepted that its inhabitants should be entitled to choose their destiny. *See,* "The Question of Western Sahara at the United Nations," *Decolonization* (UN Department of Political Affairs, Trusteeship and Decolonization, New York), No. 17, October 1980, p.5, cited by Hodges at 105, fn. 9. Morocco voted in favor of all but one of the resolutions of the General Assembly calling for a referendum passed between 1967 and 1973.

[35] *Id.,* at 607.

[36] Thomas M. Franck, *The Stealing of the Sahara,* 70 AJIL 694, 703 (1976).

Only the Saharawis themselves—who by 1973 had formed an independence movement called the *Frente Popular para la Liberacion de Saguia el Hamra y Rio de Oro* or POLISARIO—made any serious attempts during this period to see to it that these resolutions were implemented.

(3) Rise of Saharawi Nationalism

The Spanish government's professed commitment to self-determination as a way to forestall any action by the United Nations, as well as the predatory aims of Morocco and Mauritania, in turned created a "nationalist consciousness that was later to rebound against the Spanish" by the end of the 1960s.[37] As Hodges noted, the leadership of the anticolonial movement of this period was "markedly different in background and experience" from the nomads who led the Saharawi guerilla forces against the French and Spanish ten years earlier, and the aged sheikhs who presided over the *djemma*, and by and large "reflected the social and political revolutions that had characterized the "60s" in other parts of the world."[38] They were an eclectic group. Most of them were young—in their early to mid 20s, and many of them were educated—often at universities in Morocco.[39] Added to this core group were members who had military experience in the *tropas nomadas* or experience with prior Saharawi resistance movements in the early 1970s. They took their inspiration from John F. Kennedy, Woodrow Wilson, Che Guevara. They distained the tribal allegiances of old and sought to establish a new trans-Saharan allegiance based on principles of democracy and equality. Above all they believed passionately in the in the United Nations doctrine of self-determination.

Their initial aim was to free the territory from Spanish control, and initially they organized themselves in Rabat, attempting to win the support of opposition groups in Morocco. However, after being rebuffed by these groups and persecuted by the Moroccan authorities they decided to focus on creating an allegiance among groups within Western Sahara itself and among like minded Saharawis in other centers around the world, and relocated to Zouerate, Mauritania.

On May 10, 1973, these young revolutionaries formed the Polisario, and immediately launched a guerilla campaign against the Spanish whose crowning achievement was the sabotage of the Boucraa conveyor belt, which temporarily halted all phosphate deliveries to the coast, in 1974.[40]

---

[37] Hodges at 152.

[38] *Id.*, at 153.

[39] There were only a handful of Saharawi students, all male, enrolled at the Mohammed V University in Rabat, Morocco's most prestigious university, in 1970, including the founder of the Polisario, El Ouali Mustapha Sayed, and five others who formed the Polisario leadership.

[40] Hodges at 160–161.

In a manifesto adopted at their second congress, in August of 1974, the group defined for the first time their goals, declaring that "the Saharawi people have no alternative but to struggle until wresting independence, their wealth and their full sovereignty over their land."[41] As Hodges noted, the program of national action they adopted demonstrated both the historic Saharan independence from religious and political domination and the effects of the philosophical movements of the 1960s; it called for a "fair distribution of resources, to overcome the differences between the countryside and the towns" the provision of adequate housing and health facilities, the incorporation of Arabic in education and the provision of free, compulsory schooling at all levels and for all social layers. "There was a strong commitment to the principle of women's emancipation and a democratic form of government."[42]

The leaders of the Polisario movement rejected categorically the idea of integration into Morocco; that would have meant not only integration with peoples with whom they felt no communal bonds, but also integration into a type of government—a monarchy lacking in democratic institutions—that was anathema both to the traditional independence of the Saharan tribes and to the Western style principles of democracy they wished to introduce into the society. Moreover, as Hodges noted, "there was little evidence in 1974 of support among the masses of Saharawis for the idea of integration with Morocco"[43]—a fact that was to be confirmed a year later by a visiting UN commission. To emphasize their commitment to independence, the Polisario in 1974 sent a letter to King Hassan, warning him not to proceed with his claims to the territory.[44]

This letter, however, fell on deaf ears, for by the time the Polisario was created the King of Morocco had fully embraced the concept of "Greater Morocco."

(4) Rise of the Concept of "Greater Morocco"

The ambiguous and sporadic nature of the historic relationship between the tribes of Western Sahara and the Sultan of Morocco in pre-colonial days, the lack of a relationship between the people of the territory and the current government, and the total lack of enthusiasm among these people for integration with Morocco, did nothing to dampen the enthusiasm of Moroccan nationalists in the late 1950s— fueled by the success of their recent disentanglement from France—for attempting

---

[41] *Manifeste politique, adopte par le deuxieme congres,* in *Le peuple Saharoui en lutte* (Polisario Front, 1975) *supra* at 50; cited in Hodges at 163.

[42] *Programme d'action nationale, adopte par le deuxieme congres,* in *Le peuple Saharaoui en lutte* (Polisario Front, 1975), *supra,* at 42, cited in Hodges at 164.

[43] Hodges at 160–161.

[44] *Message du deuxieme congres tenu du 25-8-1974 au 31-8-1974 a Sa Majeste Hassan II, Roi du Maroc,* in *Le peuple saharaoui en lutte* (Polisario Front, 1975) at 52.

to expand the borders of the Kingdom to its farthest possible reaches. The concept of "Greater Morocco"—or a Morocco that would encompass all lands and peoples that owed any allegiance to the Sultan in pre-colonial days—was first espoused by the founder of one of Morocco's main opposition parties—the Istiqlal Party— shortly after Morocco first claimed independence from the French in 1956.[45] The Istiqlal Party had been formed during the 1950s as an anti-French liberation movement. After a brief period in the 1960s in which it became part of the government of King Hassan, it became the leading opposition party in Morocco. According to its founder—Allal el-Fassi—and based upon the alleged influence of the Alawite Sultans in the regions of the Sahara beyond the frontiers established by the colonial rulers, Morocco's true southern border was the Senegal River, and much of present day Algeria, Mauritania and, of course, Western Sahara, were properly speaking part of the lands that belonged to Morocco.[46]

At first the expansionist claims of the Istiqlalians were ignored by the King of Morocco. However, as the idea grew in popularity among the people, and not wishing to seem less patriotic than the opposition, the King began to change his position. Mohammed V officially embraced the cause of Greater Morocco toward the end of 1957, when, at the United Nations, Morocco laid claim to Ifni, Mauritania and Western Sahara.[47] On February 25, 1958, when the combined Franco-Spanish forces had finally managed to subdue the Army of Liberation, he once again endorsed this claim. Throughout the 1960s under the banner of Greater Morocco the Moroccan government continued to lay claim to these territories as well as to a large chunk of Algeria and the Spanish presidios on the Mediterranean coast. When Mauritania became independent from France in 1960, Morocco tried to block its admission to the United Nations—claiming in an argument that foreshadowed its later claims about Western Sahara that France was trying to create an artificial state in Mauritania, run by hand picked yes-men, so that it could exploit its minerals[48]—and withheld diplomatic recognition for nine years

---

[45] Allal el-Fassi, the principal leader of the Istiqlal Party, began to argue that only parts of the historic Alawite empire had been freed and so the ending of the protectorate had only been a partial victory. "So long as Tangier is not liberated from its international statute, so long as the Spanish deserts of the south, the Sahara from Tindouf and Atar and the Algerian-Moroccan borderlands are not liberated from their trusteeship, our independence will remain incomplete and our first duty will be to carry on action to liberate the country and to unify it," he proclaimed on March 27, 1956. *See,* Hodges at 85, citing Bertrand Fessard de Foucault, "La question du Sahara espangnol (I)," *Revue Francaise d'Etudes Politiques Africaines,* 10th Year, No. 119, November 1975, at 78.

[46] Allal el-Fassi was the main proponent of the idea. By June of 1956 he was insisting that Morocco's true southern border was the Senegal River and published a map of "Greater Morocco" in the Istiqlal Party's daily newsdpaper, *Al-Alam.* In a series of articles collectively called *Livre Rouge* and published in the nationalist review *Perspectives Sahariennes* in 1959–60, Allal el-Fassi sought to prove that France and Spain had deprived Morocco of its historic Saharan provinces by imposing their arbitrary colonial frontiers at the beginning of the century. Hodges at 85.

[47] United Nations Document A/C.4/SR.670.

[48] Hodges at 88. Backed by support from other Arab states, Morocco in 1960 persuaded the UN General Assembly to

on the basis of its assertion that it was rightfully part of Morocco.[49] One year after Algeria finally achieved independence after eight years of bloody war with France, King Hassan II of Morocco, who had acceded to the throne the previous year after the death of his father, led an ill-fated attempt to seize Tindouf by force.[50]

Ever the pragmatist, when the UN started to champion the cause of self determination for Spanish Sahara, Hassan tailored his policy to accommodate the UN's position, causing Morocco to endorse the UN resolutions calling for a referendum of self-determination without officially relinquishing its historic claim to the territory. Hassan may have decided to play along with the UN policy of self-determination rather than pursue Morocco's claims for tactical reasons: there was little support for Morocco's position at the UN and, at least until 1974, he may have been under the assumption that a referendum would be in Morocco's favor. His seeming equivocation over the issue in the 1960s, however, inflamed nationalists of the Istiqlal party. "We are absolutely opposed to any attitude, even one explicable for tactical reasons, which could engender confusion and put in question the integrity of Moroccan territory to the slightest extent" wrote the party paper *L'Opinion* on July 22, 1966.

The nationalists never seriously questioned the legitimacy of their position. If questioned, many of them cited as justification for their cause the participation of the Reguibat and Tekna in the Army of Liberation and the defections of several prominent Mauritanians to Morocco in 1956–58.[51] However, they made little attempt to justify it on the basis of what the inhabitants of the region desired. Indeed, they seemed to believe that what they wanted was unimportant. Allal el-Fassi, when asked about the wishes of the peoples of "Greater Morocco" wrote that the question was irrelevant, and that the King was duty bound to preserve the "unity of the homeland" from any attempts by the Saharans to reject Morocco.[52] They continued to assert a claim to parts of Algeria and Mauritania years after

---

examine the dispute over Mauritania. M'hammed Boucette, an Istiqlalian who represented Morocco, argued that France was trying to create an artificial state in Mauritania that would be dominated by powerful French companies intent on exploiting its mineral reserves. Morocco and its Arab allies briefly succeeded in postponing Mauritania's admission to the UN. *Id,* at 90. However, when Mauritania's admission was considered the following year, the western powers and the Soviet Union united to ensure its admission.

[49] With Mauritania's independence only days away, the Rabat government published a "white book" spelling out in detail the historic grounds for its claim to Mauritania. The Mauritanian government replied a few days later with a rival "green book" which rebutted the Moroccan arguments point by point. Neither these arguments nor any of the diplomatic efforts of Morocco during this period had any effect on President Charles de Gaulle's decision to grant independence to Mauritania, or dissuaded other African nations to support the fledgling government of Mokhtar Ould Daddah. *Id.* at 90.

[50] *Id.,* at 88.

[51] Hodges at 88.

[52] *Id.*

the King tacitly abandoned the claim, and despite overwhelming evidence that the peoples in those territories did not wish to be part of Morocco. By the 1970s besides a few small enclaves on the coast of Morocco, only Spanish Sahara—now rechristened "Western Sahara"—was left to claim, and they then directed the full force of their efforts towards persuading the King to annex that territory and to oppose any "referendum" that might possibly lead to the colony's independence.

(5) The Seeds of War

In 1974 the conflicting forces of Saharawi nationalism, Moroccan expansionism, and international pressures for the decolonization of the African continent and the principle of "self-determination," finally collided.

Faced with pressure from the Polisario and growing discontent among the younger, better educated Saharawis on the one hand, and the looming political threats of Morocco and Mauritania on the other, the Spanish, under the leadership of Generalissimo Franco, finally came to the conclusion that the wisest course of action was to prepare their colony for "independence"—that is, a type of independence that would not compromise Spanish interests. The first census of the inhabitants of the territory was prepared in 1974,[53] an indigenous group called the PUNS was groomed to take over after Spanish withdrawal, and in August of 1974, eight years after first being urged to do so by the UN General Assembly, the Spanish government announced that it would hold a referendum under UN auspices during the first six months of 1975.[54]

This was not welcomed news for the King of Morocco. After more than a decade during which he had downplayed Morocco's territorial claim to the territory and had paid lip service to the proposal of a "referendum" in order to cultivate good relations with Spain and the member states of the UN—much to the displeasure of the Moroccan opposition parties—King Hassan II found himself forced to take action. Over the following year the "recovery" of the Saharan "province" took top priority. The prize for success in acquiring the territory was irresistible: the glory of "reunifying" the nation, reasserting the prestige of the monarchy, outmaneuvering the opposition parties and increasing his regional and international stature. The cost of failure might well be his throne.

In a Youth Day speech in 1974 the King reasserted Morocco's historic claim to the Sahara, threatened general mobilization if necessary "to recover the usurped territories," and intensified propaganda efforts both at home and abroad to muster

[53]   According to this census the population numbered 73,497 indigenous Saharawis.

[54]   Letter dated 20 August 1974 from the Permanent Representative of Spain to the United Nations to the Secretary General, UN Document A/9714.

support for Morocco's claims. However, time for diplomatic maneuvering was running out. Shortly after Spain's announcement of its proposed referendum, sensing that he must act quickly to avoid a *fait accompli*, Hassan proposed that Morocco's claim to the territory be referred to the International Court of Justice, thereby at least securing a postponement of the referendum. After some initial reluctance Mauritania, which had also proffered claims to the territory, agreed to join the suit, and after considerable lobbying by both governments the General Assembly's Fourth Committee passed a resolution requesting the General Assembly to postpone the referendum in order to seek the Court's advisory opinion on the subject.[55]

On December 13 the General Assembly issued a resolution approving the Fourth Committee's recommendation.[56] However, in addition to mandating the postponement of the referendum and requesting the International Court of Justice to issue an advisory opinion on the claims of Morocco and Mauritania, the General Assembly agreed to dispatch a UN visiting mission to the Sahara, charged with obtaining "first hand information on the situation...including...the wishes and aspirations of the people."[57]

The Mission reached the conclusion that the indigenous peoples of the territory wished to be independent not only of Spain, but also of Morocco and Mauritania.[58]

In the report it issued on October 15, 1975 it summarized its findings as follows:

> Owing to the large measure of co-operation which it received from the Spanish authorities, the Mission was able...to visit virtually all the Main population centres and to ascertain the views of the overwhelming majority of their inhabitants...From all of these, it became evident to the Mission that there was an overwhelming consensus among Saharans within the Territory in favour of independence and opposing integration with any neighboring country."[59]

---

[55] The questions it requested to be presented to the International Court of Justice were:
1. Was Western Sahara (Rio de Oro and Saguia El Hamra) at the time of colonization by Spain a territory belonging to no one (*terra nullius*)?
2. If the answer to the first question is in the negative, what were the legal ties between this territory and the Kingdom of Morocco and the Mauritanian entity?

[56] G.A. Res. 3292 (XXIX), 29 UN GAOR Supp. 31, at 103–104, UN Doc. A/9631 (1974).

[57] The report of this Mission is entitled "The Report of the Special Committee on the Situation With Regard to the Implementation of the Declaration on the Granting of Independence to Colonial Countries and Peoples," UN Doc. A/100023/Add.5, Annex, at 26 (1975). ("The UN Mission Report")

[58] In addition to interviews with indigenous Saharawis in Western Sahara, the Mission met in Tindouf with the Polisario leadership and toured three Saharawi settlements, at Hassi Abdallah, Oum el-Assel and Tindouf, in each of which, the Mission later reported, it "was met by large and vociferous demonstrations of several thousand people in which the flags of the Polisario were prominently displayed." The UN Mission Report at 95.

[59] *Id.* at 48.

The Mission also noted the popular support for the Polisario, which had organized mass demonstrations of support wherever the mission visited,[60] commenting that in light of "the mass demonstrations of support for one movement, the Frente Polisario" it believed that its visit had brought into the open "political forces and pressures which had previously been largely submerged...."[61] The Mission concluded with the recommendation that "the General Assembly should take steps to enable those population groups to decide their own future in complete freedom and in an atmosphere of peace and security...."[62]

On the day after the publication of the Mission's report, the International Court of Justice rendered its opinion on the territorial claims of Morocco and Mauritania.[63] The question referred to the Court had been narrow: to determine whether the Territory, prior to the Spanish colonization, was *res nullius*, or without legal tie to a sovereign, or whether such ties existed, and if they existed, whether such titled vested in either Morocco or Mauritania, or both. After an examination of evidence of political, military, religious, and economic ties between the claimants and the inhabitants of the territory before Spain's arrival, the judges found that "the information before the Court does not support Morocco's claim to have exercised territorial sovereignty over Western Sahara."[64] The Court explained that while the evidence showed that the Sultan exercised "some authority" over "some, but only some," of the nomadic tribes of the region, it "does not establish any tie of territorial sovereignty between Western Sahara and that State. It does not show that Morocco displayed effective and exclusive State activity in the Western Sahara."[65] The Court's response to Mauritania's claim was essentially the same.[66]

The King of Morocco completely ignored the report of the UN Mission and his reaction to the Court's decision was to twist its findings beyond recognition. In a press release of the Permanent Mission of Morocco to the United Nations issued on

---

[60] Mass demonstrations in favor of the Polisario greeted the Mission from the moment it landed at El-Aiun airport until it departed. In many of the towns, the mission reported, the demonstrations "appeared to represent the majority of the Saharan residents." The UN Mission Report at 66. According to Hodges, more than half the population of Smara came out onto the streets to greet the Mission during its visit there on May 16, and at Boucraa almost all of Fosbucraa's Saharawi work force had demonstrated two days earlier. Hodges at 199. The Mission reported that in the manifestations in the north the "overwhelming majority" of the demonstrators carried the flags and emblems of the Frente Polisario, and that on May 13 in El Aiun, the Polisario had amassed at least 15,000 demonstrators. The UN Mission Report at 67.

[61] The UN Mission Report at 59.

[62] *Id.*, at 11.

[63] *Advisory Opinion on Western Sahara* (1975), ICJ Rep. 12.

[64] *Id*, at 48.

[65] *Id*, at 49.

[66] The Court found that although there were some legal ties between present day Mauritania and the Territory, "the materials and information presented to it do not establish any tie of territorial sovereignty." *Advisory Opinion on Western Sahara*, at 68.

October 16, 1975, Morocco claimed that the opinion of the Court meant that "the so-called Western Sahara was part of Moroccan territory…and that the population of this territory considered themselves and were considered to be Moroccans…." and that Morocco's demands had been "recognized" by the "legal advisory organ of the United Nations."[67]

By the time of the Court's opinion, the King had already moved several units of his army, including all thirty-five of Morocco's T-54 tanks in the Southern Command, to the Western Sahara border.[68] Two days later the King announced that there would be a massive march of 350,000 civilians from Morocco into Western Sahara to gain recognition of Morocco's right to national unity.[69] Although the King characterized the March as a peaceful means by which Morocco could achieve international recognition of its right to national unity and territorial integrity, it was clear that the ultimate purpose of the march was to put pressure on Spain into negotiating with Morocco and Mauritania before the General Assembly could make the necessary preparations for the referendum.[70] Spain, in response to Morocco's threat, urged the President of the Security Council to convene an emergency meeting of the Council to issue a resolution condemning the proposed action. Pursuant to Spain's request, the Security Council called upon Morocco to abandon the proposed march.[71] This was followed by Resolution 379, in which the Security Council reiterated its request.[72]

These two resolutions had little effect on Hassan, who by that time had staked his personal reputation and much of his political future to the annexation of Western Sahara. On November 6, 1975, scores of Moroccan civilians in a procession deemed the "Green March" after the holy color of Islam, crossed the frontier, to the consternation of practically the whole international community.[73] Although the march was halted only a few kilometers inside the border, Morocco warned Spain that it would continue farther unless Spain agreed to terms concerning a transfer of sovereignty over the territory to Morocco and Mauritania.[74] In actuality, the

---

[67] Quoted in UN Doc. S/PV.1849, at 11 (1975).

[68] *See*, S. Zunes & J. Mundy, WESTERN SAHARA: WAR, NATIONALISM, AND CONFLICT IRRESOLUTION (Syracuse U. Press, 2010) at 5.

[69] Letter from the Permanent Representative of Morocco to the United Nations addressed to the President of the Security Council dated October 18, 1975. UN Doc. S/11852 (1975).

[70] See Vance, *Recognition as an Affirmative Step in the Decolonization Process: The Case of Western Sahara*, 7 Yale J. World Pub. Ord. 45 (1980–1981) at 57.

[71] 30 UN SCOR, Resolutions and Decisions 8, UN Doc. S/Res./377 (1975).

[72] 30 UN SCOR, Resolutions and Decisions 9, UN Doc. S/Res/379 (1975).

[73] Among other things, the Security Council adopted Resolution S/Res/380 (6 Nov. 1975) deploring the march and calling for Morocco to withdraw all of the participants from Western Sahara.

[74] 30 UN SCOR, Supp. (Oct.-Dec. 1975), U.N. Doc. S/11871 (1975); *see also*, Vance, R., *Recognition as an Affirmative Step in the Decolonization Process: The Case of Western Sahara, supra*, at 58.

Green March was only a smoke screen and a means to exert pressure on Spain. By the last day of October Moroccan troops had already secretly crossed the border in the eastern part of the territory, igniting the first skirmishes with Polisario fighters in what was to be a long, grueling war.[75]

As a result of the deteriorating situation in Western Sahara, and despite overwhelming evidence that the population supported the Polisario's position and did not wish to be incorporated into Morocco,[76] Spain began to look for a way to exit gracefully with a minimum of negative political and economic repercussions. It decided that the best way to do this was to accede to Moroccan pressure to negotiate a political solution to the problem.[77] On November 14, the governments of Morocco, Mauritania and Spain issued a joint communiqué notifying the world of certain agreements reached as a result of negotiations on the Western Sahara issue.[78] Although the terms of these agreements—later dubbed the "Madrid Accords"—remained secret, commentators concluded that Spain had agreed to withdraw from the territory and permit it to be partitioned between Morocco and Mauritania in return for an interest in Boucraa, the 700 million dollar Saharan phosphate industry, as well as certain concessions on fishing rights off the Saharan coast.[79] Despite the fact that the agreement officially referred only to an "interim administration" which would involve Morocco, Mauritania, and the Djemma[80] as well as Spain, there was no doubt in anyone's mind that power would be transferred to Morocco and Mauritania and that a referendum would never take place.[81]

---

[75] Interview with Mohammed Bouhali, Polisario's then Minister of Defense, December 20, 2015. Morocco's General Ahmed Dlimi crossed the frontier with his troops and fighting broke out near Farsia in the eastern part of the territory on October 31, 1975. *See also,* Hodges at 220.

[76] Gomez de Salazar, the last Spanish Governor-General of the territory, was later to recall that the Djemma, the council of elderly sheikhs who were appointed during the Franco regime to have a "consultative" role but no real power "had lost prestige" and "In the end the Polisario Front represented the Saharawi people...and it was Polisario which shaped the Saharawi people's politics." Testimony in the Comision de Exteriores del Congreso, March 13, 1978 (*El Pais*, Madrid, March 14, 1978) reported in Hodges at 212.

[77] 30 UN SCOR, Supp. (October-December 1975) U.N. Doc. S/11871 (1975). There is evidence that Morocco had informed Spain that the march into Western Sahara would continue unless Spain agreed to bilateral negotiations concerning the transfer of sovereignty over Western Sahara to Morocco. *See* Vance, R. *Recognition as an Affirmative Step in the Decolonization Process: The Case of Western Sahara, supra,* at 58.

[78] Declaration of Principles on Western Sahara by Spain, Morocco and Mauritania, Annex II to UN Doc. S/11880, November 19, 1987, in Security Council Official Records, 30th Year, Supplement for October, November and December 1975, at 41.

[79] See, for instance, Franck, *The Stealing of the Sahara, supra,* at 715; Hodges at 223. Franck, T., The Stealing of the Sahara [in italics], 70 AJIL (1976) 694 at 715; Hodges at 223.

[80] In order to give the impression that the local inhabitants had some say in the governing of the colony, Spain, during the Franco regime, created a council of elderly sheikhs who would have a "consultative" role but no real power. This council was called the "Djemma."

[81] What was made public was a "declaration of principles" which stated that Spain would withdraw from Western Sahara by the end of February 1976 and in the meantime it would institute a "temporary" administration in the Territory in which Morocco, Mauritania and the Djemma would also participate. No mention was made of what

During this entire period the indigenous population of Western Sahara were never given a voice in any of these negotiations, or in discussions about any of the preceding United Nations resolutions. Nor had they been allowed to participate in the case before the International Court of Justice.[82] This did not mean, however, that they remained silent.

By the time of the Madrid Accords, the Polisario had already won the diplomatic support of a number of key African states, most prominently among them Algeria.

The relationship between the guerillas and the Algerian government started slowly. At first, President Boumedienne doubted that the Polisario enjoyed the backing of the Saharawi people. However, his appraisal began to change after the report of the Mission of the United Nations was released. In addition, by that time he had become alarmed by King Hassan II's decision to launch the Green March and by his reassertion of the principle of "Greater Morocco"—a principle which, as we have seen, could be used to claim parts of Algeria as well as Western Sahara. There are suggestions that he may have also resented what he considered to be a redrawing of the map of North Africa by Western powers without his input.[83] By the end of 1975 he had begun giving military training to Polisario fighters[84] and voicing strong opposition to Moroccan policies.[85] This began a long and close relationship between the Polisario and the Algerian government that has continued to this day.[86]

---

would transpire after this "temporary" period and there was no reference to a referendum. Rather than acquiesce in the partition of Western Sahara by Morocco and Mauritania the Djemma dissolved itself in 1975 and most of its members joined the Polisario.

[82] The Saharawis were not even accorded the right to be heard by the International Court of Justice, which can only receive evidence from "states" and "international organizations" and the Polisario expressed astonishment at a decision "to convey the destiny of our peoples before the Court of The Hague in our total absence." *Notre peuple face aux tout derniers crimes du fascisme impuni* (POLISARIO Front, 1974), at 11.

[83] *See,* S. Zunes & J. Mundy, WESTERN SAHARA: WAR, NATIONALISM AND CONFLICT IRRESOLUTION, *supra,* at 34.

[84] Emissaries from the Polisario had first solicited aid from the Algerian government in the summer of 1973. However, they were rebuffed at that time by President Boumedienne, who apparently doubted the movement's political maturity and popular support. However, by 1975, impressed by Polisario's military successes against the Spanish and evidence of its popular support among the masses in Western Sahara, Boumedienne put the weight of Algeria behind the movement, providing military aid and allowing the Polisario to install themselves at Tindouf.

[85] Among other things, in 1975 Algeria sponsored G.A. Resolution 3458A deploring the Madrid Accords and reaffirming the right of the Saharawis to self-determination and a referendum. In a memorandum sent to the UN Secretary-General on November 19, 1975, the Algerian government stated that it "does not recognize any right of the Governments of Spain, Morocco and Mauritania to dispose of the Territory of the Sahara…It therefore regards as null and void the 'declaration of principles' presented by Spain and accords no validity to the provisions contained therein." Annex to Letter dated November 19, 1975 from the Representative of Algeria to the Secretary-General, UN Doc. S/11881, November 19, 1975, *cited in* Hodges, at 225, fn. 100.

[86] Algeria was the Polisario's major diplomatic and military backer. However, it aided the military effort primarily through training troops and providing weapons. Although Morocco has claimed that Algerian troops aided in the fighting there is scant evidence that this was the case. The only time there was evidence of direct intervention by Algerian troops was on January 29, 1976, when Moroccan forces captured several Algerian soldiers at Amgala, one of the staging points for the refugees fleeing the territory. Algeria claimed that its troops were merely helping to

Even before the Green March fighting had broken out between Polisario units and Moroccan forces who were secretly infiltrating the territory; this fighting quickly escalated as Moroccan troops began advancing towards the towns of El Aiun (which they renamed Laayoune) and Smara in late 1975, following the Madrid Accords. By all accounts the Moroccan infiltration of the territory was inhospitable to the inhabitants. Occupying forces, aided by the Spanish until they departed, encircled towns with barbed wire and placed them under a state of siege.[87] A February 1976 report by the International Federation of Human Rights noted that soldiers "butchered hundreds and perhaps thousands of Sahrawis, including children and old people who refused to publicly acknowledge the king of Morocco" and that by that date 80 percent of the inhabitants of Laayoune had left.[88] During the initial stages of the conflict the Polisario were forced to concentrate on the evacuation and resettlement of the thousands of refugees who were fleeing the towns taking shelter in the eastern regions near Mudraiga, Amgala, Tifariti and Guelta Zemmour.[89] When they were later strafed by Moroccan aircraft, killing or wounding many of them,[90] Boumedienne allowed the Polisario, with the help of Algerian troops, to transport them over the border and set up camps in Tindouf, where most of them remain to this day.

The Polisario were powerless to prevent the occupation of the towns; instead, they concentrated on harassing the Moroccan and Mauritanian forces, initially on foot with no more than hunting rifles, but by the end of 1976, using vehicles and ammunition largely captured from the enemy, through the *ghazzi* raids of their forefathers—this time using bazookas and machine guns mounted on Land Rovers rather than swords on horses.[91]

When they were finally able to concentrate on fighting they concentrated

---

evacuate refugees. Algeria thereafter withdrew even its "humanitarian" direct military assistance. *See,* S. Zunes & J. Mundy, WESTERN SAHARA: WAR, NATIONALISM, AND CONFLICT IRRESOLUTION, *supra,* at 9.

[87] *Id.,* at 113.

[88] *Id.,* at 114.

[89] Spanish journalists in Laayoune were reporting that by the end of February, 1976, barely more than a fifth of the twenty nine thousand who had been registered there during the 1974 census had remained and that the other Saharawi towns were starting to look like ghost towns. The places they occupied were quickly taken over by Moroccans. A random population survey conducted by Tony Hodges in the Laayoune market in October 1978 revealed that about half of those interviewed had arrived from Morocco since 1975. The International Red Cross and the League of Red Cross societies announced in Geneva that 40,000 Saharawis had fled their homes. Other observers estimate that thirty three to fifty percent of the population fled to refugee camps in the Tindouf region of Algeria following the Moroccan occupation of the territory. When the Algerian government presented a memorandum on relief needs to the executive committee of the UNHCR in 1978 it reported that 50,000 Saharawi refugees had settled in its territory in eleven scattered camps. See Hodges at 232–233.

[90] *See,* S. Zunes & J. Mundy, WESTERN SAHARA: WAR, NATIONALISM AND CONFLICT IRRESOLUTION, *supra,* at 114.

[91] The Polisario were the first to perfect this means of warfare, which has since been a staple of desert combat.

on the weaker of their two adversaries—Mauritania. In 1976, in a brazen raid, their leader El Ouali Mustapha Sayed, led a force of fighters across 1,000 miles of Mauritanian desert to strike at the capital of Mauritania, Nouakchott. The rail line carrying iron ore from Zouerate to the coast was constantly sabotaged, leading to severe economic hardship. After several years of fierce fighting, and despite the active support of France in the battles, the President of Mauritania Mokhtar Ould Daddah was deposed, and in 1979 the Polisario persuaded the Mauritanian government to sign a peace agreement renouncing its territorial claims.

Defying all predictions,[92] the Polisario were also able to deliver successive humiliating defeats to Morocco. By 1977 Moroccan losses were rumored as high as one to two hundred men a month,[93] and the mines at Boucraa were put out of commission, not to resume normal activities until 1982. In 1978 attacks on convoys between Tan Tan and Laayoune severely disrupted supplies for months. Laayoune itself was subjected to rocket attack. After Mauritania withdrew from the conflict, such attacks intensified. In what it called the "Boumedienne Offensive," Polisario guerillas struck Moroccan outposts both within the territory and in Morocco itself. The year 1979, according to Hodges, "witnessed some of the largest and bloodiest battles of the war."[94] Polisario incursions reached deep into the heart of Morocco itself—striking military outposts such as Lebouirate, blockading Zag, and overrunning Tan Tan. Guerillas totally disrupted supplies to the city of Laayoune, and laid siege to Smara. Only by concentrating its troop strength in units of overwhelming numbers, and essentially abandoning outlying areas, was Morocco able to defend some of the territory against Polisario incursions. However, even this tactic became increasingly ineffective as the Polisario began incorporating more sophisticated armaments into its arsenal. On October 13, 1981, in one of the most devastating battles of the war, the Polisario attacked Moroccan units at Guelta Zemmour with sophisticated SAM6 surface to air missiles, downing five Moroccan aircraft. Ultimately, in 1981 the Moroccans were forced to begin building a sand wall, or "berm" across the desert to protect themselves from Polisario offensives.[95]

The Polisario were also winning battles on the diplomatic front. On February

---

[92] As was noted by Stephen Zunes and Jacob Mundy: "On paper Morocco was clearly dominant. Whereas Polisario started with 1,000 to 2,000 lightly armed guerillas, Morocco started with 80,000 soldiers. Morocco's air force and army, which were still being modernized, had been well supplied with weapons from the United States, western Europe, and the Eastern bloc." S. Zunes & J. Mundy, WESTERN SAHARA: WAR, NATIONALISM AND CONFLICT IRRESOLUTION, *supra*, at 14.

[93] *Middle East International,* Oct. 1977, cited in S. Zunes & J. Mundy, WESTERN SAHARA: WAR, NATIONALISM, AND CONFLICT IRRESOLUTION, *supra*, at 15.

[94] Hodges at 285. Hodges estimated that by 1983 the Polisario had as many as 25,000 men under arms. *Id.*, at 291.

[95] By the end of 1983 the berm enclosed roughly one sixth of the land mass of Western Sahara—the so-called "useful triangle."

27, 1976, one day after the formal termination of the Spanish administration pursuant to the Madrid Accords, the Polisario announced the formation of the Saharan Arab Democratic Republic (SADR).[96] By 1983, fifty four countries from four continents, ranging from communist Cuba and Vietnam to Mexico, Zambia and Venezuela, had granted diplomatic recognition to the SADR.

However, the Polisario gained its greatest support from its fellow Africans. Morocco's claims to Western Sahara conflicted with the two doctrines deemed most sacred by the Organization of African Unity (OAU) now the African Union (AU)—the right of colonial peoples in Africa to self determination and the preservation of the frontiers among African states inherited from the European powers in order to preserve stability in the region.

In 1976, in the midst of the fighting, the Council of Ministers of the OAU reaffirmed the inalienable right of the Saharawi people to self-determination and independence.[97] Then, in 1978, the 15th Ordinary Session of the Assembly of Heads of State and Government of the OAU adopted a resolution establishing an *ad hoc* committee of at least five heads of state to intercede between the Polisario, Mauritania and Morocco in order to end the conflict.[98] In 1979 this *ad hoc* committee recommended an immediate cease fire and "the exercise by the people of Western Sahara of their right to self determination through a general, free referendum, supervised by the OAU and the United Nations, enabling them to choose one of the two following options: a) total independence, b) maintenance of the status quo."[99] Less than one month later the government of Mauritania agreed to withdraw from the territory it had occupied. The OAU's diplomatic efforts then intensified, but after two years of unsuccessful efforts at mediation, it finally decided to take action. To the chagrin of the Moroccans, the SADR was admitted as the OAU's fifty first member in its session of February 22, 1981, prompting a walk out by the Moroccan delegation and a boycott of the organization which lasted until Morocco sought re-admission in January 2017.[100]

For a while Polisario supporters were also winning diplomatic battles in the

[96] The relevant documents and memoranda relating to the founding of the SADR can be found in T. Hultman, *Democratic Arab Republic of the Sahara,* in 5 Constitutions of Dependencies and Special Sovereignties (1978). The documents include the Constitution of the Provisional National Saharan Council, Proclamation of the Democratic Arab Republic of the Sahara, a Frente Polisario Memorandum, and the Constitution of the Democratic Arab Republic of the Sahara.

[97] Manfred Hinz, *Le droit a l'autodetermination du Sahara occidental* (Progress Dritte West Verlag, Bonn, 1978), at 63; cited in Hodges at 320 fn 4.

[98] UN Doc. A/33/337, October 31, 1978.

[99] *Jeune Afrique,* (Paris) No. 970, August 8, 1979, p. 52. On July 17–20, 1979 these proposals were endorsed by the OAU. *Le Monde,* December 17, 1979.

[100] In 2016 the Moroccan government petitioned to rejoin the organization. In January 2017 its petition was granted.

UN General Assembly. On November 21, 1979 a strongly worded resolution was adopted, by 85 votes to 6, with 41 abstentions, affirming not only "the inalienable right of the people of Western Sahara to self determination and independence" but also "the legitimacy of their struggle to secure the enjoyment of that right." The resolution deplored "the aggravation of the situation resulting from the continued occupation of Western Sahara by Morocco and the extension of that occupation to the territory recently evacuated by Mauritania" and urged Morocco to terminate the occupation of the territory. The Polisario for the first time were officially recognized as the legitimate representatives of the Saharawi people.[101]

This pro-Polisario momentum, however, did not last long. Successive additions to the berm outward from the "useful triangle" and down from southern Morocco into Western Sahara's eastern panhandle finally sealed off Dakhla and then reached the southern border with Mauritania. At its completion in 1987 it became the largest functional military barrier in the world—visible from space—and second only in length to the Great Wall of China, allowing Morocco to control roughly 80 percent of the territory. At the same time, fearing that the throne of their long standing ally, Hassan II, might be destabilized and wary of a group that counted Algeria as its main support, both the United States[102] and France intensified their military aid to Morocco, permitting it to stem the tide of Polisario's military advancements. French arms included sophisticated jet aircraft, helicopter gunships, light tanks, armored cars, artillery, and radar equipment.[103] United States arms sales grew from $33 million in 1977 to $86 million in 1978, and then to $133 million in 1979.[104] By 1980 the United States had supplied close to $1 billion in arms to Rabat, mostly in the form of sales financed by Saudi Arabia.[105] This support included clandestine shipments of U.S. arms through third parties. Following the debacle at Guelta Zemmour in 1981 this support escalated, as did the logistic support offered by the United States government to the King.

For a while the combination of the defensive barrier and the additional support given Morocco by the United States, France and Saudi Arabia effectively limited the Polisario's advances. But the Polisario eventually developed the means to overcome the berm's defenses and by 1987 began to launch a series of devastating

[101] G.A. Res. 3437, 34 UN GAOR, Supp. 46 at 203, UN Doc. A/34/46 (1979).

[102] Between 1975 and 1988 the United States supplied Morocco with over $1,000 million worth of arms, as well as $1,300 million in security and economic assistance programs. U.N. General Assembly, Special Committee Records, 1337th Meeting, 9 august 1988, pp. 2–16, report from John Zindar, Center for Defence Information.

[103] Reported in S. Zunes & J. Mundy, WESTERN SAHARA: WAR, NATIONALISM AND CONFLICT IRRESOLUTION, *supra*, at 17.

[104] *Id.* at 18, citing U.S. Department of Defense statistics (1984).

[105] *Id.*

large scale attacks along and behind the berm, so that even with the aid of their allies, the most Morocco could achieve by 1990 was a military stalemate.

Moreover, this massive infusion of military assistance to Morocco had an unintended political effect: it inflamed most of the non aligned third world, whose leaders began pressuring the United Nations into action. Beginning in 1985 United Nations Secretary General Perez de Cuellar began taking an active interest in the conflict, beginning a series of negotiations that spanned several years. Fearing that this tiny armed struggle might erupt into a conflict that would engulf the entire African continent, the world powers backed his efforts, and he was able to convince the parties in 1988 to agree to a diplomatic solution to the conflict and a cease fire, monitored by the United Nations and the AU.[106]

The diplomatic solution was dubbed "the Settlement Plan."

(6) The Long Winding Road: The Settlement Plan

As noted above, the Settlement Plan proposed by the United Nations in 1988 was seen by the major powers as the optimum solution to a conflict that was quickly escalating from a squabble between neighboring states over an obscure territory of insignificant value, to a military conflict that risked engulfing all of Africa and which had inflamed the passions of the "third world." However, if the powers thought that the Plan would quickly resolve the conflict they greatly underestimated the resolve and the diplomatic capabilities of the Moroccans.

The plan that was proposed was based loosely on proposals made by the OAU (now the AU) as far back as 1981. It called for a ceasefire between the parties and a "transitional period" followed by a "referendum of self-determination" in which the indigenous people of Western Sahara would be able to choose between independence and annexation with Morocco. During the transitional period and until the proclamation of the results of the referendum the territory would be administered by a Special Representative of the Secretary General of the United Nations, in consultation with the AU, assisted by a group of civilian and military personnel organized as the United Nations Mission for the Referendum in Western Sahara, or MINURSO.

The parties accepted the Plan in principle in 1988,[107] and on June 18, 1990 the Secretary General issued a report[108] outlining further details of the Plan. The

---

[106] The basic elements of this "Plan" had been proposed by the OAU as far back as 1981, and although King Hassan II at that time was forced to agree to it in principle, it was not implemented by the international community until 1988.

[107] On August 11, 1998 the Secretary General of the UN and a representative of the President of the AU presented an outline of a plan to both parties, which was accepted by both parties "in principle" on August 30, 1988.

[108] S/21360/1990 (18 June 1990).

Report of the Secretary General asserted their agreement that the future of the territory would be determined by a referendum conducted under the auspices of the United Nations and the AU, in which the indigenous population, defined as "all Saharawis included on the Spanish census of 1974 eighteen years of age or older," would be allowed to vote between independence and integration with Morocco.[109] The terms of the Plan were further delineated in the next Report of the Secretary General, issued on April 19, 1991,[110] again confirming the parties' agreement to a referendum and again confirming that all Saharawis listed on the Spanish census who were 18 years or older would be allowed to vote between independence and integration with Morocco. On April 29, 1991 the Security Council, in resolution 690, approved the Plan, established MINURSO, and established an estimated timetable for the transitional period preceding the referendum,[111] which was expected to last no more than 20 weeks. On September 6, 1991 the ceasefire went into effect.

However, it quickly became apparent that the conditions for the transitional period to commence would not easily be fulfilled, and the United Nations decided to commence voter registration before it began, while Morocco was still in control of most of the territory. This was the first of many decisions of the United Nations that were to have disastrous consequences.

Also, almost immediately after the ceasefire Morocco began to lobby for changes in the terms of the Settlement Plan that would enhance its position. Rather than accept the definition of voters eligible to participate in the referendum—which had been limited in the Plan to Saharawis who had been included in the 1974 Spanish census[112]—Morocco lobbied to have the criteria for eligible voters expanded, and began placing thousands of potential applicants from southern Morocco in settlement camps in the territory for the purpose of voting. Bowing to these pressures, the Secretary General in his Report of December 19, 1991[113] proposed broadening the definition of voter eligibility in a manner that would potentially include thousands of voters who had not been present in the territory in 1974, some with arguably tenuous ties to the territory.[114] The Polisario were alarmed

---

[109] *Id*, at 5.

[110] S/22464/1991 (April 19, 1991).

[111] The transitional period included a timetable for the reduction of Moroccan troops in the territory, the exchange of prisoners of war and the repatriation of refugees. The United Nations was to be responsible for monitoring law and order and have the right to suspend all laws that inhibited a free and fair referendum.

[112] S//21360/1990 at 5.

[113] S//23299/1991.

[114] The Secretary General proposed including in the voters' list not only individuals on the Spanish census who were 18 years or older (Category 1), but also persons who could prove that they were living in the territory as members of a Saharan tribe at the time of the 1974 census but were not counted (Category II), persons who were members of the

by this proposal, which they considered to be a blatant attempt by Morocco to pad the voters' list, and were even further alarmed when the Secretary General proposed relaxing the evidentiary requirements so as to permit eligibility to be established by oral testimony, which they considered to be an open invitation to fraud.[115]

For a number of months the Polisario resisted these proposals. Finally, in 1994, convinced that they had no other recourse than to rely upon the fairness of MINURSO officials in applying the definitions and procedures to determine eligibility proposed by the United Nations, they reluctantly agreed to them, and three years after the Settlement Plan was first negotiated the task of identifying eligible voters began. Citing slow progress in the voter identification process, and a resulting inability to meet other deadlines that were dependent upon this process, the Secretary General repeatedly recommended the postponement of the transitional period, delaying the assumption of essential powers the United Nations was to have exercised. As a result, the Moroccan government continued to exercise unfettered power within the territory, and unfettered influence over the identification process.

Moreover, from the very start of the process the UN adopted a number of policies that were to rebound with disastrous consequences. Instead of interpreting broadly its authority under the mandate conferred upon it by the parties, the UN hierarchy failed to put into place a mechanism that would ensure a free and fair referendum, and deferred to the will of the parties over every decision. Rather than take control of the application process, the UN placed control over the process into the hands of the parties. MINURSO officials had virtually no direct contact with potential applicants in the territory occupied by Morocco.[116] The parties were allowed to collect applications themselves and to control all access to potential

---

immediate family of individuals in Categories I or II (Category III), persons born of a Saharan father born in the territory (Category IV), and persons who were members of a Saharan tribe and who resided in the Territory for six consecutive years or intermittently for 12 years prior to the Spanish census (Category V). The last criterion caused the most concern to the Polisario, particularly since the "tribes" that were considered to be "Saharan" included, according to the proposed definition, all the tribal groups that had at least one member on the Spanish list—thus throwing the doors open to demands from applicants who were from tribes that in their eyes were not truly indigenous to the region.

[115] Their misgivings were not misplaced. As early as 1976 one commentator familiar with the demographics of the region noted that "Under the 'right' arrangements, the polling could easily be skewed by imported Moroccans and Mauritanians posing as Sahrawis." Franck, *The Stealing of the Sahara, supra,* 70 AJIL (1976) 694 at 697.

[116] Although the Secretary General in his reports maintained that applicants were free to contact UN officials to register to vote, in reality this was a sham. Armed guards prevented applicants from reaching UN premises and all applications in the Moroccan controlled areas were channeled through Moroccan officials. Moreover, the UN was prohibited from publicizing the referendum in the Moroccan controlled areas and all publicity concerning the referendum emanated from the Moroccan authorities, who consistently referred to it as a referendum to confirm Moroccan sovereignty in the area.

voters. Information about the referendum was disseminated by the parties, not the UN. There was no way to tell whether potential applicants were being excluded. Morocco, which exercised nearly total control over the applications submitted by persons within Western Sahara, submitted applications from over 180,000 applicants, including the thousands of Moroccans it had placed in settlement camps in the territory in the last three months of 1991, most of whom claimed eligibility under one of the "relaxed" criteria.[117] Many experts in the region doubted that such a large number—more than twice the number of individuals who were counted on the Spanish census of 1974—could be eligible,[118] and the eligibility sessions were fraught with charges of fraud and intimidation. On May 29,1996, amidst charges of Moroccan pressures to bias the referendum[119] and despite the fact that the eligibility determinations for the majority of applicants had been completed, the voter identification process was suspended,[120] not to resume again until the appointment in 1997 of former US Secretary of State James Baker III to be the Personal Envoy of the Secretary General on the Western Sahara docket.

Baker's dossier was clear—he was to settle once and for all what had become a protracted and painful diplomatic and legal quagmire for the United Nations and the major powers. For a while it looked as if he would succeed. In 1997 he brokered an agreement between the two parties, known as the "Houston Accords," that resolved an impasse between them over applications from members of tribes whose ties to the Territory were disputed, settled some outstanding issues concerning the powers of the United Nations during the "transitional" period, and promulgated an agreed "Code of Conduct" for the parties during the referendum process. The

---

[117] Out of approximately 180,000 applications submitted by Morocco, approximately 100,000 were on behalf of individuals who resided outside the territory in 1974. The Polisario submitted only 40,000 or so applications, the majority of which were from individuals on the Spanish census or their immediate family.

[118] Morocco's principle argument was that a significant number of Saharawis fled the territory in the 1957–58 uprisings and re-settled in southern Morocco. However, Spain's most intensive demographic studies in 1942 and 1967, which measured the population before and after the 1957–58 conflict, revealed an insignificant change in the native population, and experts in the region doubt that the territory could have sustained such a large population. *See*, S. Zunes & J. Mundy, WESTERN SAHARA: WAR, NATIONALISM AND CONFLICT IRRESOLUTION, *supra*, at 191.

[119] In 1995 the highest ranked United States citizen on MINURSO's Commission, Frank Ruddy, was summarily dismissed for voicing concerns about Morocco's domination of the voter identification process and testified before the U.S. House Appropriations Committee, which promptly voted to withhold funding from the Mission. At the same time Human Rights Watch, after an on-site investigation, issued a report entitled "Keeping it Secret: The United Nations Operation in Western Sahara" (September 30, 1995) charging that "Morocco...has regularly engaged in conduct that has obstructed and compromised the fairness of the referendum process" and that "a lack of UN control over the process has seriously jeopardized its fairness" and severely criticizing other aspects of the UN's conduct of the Mission. *See*, Report at 2. Negative reports on the Mission began to appear in publications such as the *New York Times* and the *Washington Post*. The emerging scandal led the Security Council to conduct an investigation. However, the various reports of the Security Council and Secretary General which followed this investigation failed to criticize Morocco or suggest any steps that would eliminate the potential for pressure and bias.

[120] S/Res/1056–1996.

voter identification process was resumed. In October of 1998 the Secretary General proposed a package of measures to speed up the referendum process and even scheduled a date for the referendum—December 1999.[121]

However, this progress came to a screeching halt on July 15, 1999 when the initial provisional voters' list established by MINURSO was published.[122] Showing remarkable resolve in the face of considerable pressure, MINURSO's Identification Commission rejected over 100,000 of the applicants put forth by Morocco.[123] It was clear to all that if the referendum were conducted on the basis of the 84,251 or so voters deemed eligible by the Commission as of that date, (later, on December 30, 1999, after interviews with applicants from the remaining 3 contested tribal groups,[124] the number was raised to 86, 386 out of a total of 198,469 applicants[125]) the result would most likely be a vote for independence.

Morocco's first strategy upon hearing the results of voter identification was to use the appeal process to regain the upper hand—and it lodged over 130,000 appeals[126]—but it soon concluded that this strategy would fail.[127]

Faced with the prospect of a referendum that would go against it, and the loss of King Hassan II, who died on July 23, 1999, just days after the provisional voters' list was published, Morocco simply decided to abandon the referendum all together.

The year 2000 saw Morocco admit publicly for the first time what had been obvious to most observers for a long time—that it would only permit a referendum if an outcome in its favor were preordained[128]—and the emergence of political

---

[121] S/1999/307.

[122] An initial provisional voters' list excluding applicants from the contested tribal units, was published in June, later in the year this list was supplemented with lists of approved applicants from the contested units. The list was considered provisional because the inclusion or non-inclusion of applicants could be appealed and a final voters' list would only be published following the appeals process.

[123] The Commission declared eligible 84,251 applicants out of the 147,249 applications received from individuals from the non-contested tribes and 2,135 applicants out of the 51,220 applications from the three contested groups. S/2000/131 (17 February 2000) at 2.

[124] These groups, designated as the H61, H41 and the J51/52 after their description in the Spanish census of 1974, were considered non indigenous to Western Sahara by the Polisario. Nonetheless, individuals from these groups were interviewed by the Commission and if they satisfied one of the five eligibility criteria, they were put on the voters' list.

[125] The three tribes considered not indigenous to the region by the Polisario represented 51,220 possible voters all but a fraction of whom were declared ineligible by the Commission.

[126] The total number of appeals as reported in S/2001/148 (20 February 2001) at 2 was 131,038, all but a few of which were from applicants filing through Morocco.

[127] The Moroccan appeals, with the relaxed evidentiary requirements advocated by Morocco, if permitted, would have resulted in a second round of identification taking years, something even the pro-Moroccan members of the Security Council would not permit.

[128] In an interview with former Moroccan Minister of the Interior, Driss Basri, who was in charge of the Western Sahara dossier, reported in the Moroccan weekly Al-Ayam, he acknowledged that he "was for the referendum only

pressures to find a solution outside the rubrics of the Settlement Plan—the so-called "third way."

For the first time the Secretary General in his report of February 17, 2000 emphasized the lack of means to enforce the result of a referendum,[129] suggested that it was the time to "consider other ways of achieving" a resolution of the dispute,[130] and started placing pressure on the parties to accept a settlement based on "quasi autonomy" for the region.[131] For the first time the Security Council adopted a resolution calling for the discussion of a mutually acceptable "political solution."[132]

The abrupt shift in position of the United Nations "coincided" with a similar shift in the strategy of the Moroccans. In early 2000, according to news sources,[133] a royal commission headed by former Moroccan opposition leader Abraham Serfaty, who until then had strongly supported the Saharawis' claim to independence, advanced the concept of autonomy for Western Sahara within the Kingdom of Morocco, taking as a model the autonomous regions of Catalonia and Andalusia in Spain. By February of 2001 the Moroccan Minister of Foreign Affairs, Mohamed Benouisa, had announced publicly that Morocco was ready to "present a paper setting out a global conception for a practical solution to the conflict in the Sahara, based on...decentralisation and democracy in the context of Moroccan territorial unity and sovereignty."[134] and later that month the Moroccan Minister of the Interior Midaoui confirmed that Morocco would refuse any solution that put national sovereignty into question. In April of that year the *Diario de Avisos* (Spain) reported that Morocco was working on a plan to offer the inhabitants of Western Sahara quasi autonomy.

---

in a tactical way" and that the King had assured him that he would not have agreed to a referendum if he had not been sure that Morocco would win it. *http://www.wsahara.net/03/alayambasrieng.html.*

[129] Noting that the developments over the last nine years constituted a "real source of concern and raise doubts about the possibility of achieving a smooth and consensual implementation of the settlement plan" and that "even assuming that a referendum were held...no enforcement mechanism is envisioned by the settlement plan, nor is one likely to be proposed, calling for the use of military means to effect enforcement...." Annan announced his intention to ask Baker "to explore ways and means to achieve an early, durable and agreed resolution of their dispute...." S/2000/131 (17 February 2000) at 10; The lack of any enforcement mechanism in the settlement plan was repeated in the Secretary General's next report, S/2000/461 (22 May 2000) and emphasized again in his report of July 12, 2000 (S/2000/683), after attempts to persuade the parties to negotiate on the basis of a political settlement failed.

[130] S/2000/461 (22 May 2000) at 4.

[131] In the last Report of the Secretary General for 2000 after face to face meetings between the parties in London and Berlin failed to show any progress in resolving the conflict he suggested that further face to face meetings of the parties would be counterproductive unless Morocco was prepared to offer "some devolution of governmental authority" for the area. S/2000/1029 (26 October 2000) at 6.

[132] S/Res/2000/1309 (25 July 2000); S/Res/2000/1324 (30 October 2000).

[133] According to an article by Yahia H. Zoubir and Karima Benabdallah-Gabier in Middle East Reports (No. 227) entitled *Westen Saharan Deadlock* at 2.

[134] According to an article in Acharq Al Awsat, an Arabic daily printed in London on February 6, 2001.

According to published reports, early in 2001 Morocco presented to the United Nations such a plan—dubbed the "third option"—proposing a ten year period of "substantial devolution of authority" in Western Sahara during which the implementation of a referendum would be "studied."[135]

The Moroccan proposal was quickly embraced by Baker. Instead of placing pressure on the Moroccans to go ahead with the referendum, Baker, during a secret visit to the Polisario refugee camps in May of 2001, championed a slightly modified version of the "third option" called the Framework Agreement,[136] under which Morocco, recognized as the "administrative power" in the Territory, would "delegate" certain powers[137] to the "inhabitants of the Territory" for a period of five years, after which a referendum would take place in which not only the individuals on the voters list established by MINURSO, but *all* people living in Western Sahara for more than one year prior to the referendum would be allowed to vote (including the hundreds of thousands of Moroccans who had come to reside in the Territory since it was occupied by Morocco, or who had been resettled by Morocco in Moroccan built settlement camps in the Territory for the purpose of voting in the referendum, and any others who might decide to settle in the region) and the voting options would include the continuation of such an autonomous state within Morocco.

It was clear that the "Framework Agreement" was little more than the repackaging with slight modifications of the proposal that emanated earlier from Morocco whose purpose was to overcome the legal obstacles presented by the Settlement Agreement, and the internationally recognized right of the Saharawis to self-determination on the issue of independence, as well as to facilitate the international acceptance of Moroccan *de facto* control over the territory. King Mohammed VI was later to comment to the French newspaper *Le Figaro* that he had "…settled the question of the Sahara which has been consuming us for the past 25 years…we have worked hard and in the strictest confidentiality for 18 months to ensure that the 11 members of the United Nations Security Council recognize the legitimacy of Moroccan sovereignty over Western Sahara…We agree

---

[135] According to an article appearing in the Madrid daily *El Pais*, on May 16, 2001. According to this plan the administration of the territory would be committed to a council composed of members of the Polisario and Saharawis who had lived for 25 years in Western Sahara. This institution would have at its disposal 20% of the phosphates and fisheries incomes and would manage cultural and social affairs and participate in the administration of justice, but Rabat would control the police, defense, foreign affairs and communications. The Secretary General alluded to such a proposal when, in his report S/2001/398 (24 April 2001) at 4 he suggested that "substantial progress" had been made towards determining whether Morocco was prepared to offer some devolution of authority to the inhabitants.

[136] Referred to in an Annex to the Report of the Secretary General S/2002/41, released on January 11, 2002.

[137] Like the "third option" proposed by Morocco, the administration of the Territory would be administered by a Council composed of members of the Polisario and of Saharawis living for at least 25 years in the Territory. It would have certain authority over local affairs but less independence than that of any Spanish autonomous community.

that an equitable solution should be found within the framework of Moroccan sovereignty…"[138]

In June of 2001 United Nations Secretary General Kofi Annan officially proposed that the UN abandon the Settlement Plan and thirty years of policies supporting the rights of colonial peoples to exercise self-determination in determining their future, in favor of this "Framework Agreement."[139] This proposal was made the more striking because, ironically, it contrasted with the establishment at that time of an independent state following a UN sponsored referendum in another former colony, East Timor.

However, if the supporters of Morocco thought that they would be able to "persuade" the Polisario to renounce their rights under the Settlement Plan, or convince the Security Council to embrace the Framework Agreement without the Polisario's support they were disappointed. The Polisario resolutely refused to budge on their demands for the implementation of the Settlement Plan,[140] and the Security Council refused to take measures to force the Framework Agreement upon them,[141] leading to a stalemate and an escalating level of friction among parties to the dispute and international officials alike.[142]

---

[138] *Le Figaro*, September 4, 2001.

[139] S/2001/613 (20 June 2001). In this report the Secretary General noted the various attempts Baker had made to get the parties to arrive at a political solution to the problem, noting that a political agreement would most likely produce a solution somewhere between total independence and total integration and further noting that self-determination could be achieved through "agreement" as well as through elections. (at 7) He supported continuing discussions on the proposed "framework agreement" and in the interim putting the settlement plan "on hold." (at 10).

[140] In a statement issued on June 20, 2001 the European representative of the Polisario commented that Baker had shown the Moroccan proposals for a plan of autonomy which had been rejected "categorically and definitively." Under this plan "the currency, the flag, customs, foreign policy, home affairs, communications, defence, police and justice would all remain within the competency and authority of the Moroccan state." At the end of four years "Morocco could organise, if it so wished, a consultation designed to give a blessing to the integration of Western Sahara within it… The electors called to vote would in fact be a majority of Moroccans, sent over the preceding years to the territory to contribute to the colonisation of Western Sahara, and to reduce the Saharawis to a simple minority."

[141] Following the Report of the Secretary General outlining the "Framework Agreement" and despite lobbying by the U.S. and others to have it endorsed by the Security Council, the most the Security Council would agree to do was to "encourage" the parties to discuss it. S/Res/1359 (29 June 2001). In April of 2002 the U.S. backed a Security Council resolution which would have imposed a solution of autonomy upon the parties. When it failed to win majority support it was withdrawn in favor of a resolution which simply extended MINURSO's mandate by three months. In July of that year the U.S., UK and France presented a draft resolution which would have charged Baker with revising the Framework Agreement and abandoning the Settlement Plan. This also failed to win majority support and was abandoned. Instead, the Security Council in S/Res/1429 (July 30, 2002) reaffirmed the validity of the Settlement Plan and gave itself a period of three months to "study" the various options proposed by the Secretary General in UN Doc. S.2002/41.

[142] Baker met with the Polisario several times during this period to try to persuade them to agree to the Framework Agreement, to no avail. Besides being against any departure from the Settlement Plan on principle, the Polisario were concerned that the Framework Agreement permitted Morocco to retain too much power over police and the administration of justice and the appointment of legislative officials during the period leading up to voting on the future of the territory and that additional masses of Moroccans could be settled in the territory by Morocco ensuring Morocco's victory at the polls. To them the Framework Agreement would virtually hand the territory over to Morocco under a pretext of "self determination." *See*, Memorandum from the Frente Popular para la Liberacion

On February 19, 2002, faced with a political impasse, the Secretary General outlined four options and asked the Security Council to make a choice.[143] These were: (1) try to implement the Settlement Plan without requiring the concurrence of the two parties, (2) adopt the Framework Agreement and present it to the parties on a non-negotiable basis, (3) explore with the parties the possibility of dividing the territory between them, and (4) terminate MINURSO and admit defeat in resolving the dispute. The issuance of this report was coupled with intense lobbying by the US government and others to have a Security Council resolution passed that would impose the Framework Agreement upon the Polisario.

Once again, however, efforts by the major powers to force a politically attractive solution upon the Polisario failed. Instead of acquiescing to pressure from the United States, the Security Council demurred, reiterating its commitment to the Settlement Plan and its willingness to consider any approach—as long as it provided for self-determination.[144]

In January of 2003, in a final attempt to surmount this political impasse Baker submitted to the parties a more finely tuned version of the Framework Agreement dubbed the "Peace Plan".[145]

At first blush the Peace Plan did not seem to be radically different from the Framework Agreement—both essentially abandoned the provisions of the Settlement Plan and the voters' list established by MINURSO in favor of a provisional period of "autonomy" for the Territory followed by a "referendum" in which Moroccans as well as Saharawis would be allowed to vote. However, as one writer put it "the devil is in the details" and the details of the Peace Plan corrected some of the more glaring pro-Moroccan provisions of the Framework Agreement.[146] For one thing, a residency cut off date of December 30, 1999 was established for voter eligibility, thus reducing the ability of Morocco to flood the territory with new "voters" prior to the referendum. The Peace Plan made it clear that the local

---

de Saguia el-Hamra y del Rio de Oro (Frente POLISARIO), Annex II to the Report of the Secretary General, UN Doc. S/2001/613 (20 June 2001) and Annex I to the Report of the Secretary General, UN Doc. S/2002/41 (10 January 2002).

[143] UN Doc. S/2002/178 (19 February 2002).

[144] S/Res./1429 (30 July 2002). Although the Security Council stressed that the search for a political solution was "critically needed" it fell short of endorsing the Framework Agreement, instead indicating its determination to secure a mutually acceptable political solution that would provide for the self-determination of the people of Western Sahara "in the context of arrangements consistent with the principles and purposes of the Charter of the United Nations" and indicating its willingness to consider "any approach which provides for self-determination."

[145] Reprinted in UN Doc. S/2003/565, Annex II.

[146] As one writer familiar with the issue put it: "Baker's current proposals define the contours of Saharawi autonomy more clearly, as well as suggesting that the two parties would not be intimately involved in every aspect of developing the eventual referendum." Toby Shelley, *Behind the Baker Plan for Western Sahara*, Middle East Report, August 1, 2003.

authority in Western Sahara—which would be elected by the Saharawis deemed eligible to vote by MINURSO—would control the police and local courts during the transitional phase, and that internationally accepted standards of human rights would be applied. The Peace Plan also made it clear that Morocco and the local government would be expected to work closely on most issues—including every aspect of the eventual referendum—and that Morocco would not be able to exert unilateral veto power over adopted measures.

In May of 2003 the Secretary General publicly announced his support of Baker's revised Framework Agreement—now dubbed the "Peace Plan"[147]—and on July 31, 2003 the Security Council voted unanimously to "support strongly" what it described as "an optimum political solution on the basis of agreement between the two parties" and called upon the parties "to work with the United Nations and with each other towards accepting implementation of the Peace Plan."[148]

To most observers' surprise, despite initial reluctance, the Polisario eventually gave a qualified approval to the Peace Plan.[149] However, in an equally surprising twist, despite the fact that Baker had gone out of his way to craft a solution that would cater to Morocco's interests, Morocco rejected it. According to the Secretary General, Morocco's main objection to the Plan was that one of the ballot choices on the referendum was independence.[150] Moreover, any real autonomy for the Saharawis was apparently more than the Moroccan government could stomach,[151] and, somewhat ironically, the government seemed unwilling to gamble on the loyalty of the very Moroccans it had fought for years to get on the election rolls.[152] On April 15, 2004 Morocco delivered its final response to the Plan, indicating that

---

[147] UN Doc. S/2003/565 (23 May 2003).

[148] Press Release SC/7833, July 31, 2003.

[149] July 2003. The Polisario accepted the proposal that the notion of self-determination on the issue of independence would be maintained and that the Moroccan administration of the territory would end, but indicated that everything else would have to be negotiated with the UN. The Polisario expressed reservations, in particular, about the proposed voter rolls and the length of the transition period.

[150] UN Doc. S/2002/565 at 10. As the Secretary General commented: "It is difficult to envision a political solution that...provides for self-determination but that nevertheless precludes the possibility of independence as one of several ballot questions. This is particularly difficult to envision given (a) the stated commitment of Morocco to the settlement plan...over so many years; and (b) the inclusion in the electorate for the referendum...of all those who have resided continuously in Western Sahara since 30 December 1999, as opposed to only those who would be included in the voter list, which was created on the basis of the work of the Identification Commission." at 10–11.

[151] As Baker noted in an interview with PBS Wideangle on August 19, 2004: "...it's very much in Morocco's interest at the very least to offer some meaningful proposals on autonomy or self-government for [the Saharawis]. And yet they'll get right up to the bar, they'll talk about wanting to grant autonomy, but they're never willing to put an autonomy plan on the table."

[152] As Baker also noted in the interview with PBS Wideangle, supra, "...my plan...called the Peace Plan.... broadened the electorate so that everyone in Western Sahara would have the right to vote on this issue of self-determination on the referendum and not just the people who were identified in the Spanish census of 1975 or 1976. And...the Moroccans concluded that they weren't even willing to risk a vote under those circumstances. And of course that made it impossible to reach a solution to which both parties would agree."

it would only agree to a plan that provided for "autonomy within the framework of Moroccan sovereignty," that is, that ruled out once and for all the option of independence for the territory.

In apparent total frustration on April 11, 2004 Baker resigned as Personal Envoy of the Secretary General.

(7) Direct Negotiations

Baker's departure ushered in a period of stalemate and a new policy direction. In a resolution issued on July 31, 2003 the Security Council had again reiterated its commitment to the pursuit of arrangements whereby the people of Western Sahara could exercise their right to self-determination in a manner that would be "consistent with the principles and purposes of the Charter of the United Nations."[153] However, by the time of his General Report in April of 2004, Secretary General Kofi Anan confirmed that "Morocco does not accept the Settlement Plan to which it had agreed for many years…and it also now does not accept essential elements of the Peace Plan (of Baker). It accepts nothing but negotiations about the autonomy of Western Sahara 'in the framework of Moroccan sovereignty'".[154]

In April of 2006, in a departure from previous United Nations statements and policy, he recommended that the United Nations "step back" from its attempts to formulate a plan for self determination for Western Sahara in favor of direct negotiations between the parties.[155] The Secretary-General's recommendation followed the briefing to the Security Council in January 2006 by his Personal Envoy Peter van Walsum. Van Walsum concluded that, due to Moroccan opposition, holding a referendum that included the option of independence was no longer possible, and that a new approach of direct negotiations was necessary as "the only alternative to the indefinite prolongation of the impasse."[156] In that year the United States placed pressure on the Moroccans to make a serious proposal to help solve the conflict. Gordon Gray, Deputy Assistant Secretary of State for Near Eastern Affairs, declared that the United States was seeking "an acceptable political

---

[153] On self-determination norms and Western Sahara, see Beth A. Payne, *The Western Sahara: International Legal Issues*, INTERNATIONAL DIMENSIONS OF THE WESTERN SAHARA CONFLICT, (Zoubir and Volman (eds) Westport, Praeger (1993).

[154] Report of the Secretary-General on the Situation Concerning Western Sahara, UN Doc. S/2004/325.

[155] Report of the Secretary-General on the Situation Concerning Western Sahara, UN Doc. S/2006/249, 19 April 2006. *See also*, the discussion of this issue by Catriona Drew in *The Meaning of Self-Determination: "The Stealing of the Sahara" Redux?*, INTERNATIONAL LAW AND THE QUESTION OF WESTERN SAHARA, (Karin Arts and Pedro Pinto Leite (eds) IPJET (2007) at 88.

[156] *See*, "Briefing to the Security Council", 18 January 2006, summarized in "Report of the Secretary-General on the Situation Concerning Western Sahara," UN Doc S/2006/817, 16 October 2006, para. 14.

solution" to the conflict and had encouraged Morocco to present a "credible" autonomy proposal.[157]

This encouragement apparently had results, for in April of 2007 both the Polisario[158] and the Moroccans[159] presented to the Security Council proposals for consideration.

Within weeks of the submission of these proposals the Security Council adopted Resolution 1754, calling upon the parties:

> "[t]o enter into negotiations without preconditions in good faith, taking into account the developments of the last months, with a view to achieving a just, lasting and mutually acceptable political solution, which will provide for self-determination of the Western Sahara."[160]

In a step that was hailed as a "new phase in the search for a solution to the conflict," the parties commenced direct talks in June 2007 in Manhasset, New

---

[157] Y. Zoubir, *Geopolitics and Realpolitik as Impediments to the Resolution of Conflict and Violations of International Law: The Case of Western Sahara*, INTERNATIONAL LAW AND THE QUESTION OF WESTERN SAHARA, *supra*, at 292.

[158] The Polisario declared its readiness to negotiate directly with Morocco the modalities for implementing the Baker Plan as well as those relating to the holding of a "genuine" referendum on self-determination "in strict conformity with the spirit and letter of the UN General Assembly resolution 1514 (XV) and within the format envisaged in the framework of the Baker Plan, namely the choice between independence, integration into the Kingdom of Morocco and self-governance." *Proposal of the Frente Polisario for a Mutually Acceptable Political Solution That Provides for the Self Determination of the People of Western Sahara*, April 10, 2007, para. 7. The Polisario furthermore indicated that it was prepared to grant to the Moroccan population residing in Western Sahara for 10 years as well as to Morocco certain "guarantees" should a referendum lead to independence, including respect for the borders "inherited from the independence period," the guarantee of rights of Moroccans in Western Sahara to participate in the political economic and social life of the country, an agreement on the joint exploitation of natural resources, economic cooperation in different sectors, the renunciation of compensation for any material destruction that has taken place, security arrangements, cooperation in bringing to a conclusion the integration of the Maghreb, and cooperation in efforts to maintain peace and stability in the region. *Id*. Para. 9.

[159] The *Moroccan Initiative for Negotiating an Autonomy Statute for the Sahara Region* of April 11, 2007 set forth the powers that would be conferred upon inhabitants of the region, should it become an "autonomous" region of Morocco, and the powers that would be reserved for the central authority. Among the powers that would be conferred upon the inhabitants of the region would be power over the region's local administration and local police, regional economic development, local budget and taxation, local infrastructure, social services and cultural affairs, and the local environment. *Id*. para. 12. Reserved to the local authority would be the attributes of sovereignty (flag, currency, etc.), the constitutional and religious prerogatives of the King, national security, external relations and the judicial order. *Id*. para. 14. The financial resources made available to the territory would include the proceeds from local taxes, the exploitation of natural resources allocated to the region, a share of proceeds collected by the central authority from the exploitation of natural resources located in the region, certain "necessary funds" allocated in keeping with the principle of national solidarity, and proceeds from the region's "assets." *Id*. para. 13. Other provisions concerned the method of electing members of the region's legislative body and chief executive, the role of the local courts, and the creation of an Economic and Social Council. *Id*. paras. 19–26. Finally, there are provisions for the negotiation of the region's "autonomy statute", which is to be submitted to the populations concerned in a "free referendum," as well as for the autonomy provisions to be incorporated into the Moroccan constitution. *Id*. paras. 27–35.

[160] S/Res/1754 (30 April 2007).

York. As of 2017, there had been numerous rounds of such "talks" with few concrete results,[161] leading to the resignation of Christopher Ross, the Special Envoy of the Secretary General to Western Sahara in March of 2017, and the appointment of his replacement, former German President Horst Koehler, in June of that year.

For two years Kohler led a number of roundtable discussions with the parties as well as Algeria and Mauritania, but despite his efforts the political situation remained relatively unchanged. Kohler resigned his post on May 22, 2019, and the Secretary-General has yet to appoint a new Personal Envoy.

The reason for the most recent Personal Envoy's resignation, according to Ross, was "likely out of disgust for Morocco's lack of respect and efforts to impede his work (as they did with me)…" He noted that those approached to date to take on the role have demurred, "probably because they recognize that Morocco wants someone who will in effect become its advocate instead of remaining neutral…"[162]

Meanwhile, the situation on the ground remained tense. In July 2019, King Mohammed VI of Morocco again declared in a speech that Western Sahara is part of Morocco,[163] urging the international community to work on Morocco's autonomy plan, intensifying friction between the parties. Then, on the anniversary of the Green March on November 6, 2019 the King reiterated his position, adding to the friction.[164] Also, after intense lobbying by the Moroccan government, Burundi, Central African Republic, Comoros, Côte d'Ivoire, Gabon, The Gambia, Guinea, Liberia, and São Tomé and Príncipe all recently opened consulates in Laayoune and Dakhla, further escalating tensions. Special Representative Colin Stewart, head of MINURSO, briefed Council members on October 16, 2019, highlighting his concerns about the humanitarian situation and rising frustration

---

[161] As of April 14, 2008 the most that could be said about the progress of these four rounds of talks was that the parties had reached an "exchange of views on the implementation of Security Council resolutions" and unspecified "thematic subjects." Report of the Secretary General, UN Doc. S/2008/251, April 14, 2008.

[162] Facebook, December 13, 2020.

[163] In a speech commemorating Throne Day, the King proclaimed: "The celebration of the glorious Throne Day is a most fitting occasion to reiterate our unwavering commitment to the Moroccanness of the Sahara, to our national unity and territorial integrity, and to full sovereignty over every inch of the Kingdom's territory…. I am proud of all that our country has achieved at the United Nations and at African and European levels. We need to remain mobilized across the board to consolidate these achievements and face up to the plots of our adversaries. Morocco remains resolutely and earnestly committed to the political process, under the exclusive aegis of the United Nations Organization. Morocco is also clear in terms of its fundamental convictions: the way to achieve the desired settlement can be none other than through Moroccan full sovereignty and within the framework of the autonomy initiative." *See*, King Mohammed VI Speech on Throne Day, July 29, 2019 moroccoworldnews.com.

[164] The King said: "The momentum that made the recovery of the Sahara possible in 1975 continues today…The Autonomy initiative is the concrete translation of the solution sought. In fact, it is the only possible way to achieve a settlement of the conflict…." https://beninwebtv.com/en/2019/11/morocco-green-march-full-speech-of-king-mohammed-vi-to-the-nation-video/.

among Saharawi youth because of the lack of opportunities and of any final settlement of the issue.

In the midst of these developments, on 30 October 2019, the Council adopted resolution 2494 renewing the mandate of MINURSO for one year.

The year 2020, however, saw a continued deterioration of both the political situation and the situation on the ground. On the political front, nothing occurred to end the stalemate, and the worldwide pandemic obliterated any meager attempt at negotiations. On October 30,[165] the Security Council renewed MINURSO's mandate for an additional year without any realistic hope that progress would be made.

At the same time Saharawi civilians, incensed by the fact that Morocco had built a road at the Guerguerat crossing between Western Sahara and Mauritania in the buffer zone that was supposed to be off limits to both parties, staged a blockade preventing traffic from using what had become a major commercial route between Morocco and the rest of Africa. In response, on November 13, Moroccoan troops advanced into the buffer zone and fired upon the protesters. The Polisario retaliated by declaring an end to the ceasefire and attacking the Moroccan troops and Moroccan positions at several points along the berm. Following the announcement of the end of the ceasefire, Saharawi civilians in Western Sahara staged pro-independence demonstrations in most major towns. This in turn led to widespread beatings and arrests by Moroccan police, and gave Morocco an excuse to clamp down on Saharawi activists and place some of them, such as Aminatou Haidar, under house arrest.

In the midst of this turmoil, U.S. President Donald Trump, on December 10, 2020, shortly before he was to relinquish the Presidency to his successor Joseph Biden, announced that the United States would recognize Morocco's sovereignty over Western Sahara in exchange for Morocco establishing diplomatic ties with Israel, adding fuel to the fire.

Undoubtedly, the resumption of these hostilities—even if short lived—will prompt UN and U.S. diplomats to pay greater attention to this conflict than they have in recent years.

But these hostilities may not be short lived. Indeed, they are the culmination of frustrations that have been percolating for years, particularly among Saharawi youth. It is difficult to predict the turn they may ultimately take, or the blood that may be shed before it is over.

---

[165] S/Res/2548 (October 30, 2020).

(8) Future Prospects

(a) Western Sahara Today

Western Sahara is not today the same country it was in 1974. As was noted previously, when the Moroccan troops first invaded the country in 1975 the Saharan civilian population began an exodus that resulted in over 50,000 inhabitants—some suggest the majority of the Saharan population—settling in refugee camps near Tindouf, Algeria. Throughout the years of Moroccan occupation the Moroccan government pursued a campaign designed to entice Moroccan settlers to replace these inhabitants. Moroccans who chose to migrate to Western Sahara were given tax credits and other benefits not enjoyed by others in Morocco. This resulted in an enormous demographic shift in population. In an informal census conducted in 1981, the population of Western Sahara was estimated to be approximately 162,000 only a small number of whom were individuals who were on the Spanish census of 1974 or their families.[166] This effort was intensified after the 1991 ceasefire, and today it is estimated that of the 500,000 or so residents of Western Sahara only 25% are native Saharawis.[167]

As was noted in a 2003 report of the NGO the French Association of Friendship and Solidarity with the Peoples of Africa (AFASPA) upon investigating human rights abuses committed by Morocco:

> "Since the implementation of the 1991 UN ceasefire, Morocco embarked on a policy aiming at settling Moroccans in Western Sahara, in addition to some 200,000 members of the Moroccan security forces already stationed in the territory since the beginning of the conflict. This is why, today, the Saharawi population is a minority in the territory."[168]

This effort reached its peak during the period of MINURSO's registration of potential voters, when the Moroccan government established "tent cities" where thousands of settlers from southern Morocco who submitted applications to vote were housed and fed—some say against their will.[169]

Likewise, the Moroccan government has not allowed the resources of Western

---

[166] Human Rights Watch Report, *Keeping It Secret: the United Nations Operation in Western Sahara, (supra)* at 25.

[167] U.S. Country Report on Human Rights Practices in Western Sahara, 2015, at 2.

[168] International Mission of Investigation in Western Sahara, January 2003, *www.france-libertes.fr* (Part II).

[169] Human Rights Watch, *Keeping It Secret: The United Nations Operation In The Western Sahara, supra,* at 27, citing among other evidence reports from MINURSO staff members and the testimony of Jarat Chopra before the Subcommittee on Africa of the U.S. House of Representatives' International Relations Committee in 1993.

Sahara to remain idle. Morocco is one of the largest exporters in the world of a certain grade of phosphates used to make fertilizers for crops and, more recently, for the production of alternative fuels. Western Sahara's Boucraa mine also produces such phosphates. According to a report by the UN Environment Programme in 2008, satellite imagery taken between 1987 and 2007 revealed that Morocco had expanded the size of the Boucraa mine more than three times. Certain observers estimate that Morocco is possibly earning $80 to $150 million from these mines per year.[170] Phosphates from Boucraa have been exported to countries throughout the world, including the United States.

Moreover, with some of the richest fishing grounds on the west coast of Africa along its coast, fisheries from Western Sahara have contributed greatly to the Moroccan economy during the past thirty years, accounting for an estimated two thirds of the revenue Morocco receives annually from its fishery exports.[171]

In 2001 the Moroccan government entered into an agreement with Kerr-McGee and France's Total to explore the possible offshore Western Saharan oil reserves. It was only after the publication of a legal opinion of the Undersecretary and Legal Advisor of the United Nations which held that the exploitation of the natural resources of Western Sahara by Morocco without the consent of the Saharawis and without inuring to their benefit would violate international law (the "Corell Opinion"),[172] followed by considerable pressure from NGO's and the decision of the government of Norway to divest itself of stock in companies conducting activities in Western Sahara, that Kerr-McGee and Total discontinued their activities. However, this did not stop Morocco's exploitation efforts. Other firms entered the market—including Total again briefly—and by the beginning of 2017 at least eight international firms were involved in some aspect of mineral exploration or exploitation in the territory.[173] And Morocco has also benefitted from the territory's agricultural produce and potential for renewable energy programs.

In the meanwhile, the majority of the Saharawis who had remained in the territory following the Moroccan occupation saw their independence severely curtailed. According to Hodges, during the early war years the movements of the Saharawis were carefully monitored. By the spring of 1976 they had lost all freedom of movement beyond the towns and could only travel between the

---

[170] Reported in S. Zunes & J. Mundy, WESTERN SAHARA, WAR, NATIONALISM AND CONFLICT IRRESOLUTION (*supra*) at 35.

[171] *Id.*

[172] Letter dated January 29, 2002, from Undersecretary of the United Nations for Legal Affairs Hans Corell to the President of the Security Council, UN Doc. S/2002/161 (12 February 2002). ("Corell Opinion")

[173] 2016 Annual Report of Western Sahara Resource Watch ("WSRW"), an NGO based in Belgium which monitors Morocco's use of the resources of Western Sahara.

Moroccan controlled areas in military convoys or leave by plane for Morocco or the Canary Islands—if they were lucky enough to be granted the necessary travel documents.[174] He reported that despite the Moroccan occupation, support for the Polisario "remained strong" because of an "effective clandestine network" that the Polisario was able to maintain in the territory, but that overt expression of hostility to the Moroccan presence was "almost suicidal under such extreme conditions of military occupation, where the Moroccan troops almost outnumbered the towns' civilian population." As he noted in 1983:

> "There were periodic waves of arrests, in which known or suspected Polisario sympathizers were rounded up, detained and often tortured,[175] though the number of detainees was difficult to gauge as they were never brought to trial and there were seldom independent journalists in the territory to record or report arrests."[176]

Indeed, not long after Spain acquiesced in the Moroccan takeover of the territory, Morocco initiated a campaign designed to wipe out any semblance of opposition among its inhabitants. The early waves of state terror focused primarily on the remaining Polisario activists and their families, those who could not or chose not to flee. Morocco's favored method for dealing with suspected pro-independence militants was simply to "disappear" them.[177] A number of Saharawis were incarcerated, often for years, many without even the semblance of a trial, or were executed.

---

[174] Hodges, *supra*, at 281.

[175] Documented torture methods in Morocco include beatings all over the body, often with stones, whips, chains, and metal rods; beatings on the bottom of prisoners' feet, a method known as *falaqa*; partial suffocation by either forced near drowning or the stuffing of rags soaked in bleach into the mouth; suspension of prisoners by hands and feet tied behind their back and then the application of beatings or pressure to their backs; the hanging of prisoners by their hands and feet tied together in front of them, followed by beatings or partial suffocation; and the hanging of prisoners by the hands so that only their toes touch the ground, causing massive swelling of the hands and feet. *See,* S. Zunes & J. Mundy, WESTERN SAHARA: WAR, NATIONALISM & CONFLICT IRRESOLUTION, *supra,* at 146 (quoting the report of Amnesty International, 1991, at 23–25).

[176] He goes on to cite the case of fifty civilians arrested in Laayoune on May 20, 1978, the fifth anniversary of Polisario's first guerilla attack against the Spanish army, seven of whom had been hospitalized following electric shock "torture." See, Hodges, *supra*, at 281. Recent articles confirm the uncovering of mass graves of Saharawi civilians from this era. *See,* for instance, the article by Moroccan filmmaker and human rights advocate Nadir Bouhmouch, February 5, 2014, in *Pambazuka News*. The *New York Times* in 2005 reported the discovery of mass graves of persons who disappeared during this era, and estimated that the number of such persons could be as high as 600. (N.Y. Times, October 9, 2005).

[177] The International Federation of Human Rights Leagues has claimed that the number of Saharawi "disappeared" may be as high as fifteen hundred. The Association of Families of Sahrawi Prisoners and Disappeared (AFAPREDESA), a Saharawi human rights organization based in the camps, has registered roughly 890 Saharawi "disappeared" since 1975. Amnesty International (1990) cites a slightly lower figure, 488. See S. Zunes & J. Mundy, WESTERN SAHARA: WAR, NATIONALISM & CONFLICT IRRESOLUTION, *supra,* at 145.

Most of the Saharawi population of southern Morocco was also politically suspect during this period, and so there were also numerous arrests of presumed Polisario sympathizers in the regions of Zaag and Tan Tan.[178]

The investigation of the French NGO AFASPA documented in depth the human rights violations that Moroccans have committed in Western Sahara. Its 2003 report is "replete with testimonies from Saharawis about the violations of their basic human rights: no right to equitable trial and reparations, torture—even of pregnant women—mutilations, forced disappearances, arbitrary arrests, and no access to a useful appeals procedure."[179]

As of 1995—the period of voter identification by MINURSO—the situation in Western Sahara for the Saharawis, according to Human Rights Watch, had not improved significantly. In its report *Keeping It Secret: The U.N. Operation in The Western Sahara*, published in 1995 after an on site investigation, Human Rights Watch noted reports of the arrest and detention—as well as "disappearance"—of hundreds of Saharawis, whose whereabouts were still unaccounted for, and the continued curtailment of movement and freedom of speech in the territory.[180]

Although the brunt of the war with Morocco—both militarily and politically— was borne by the Polisario and the Saharawis who had managed to escape to the Tindouf camps, the Saharawis who remained in the territory—as well as others residing elsewhere—did not remain quiet during the war years or those which followed the ceasefire. During the war, cells of sympathizers located in every corner of the territory as well as in southern Morocco and the Canary Islands helped the war effort by smuggling letters and cassettes from relatives and providing intelligence and logistic support. Following the ceasefire there were sporadic demonstrations in the territory by Saharawis who were literally risking their lives to speak in support of independence. There arose a number of key activists such as Aminatou Haidar, who, despite being imprisoned for years and tortured, continued pro-independence activities.

However, large scale demonstrations in the territory did not begin until September of 1999, when a series of unprecedented uprisings marked the beginning

---

[178] Amnesty International reported in 1981 that it could "confirm the 'disappearance' of approximately 100 individuals from towns in southern Morocco since 1975, "in the context of the dispute over Western Sahara" and that "this figure probably substantially underestimates the true number of individuals taken into custody in this region by the Moroccan security forces whose arrests have not been officially admitted by the authorities." *Report of an Amnesty International Mission to the Kingdom of Morocco*, February 10–13, 1981 (Amnesty International, London 1982), p.42. Reported in Hodges, *supra*, at 282–283.

[179] Y. Zoubir, *Geopolitics and Realpolitik as Impediments to the Resolution of Conflict and Violations of International Law: the Case of Western Sahara*, in INTERNATIONAL LAW AND THE QUESTION OF WESTERN SAHARA, *supra*, at 282–283.

[180] *See, Keeping It Secret: The U.N. Operation in The Western Sahara*, *supra*, at 27–28.

of what has been referred to as the Saharawi "intifada." By May of 2005 these waves of demonstrations reached their peak, spreading to cities in southern Morocco such as Tan Tan and Assa, and including, besides Saharawis living in Western Sahara, ethnic Saharawis living in southern Morocco. Although this uprising was quickly repressed, sporadic incidents of disobedience, ranging from nightly skirmishes between Saharawi youth and Moroccan police, to protests in secondary level school years, and isolated demonstrations from 2005 to 2010, continued to frustrate the government and served to illustrate the continued support among the Saharawis in Western Sahara for the idea of independence.[181]

In 2010 tensions boiled over when in October an estimated twenty thousand Saharawis amassed more than 6,000 makeshift tents—some of them sewn together from the robes the women were wearing—at a place called Gdeim Izik in the outskirts of Laayoune, to champion independence and protest their treatment at the hands of the Moroccan government. On November 8 the protest was forcefully put down by government forces who bombarded the camp with tear gas and water hoses. Violence escalated as the Saharawis, armed with no more than sticks and stones, attempted to prevent the approach of the advancing troops. Although the government had imposed a total news blackout of the incident, two Spaniards, masquerading as Saharawis,[182] managed to capture the confrontation on a video which they posted on YouTube, and individuals in the camp were able to send messages and pictures of the ensuing carnage via their smartphones. The violence in the camp quickly spilled over into Laayoune, where there were reports of gangs of Moroccan citizens and security forces enacting retribution vigilante style by invading the houses of Saharawis, beating their inhabitants, looting their contents and setting fire to their vehicles.[183] Widespread arrests of Saharawis were made (but no Moroccans), and eleven Moroccan police officers and a number of Saharawis were reportedly killed in the incident. Although this was the last large scale demonstration, smaller protests have continued sporadically throughout the past ten years.

The repression of those who advocated for an independent Western Sahara has not been limited to Saharawis. Indeed, following its occupation of the territory the Moroccan government stifled debate on its policies towards Western Sahara even among its own citizens, making it difficult to gage the depth of public sentiment

---

[181] *See*, S. Zunes & J. Mundy, WESTERN SAHARA: WAR, NATIONALISM, AND CONFLICT IRRESOLUTION, *supra*, Introduction at xxxxii, and 154–155. The authors cited a number of demonstrations not only in the Western Saharan cities of Laayoune, Dakhla and Smara, but in the Moroccan cities of Tan Tan and Assa, and the universities in Agadir, Marrakech, Casablanca, Rabat, and Fez.

[182] Antonio Velazquez and Isabel Terraza. Their video is currently on YouTube.

[183] Human Rights Watch, "Western Sahara: Beatings, Abuse by Moroccan Security Forces," November 26, 2010.

on the subject.[184] As the Moroccan Association of Human Rights (AMDH), in an addendum to a report it issued in 2001, wrote: "As for the problem of Western Sahara raised by the report, international bodies are better able to judge its progress since the Moroccan people do not have the right to express an opinion contrary to the official position; worse still we note continual repression of any opinion contrary to that of the official position…."

Throughout the period of the war, Moroccan officials steadfastly denied that they were engaging in human rights violations. Following the ceasefire, however, King Hassan established the Conseil Consultatif des Droits de l'Homme (CCDH), to examine allegations of illegal detentions and the disappearance of Saharawis and Moroccans, and in 1991, Morocco announced the release of hundreds of political prisoners as a gesture of "good will."[185] However, it was not until 1998 that the King accepted the findings of the CCDH which acknowledged 112 cases of "disappearance," 56 of whom had died in prison, and it was not until Mohammed VI replaced his father on the throne in 1999 that the government formally acknowledged its responsibility for such "disappearances," and attempted to compensate some of its victims.

These measures did not go far enough for the families of many of the imprisoned and "disappeared," a significant number of whom had still not been accounted for,[186] and there were repeated calls for greater transparency and accountability for past and continuing human rights violations on the part of the Moroccan government. Moreover, despite the government's attempt to stem the more horrific abuses, the repression of any opinion on this issue contrary to the official government position continued unabated.

Morocco, for its part, accused the Polisario of its own human rights abuses, alleging that refugees in the camps at Tindouf were being forced to remain against their will and were treated harshly,[187] that the Polisario had exaggerated the number

---

[184] *See,* S. Zunes, *East Timor and Western Sahara: A Comparative Analysis on Prospects for Self-Determination,* in INTERNATIONAL LAW AND THE QUESTION OF WESTERN SAHARA, *supra,* at 117.

[185] According to a State Department report published in 1994, roughly three hundred "disappeared" Saharawis were among those freed, including whole families and some persons missing since 1975. See S. Zunes & J. Mundy, WESTERN SAHARA: WAR, NATIONALISM, AND CONFLICT IRRESOLUTION, *supra,* at 148.

[186] The AFAPREDESA claim that out of 890 "disappeared" Sahrawis, 50 died in custody, 310 have been released, and 526 are still unaccounted for. Amnesty International cited 450 Sahrawis whose fate remained unknown. In 2004 the King created the Equity and Reconciliation Commission whose mandate was to offer specific details about the fate of the hundreds of disappeared persons by 2005. By April of that year the commission had received more than twenty thousand petitions for redress covering acts committed between 1959 and 1999. See S. Zunes & J. Mundy, WESTERN SAHARA: WAR, NATIONALISM AND CONFLICT IRRESOLUTION, *supra,* at 145, 150–151.

[187] See, for instance, *Western Sahara Conflict Traps Refugees in Limbo,* New York Times, June 4, 2008, in which the author, Cara Buckley interviewed several Saharawis who claimed that they had been prevented from leaving the refugee camps at Tindouf. More recently an independent film crew claimed to have evidence that slavery existed in the camps. However, in 2004 Ali Lmrabet, a journalist for the now defunct Moroccan newspaper, *Le Journal*

of refugees in order to profit on the black market from the aid they were given by NGOs,[188] and that the Saharawis in Western Sahara actually wish to have the territory incorporated into Morocco.

In support of the last argument, Morocco points to the number of Saharawis who enjoy prominent positions in the territorial government. For many years the main body for Saharawi representation outside of elected officials was the Conseil Royal Consultatif Pour les Affaires Sahariennes (CORCAS), a council created by King Hassan largely filled by pro-Moroccan tribal leaders. Defunct for a time, it was revived in early 2006. In addition to members of this Council there are a number of Saharawis in elected or appointed government positions throughout the territory. Also claiming to represent Saharawis inside the territory and in the camps are a handful of Polisario defectors. However, those allowed to rise to prominence must swear allegiance to the King, and many are rewarded handsomely for doing so.[189]

Throughout the years a number of prominent international human rights organizations conducted investigations of the allegations of both parties.[190] The reports they issued cited some problems in the refugee camps, but were mostly critical of Morocco. In 2006 the United Nations finally conducted its own investigation: the Office of the United Nations High Commissioner for Human Rights (OHCHR) sent a mission to both Western Sahara and the refugee camps to investigate allegations of restraints on free speech and assembly and other human rights abuses. After interviewing residents and officials in both the Moroccan occupied and Polisario occupied territories, the members of this mission issued a Report to the High Commissioner.[191] In this Report they noted no complaints about violations of the right to freedom of speech or assembly, or any other serious human rights abuses, on the part of residents of the Polisario camps. On the other

---

Hebdomadaire, visited the Polisario camps and wrote articles challenging the Moroccan government's claims about the camps being "prisons.' For this act he was banned from working as a reporter in Morocco for ten years. *See,* S. Zunes & J. Mundy, WESTERN SAHARA: WAR, NATIONALISM, AND CONFLICT IRRESOLUTION, *supra,* at 162. On February 5, 2014 a Moroccan film maker and human rights advocate, Nadir Bouhmouch also wrote an article in *Pambazuka News,* claiming that many of the Moroccan allegations were false.

[188] Jarat Chopra, *United Nations Determination of the Western Sahara Self,* (Oslo: Norwegian Institute of International Affairs, 1994) p. 21, referring to discussions with Moroccan foreign ministry officials, cited in *Keeping It Secret, supra,* at 36, fn 137.

[189] *See,* S. Zunes & J. Mundy, WESTERN SAHARA: WAR, NATIONALISM AND CONFLICT IRRESOLUTION, *supra,* at 157.

[190] Besides the Human Rights Watch Report issued in 1995, there are two reports from Amnesty International issued in 1993: "Continuing Arrests, 'Disappearances' and Restrictions on Freedom of Expression and Movement in Western Sahara" (London) AI Index MDE 29/03/93, February 1993 and "Breaking the Wall of Silence: The Disappeared in Morocco" (London), AI Index MDE 29/01/93, April 1993.

[191] Report of the OHCHR Mission to Western Sahara and the Refugee Camps in Tindouf, May 15–23 and June 19, 2006 (OHCHR Geneva, September 8, 2006)

hand, they cited reliable evidence that Moroccan officials had recently arrested and abused persons in Western Sahara who advocated its independence from Morocco,[192] and had curtailed their freedom to establish associations.[193] Although they refrained from drawing any conclusions about the human rights situation in the Polisario camps,[194] they were not hesitant in drawing conclusions about the situation in the Moroccan territories, noting:

"Overall, the human rights situation is of serious concern, particularly in the Moroccan-administered territory of Western Sahara. Currently, the Sahrawi people are not only denied their right to self-determination, but equally are severely restricted from exercising a series of other rights, and specially rights of particular importance to the very right of self-determination, such as the right to express their views about the issue, to create associations defending their right to self-determination and to hold assemblies to make their views known. In order to comply with its international obligations, particularly under the Covenants on Civil and Political Rights and on Economic, Social and Cultural Rights, serious changes to both legislation as well as government practice on the issue of Western Sahara are required."[195]

Saharawi human rights groups, both within and outside the territory, leant support to these findings.[196]

The members of the mission were also not hesitant in drawing a link between the denial of the right to self-determination and human rights abuses, noting:

"Realization of the right to self-determination of the people of Western Sahara is the responsibility not only of Morocco as administrative authority but also of the international community. Almost all violations of human rights noted above stem from the non-realization of this right, including civil and political rights as

---

[192] In the words of the OHCHR Report: "It has been confirmed in several meetings, both with governmental as well as non-governmental counterparts, that the sovereignty of Morocco over Western Sahara may not be questioned. Such limitations, especially in view of the internationally recognized right of the people of Western Sahara to self-determination, cannot be interpreted as falling with the permissible restrictions under article 19 of the ICCPR...." Report, para. 28.

[193] In the words of the OHCRH Report: "The freedom to establish associations equally has been curtailed in the territory of Western Sahara in significant aspects." Report, para 31.

[194] This was apparently due to a feeling that they lacked the means to carry out an adequate investigation. The conclusion of the Mission was "Despite the level of cooperation extended to the delegation during its visit of some of the camps, it was unable to obtain sufficient information to draw extensive and well-founded conclusions with regard to the de facto enjoyment of human rights by the refugees in the camps. Therefore, serious further inquiries are required." Report, para. 54. The Report did, however, conclude that Algeria had the responsibility of ensuring that the Polisario upheld the requirements of pertinent human rights conventions to which it was a party.

[195] OHCHR Report, para. 53

[196] The Saharawi human rights organization AFAPREDESA has collected and published through the years numerous case histories of "disappeared" and tortured Sahrawi individuals as well as pictures and stories of inhuman conditions faced by Sahrawi prisoners in Moroccan prisons.

well as economic, social and cultural rights of the people of Western Sahara in all locations where they currently reside. In accordance with international obligations with respect to the question of Western Sahara, the international community should take all necessary measures to ensure the right of self-determination of the people of Western Sahara…."[197]

That plea to the international community in 2006 has so far remained unanswered.

According to a number of international human rights organizations, the Saharawis living in Western Sahara have continued to have their political views suppressed by the Moroccan government. As noted previously, in 2010 a mass protest of Saharawis was forcefully put down by government forces, resulting in widespread violence in Laayoune. In August of 2012 a number of human rights experts were sent by the RFK Center for Justice and Human Rights to investigate human rights violations in the Territory and found themselves and those they interviewed harassed by plainclothes police. In their report, "Nowhere to Turn: The Consequences of the Failure to Monitor Human Rights Violations in Western Sahara and the Tindouf Refugee Camps," they noted:

> "There is near-absolute impunity for human rights violations against the Sahrawi people, who live in a state of fear and oppression under the impassive watch of the UN peacekeeping mission. In Moroccan-controlled Western Sahara, the overwhelming presence of security forces, the violations of the right to life, liberty, personal integrity, and freedom of expression, assembly, and association create a state of fear and intimidation that violates the rule of law and respect for human rights of the Sahrawi people."[198]

Most recently, in a military trial conducted by the Moroccan government, a number of Saharawis were convicted of crimes and sentenced to long prison terms for activities related to the 2010 protests. Twenty five of them won a retrial in a civilian court after the Moroccan Court of Cassation on July 27, 2016 quashed their 2013 conviction before a military court. The military court had imposed on 23 of them prison sentences of between 20 years and life. The men, who include a few well-known activists, had been charged with the death of the eleven Moroccan officers. However, the Court of Cassation charged that the military court had failed to investigate allegations that police had tortured or coerced them into signing false

---

[197] OHCHR Report, para. 52.

[198] *Id*, at 3–4.

statements, which were the only concrete pieces of evidence produced against them. Their trial in a civil court was held in January 2017.[199] After expelling the French attorneys who were representing them, and rejecting the evidence they produced, the civil court again imposed harsh sentences upon them.

For over twenty years there have been continuing calls among human rights advocates for an extension of the mandate of the UN's peacekeeping force in the Territory, MINURSO, to report human rights violations.[200] MINURSO has been one of the few UN peacekeeping missions that does not include such monitoring in its mandate. In 2010 and again in 2013, 2015 and 2017 the Association of the Bar of the City of New York wrote to the United Nations Secretary General in support of the expansion of MINURSO's mandate, noting:

> "Throughout the 19 years since the establishment of MINURSO there have been consistent reports of human rights violations…I its 2006 Country Reports on Human Rights Practices in Western Sahara, the United States Department of State acknowledged a number of allegations of human rights abuses in the territory as well as the fact that '[t]he Moroccan government restricted freedom of expression, assembly and association.'…Despite these reports of human rights abuses…MINURSO personnel have been unable to take steps to monitor and report on their existence, because their mandate contains no provisions relating to human rights. This is particularly unfortunate because the United Nations Department of Peacekeeping Operations considers international human rights law to be 'an integral part of the normative framework for United Nations peacekeeping operations'…."

The letter noted that all of the peacekeeping missions initiated within the past decade had included such provisions.

Morocco has opposed such a modification while the Polisario has welcomed it. Largely because of vetoes by the United States and France, the measure has never been endorsed by the Security Council. In May of 2013, Saharawis in Western Sahara cities amassed in large numbers to protest the decision of the United Nations not to expand the mandate of MINURSO to include the monitoring of human rights abuses.

---

[199] Human Rights Watch 2017 World Report, Events in Morocco and Western Sahara.

[200] *See, for instance,* Human Rights Watch Letter to Members of the Security Council, April 14, 2014; Amnesty International Letter to Members of the Security Council, April 24, 2014; RFK Center for Justice and Human Rights Letter to Members of the Security Council, April 24, 2014.

And despite some recent improvements in Morocco's overall human rights policies, abuses have continued, particularly with respect to those who advocate the Saharawis' right to self-determination.

An effective ban was imposed by Morocco in 2015 on research missions by Amnesty International and Human Rights Watch.[201] However this did not prevent the two organizations from publishing reports on the situation in Western Sahara.

According to Eric Goldstein, Deputy Director for the Middle East and North Africa at Human Rights Watch, as of 2017 "overall progress has stagnated." He explained that while Morocco has implemented some positive reforms in many ways the country's human rights situation has deteriorated amid crackdowns on reporters and activists.

In its 2017 World Report, Human Rights Watch noted that "Many persons continued to serve long prison terms after unfair trials for politically motivated offenses. While authorities often tolerated protest demonstrations, in Western Sahara they systematically prevented gatherings supporting self-determination for the contested territory."[202]

And the situation apparently has not improved. Despite the promulgation in 2016 of a new Press and Publications Code which liberalizes somewhat free speech on most topics, according to Human Rights Watch's 2020 World Report, the penal code continues to maintain prison as punishment for speech that "causes harm" to Morocco's "territorial integrity,"—a reference to the speech of those who advocate independence for Western Sahara, or even support the idea of a referendum to decide the issue.

This Report further noted:

"Moroccan authorities systematically prevent gatherings in the Western Sahara supporting Sahrawi self-determination, obstruct the work of some local human rights nongovernmental organizations (NGOs), including by blocking their legal registration, and on occasion beat activists and journalists in their custody and on the streets."

The Report went on to cite the 25 Sahrawi men who were "convicted in unfair trials in 2013 and 2017 for the killing of 11 security force members" during clashes at Gdeim Izik, and noted that the courts "relied almost entirely on their confessions to police to convict them, without seriously investigating claims that the defendants had signed their confessions under torture without being permitted to read them."

And prison often does involve torture. According to a May 19, 2015 report by

---

[201] Human Rights Watch World Report 2017, *supra*.

[202] *Id.*

Amnesty International called *Shadow of Impunity: Morocco and the Western Sahara*, cited by the 2015 U.S. Country Report on Human Rights Practices in Morocco, while torture may no longer be an officially state sanctioned practice "an array of torture techniques are used by Moroccan security forces to extract confessions to crimes, silence activists, and crush dissent." Amnesty International goes on to note "There is a gap between what's on paper and what's in practice."

In 2013 the UN Working Group on Arbitrary Detention visited prisons in Morocco and Western Sahara. The group's report, released in August 2014,[203] stated that in cases related to state security, such as supporters of independence for Western Sahara, there was "a pattern of torture and mistreatment…by the police, in particular agents of the National Surveillance Directorate."

And, as was indicated previously, the courts often turn a blind eye to these abuses, sentencing accused persons to long prison sentences based on scanty evidence—often confessions coerced through torture—and through trials lacking in procedural fairness. The trials of the 25 men put on trial for participating in the Gdeim Izik demonstration are glaring examples of this. On November 25, 2020, the Moroccan Court of Cassation upheld the decision of the Court of Appeals in 2017, thereby affirming sentences for 19 of them ranging from 20 years to life.[204] The statement in the State Department's 2015 U.S. Country Report on Human Rights Practices in Morocco, "The judiciary lacked independence and sometimes denied defendants the right to a fair public trial" is probably an understatement.

According to the 2015 U.S. Country Report on Human Rights Practices in Western Sahara, the "Principal human rights concerns in the territory were governmental restrictions on the civil liberties and political rights of pro-independence advocates, limitations on freedom of speech, press, assembly and association; and the use of arbitrary and prolonged detention to quell dissent."

In March of 2020 the State Department released its 2019 U.S. Country Report on Human Rights Practices in Western Sahara. It noted few changes in the overall situation. In particular it confirmed that the penal code continues to maintain prison as punishment for speech that "causes harm" to Morocco's "territorial integrity," and that the Moroccan government denies official recognition to NGOs that advocate against the government's policy on that issue. It also cited an Amnesty International report that Moroccan authorities routinely reject the registration applicants of Saharawi human rights groups.[205]

---

[203] A/HRC/27/48/Add.5

[204] Western Sahara Resource Watch, November 26, 2020. A description of the trials which led to this decision can be found at Western Sahara Resource Watch, September 8, 2020.

[205] 2019 U.S. Country Report on Human Rights Practices in Western Sahara, Section b.

Today, while Morocco continues to utilize the land and resources of the Territory, the Saharawis in Western Sahara, according to reliable reports, have become second-class citizens and a minority in their own country and subjected to continuous violations of their human rights, particularly their freedom to advocate for a referendum and the independence of Western Sahara.

(b) The Refugees

As noted previously, over 50,000 Sahrawi's fled the Moroccan occupation in 1975–76, and after having been attacked by Moroccan aircraft while in camps within the territory,[206] were permitted by the Algerian government to establish camps near Tindouf, Algeria, a small oasis settlement near the border between Algeria and Western Sahara most noted for its military base.

When they arrived at Tindouf they found themselves at the edge of the *hammada*—a vast and desolate plain extending from eastern Western Sahara to the center of Algeria, devoid of most vegetation except for the occasional acacia tree, where temperatures could rise to over 100 degrees during the summer day and drop to well below zero in the winter night. There was no source of food or water for miles, and most of the arrivals carried few provisions with them.

Rather than succumb to the destitution that has beset other refugees faced with similar obstacles, however, the Saharawis slowly and determinately set about creating an organized and disciplined environment. With initial aid from the Algerian Red Crescent, the UNHCR and other relief agencies, the refugees began to transform their barren landscape into a camp structure that today is considered by many to be a marvel of self-achievement.

The population was initially assigned to one of three separate sub units called *wilayas*, each one named after a town in Western Sahara. After a number of years a fourth was added. In the beginning the inhabitants lived in tents, provided by relief organizations. But over time the refugees built mud brick structures to attach to these tents or to serve as schools, hospitals, or administration buildings. From the very beginning the refugees assumed the responsibility for organizing and maintaining the *wilayas* themselves. While their policy for external affairs, including relations with other states, proceedings at the UN, and the conflict

---

[206] In December of 1975, refugees who had amassed near the tiny enclave of Mudraiga were strafed by Moroccan aircraft, using napalm and white phosphorous bombs, killing or wounding hundreds of women and children. Refugee camps at Guelta Zemmour, Amgala, Tifariti and Bir Lehlou were also attacked by Moroccan forces. Pictures of the aftermath of some of these attacks and the injuries inflicted on the refugees are prominently displayed at the War Museum in the refugee camps and corroborated by numerous refugees located there. These attacks were repeated for several months and led President Boumedienne of Algeria to grant the Polisario permission to utilize grounds near the army base at Tindouf for a refugee camp.

with Morocco, was the domain of the initial leaders of the movement, the day to day management of the camps and distribution of food and other aid was run on an essentially democratic basis through a sophisticated organizational structure. The grassroots level of decision making and management was entrusted to the *hayy*, each one comprising around two hundred tents, and a number of twelve to fifteen person cells called *khaliyah*. The *khaliyahs* were responsible for organizing specific activities, such as dealing with floods and other emergencies, and was the mechanism though which its members would discuss the political or social initiatives that they wished to bring to the attention of the higher officials.

Four *hayys* formed a *dairah* or "district," which had a council composed of elected representatives, ministry representatives, and an elected executive who represented the *dairah* at higher levels. On a yearly basis the six to seven districts within each *wilaya* would hold a Base Congress to elect the *dairah* executive and to assign positions on the local committees. Those committees covered five areas of social life: children's education, health/sanitation, justice, food/provisions, and production/crafts. A Parliament, comprised of elected officials, supervised the overall management of the camps.

Strategic decisions were made at General Congresses, held intermittently when important issues arose. One month before each Congress, Primary Popular Congresses would be held in every local area. Everyone would come to discuss the political and military situation, social and economic problems, and ideological issues, following which representatives to the General Congress would be elected.

Over the years, this structure became increasingly democratic. Initially, most important foreign policy and military decisions, including the day to day operation of the war effort, were not entrusted either to the Parliament or the General Congresses. Rather, they were made by the President and a small group of veteran Polisario leaders who comprised an Executive Committee. However, as the emphasis in the camps began to shift away from the war effort to more political issues, this concentration of power began to erode.

In 1991, after the ceasefire with Morocco, there were calls for greater democracy at the upper echelons of government and laws that would define more clearly the rights and responsibilities of citizens and the type of government that would be established when independence was obtained. The Executive Committee was abolished and replaced with an elected National Secretariat, and a new Constitution was adopted. The Congress also adopted a platform calling explicitly for multiparty democracy and a free market economy following independence. At the next Congress, in 1999, among other things a consultative council of Sheikhs was added to the Parliament, making it a bicameral institution.

Throughout the years residents were able to overcome seemingly impossible obstacles. From the inception of camp life there was an emphasis on education, not only of children, but of the women who had been largely denied access to education when Western Sahara was a Spanish colony. With virtually no funding from outside sources they were able to increase the number of schools in the camps over the years incrementally until today there are six primary schools in each *dariah*, as well as a "women's school," the February 27 School, where adult women are taught to read and write as well as other skills. There are also two national secondary schools for boys and girls, and students have been sent abroad for medical and other training. Due to the emphasis the refugees placed on education, they have attained a literacy rate of nearly 95%—a rate far in excess of that achieved by any of their neighboring states, including Morocco.[207]

Health care improved throughout the years. The first months of the camps witnessed widespread outbreaks of tuberculosis, bronchitis, and dysentery. Epidemics ravaged the camps in 1975 and 1976, killing thousands of children. Due to lack of refrigeration badly needed vaccines were not available. Since then, solar powered generators became available, and vaccines to combat most of these ailments virtually eliminated many of these diseases. Also, a number of Saharawis studied medicine abroad in order to return to the camps and provide medical assistance.

From scratch they were able to draft a comprehensive framework of laws, based for the most part not on *sharia* or the models of their neighboring states, but on Western concepts of secularism, justice and democracy. These laws, including their most recent Constitution, are a reflection of the philosophy that guided the Polisario leadership since its inception. The "program of national action" they adopted as early as 1974 to define their ambitions for an independent Western Sahara, found its genesis in the movements that shaped the politics of other parts of the world during the 60's and 70's. It called for a "fair distribution of resources, to overcome the differences between the countryside and the towns" the provision of adequate housing and health facilities, the incorporation of Arabic in education and the provision of free, compulsory schooling at all levels and for all social layers. There was a strong commitment to the principle of women's emancipation and a democratic form of government.[208]

---

[207] Adult literacy in Morocco was estimated by the UNDP's 2000 Human Development Index to be 47 percent, while literacy among women was pegged at 34 percent. Cited in S. Zunes and J. Mundy, WESTERN SAHARA: WAR, NATIONALISM AND CONFLICT IRRESOLUTION, *supra*, at 52.

[208] *Programme d'action nationale, adopte par le deuxieme congres*, in *Le peuple Saharaoui en lutte* (Polisario Front, 1975), *supra*, at 42. Cited in Hodges, *supra*, at 164.

Their most recently published "Constitution",[209] incorporates these principles. It establishes checks and balances as well as a bill of rights that guarantees freedom of expression,[210] association,[211] and movement as well as the rights of privacy,[212] due process,[213] and equal protection before the law.[214] It also creates a presumption of innocence[215] and contains explicit prohibitions against unlawful detention.[216] It includes guarantees of democracy, private enterprise,[217] religious freedom[218] and laws which uphold the rights of women and minorities,[219] as well as guarantees that every citizen shall have the right to vote in elections and hold office.[220]

But words on paper are cheap unless there is a strong commitment to abide by them. Perhaps the greatest indication of their intention to achieve their goals concerns the status of women in the society they created. The position of women in the camp society is unique in the Moslem and Arab world.[221] Women had

---

[209] The Constitution of the Sahrawi Arab Democratic Republic, Adopted by the 12th Congress of the Frente Polisario, 14–20 December 2007.

[210] Article 30: "Freedom of expression shall be guaranteed and shall be exercised according to the law."

[211] Article 31: "The right to form associations and political parties is recognized and shall be guaranteed after the attainment of independence."

[212] Article 28: The domicile of every citizen shall be inviolable; Access to a citizen's home shall be upon the orders of a competent judicial authority."

[213] Article 27: "Individual freedoms shall be guaranteed by the law. No one shall be denied the exercise of his/her freedom except according to the law."

[214] Article 25: "All Sahrawi citizens shall enjoy the rights and freedoms recognized and guaranteed by the Constitution without any discrimination as to ethnicity, race, colour, gender, language, religion and political or any other opinions." Article 26: "All citizens shall be equal before the law in terms of both protection and sanctions."

[215] Article 27: "Every citizen shall be presumed innocent until proven to the contrary by law.

[216] Article 27: "The right to defence shall be guaranteed including the choice of a legal representative; No one shall be arrested and detained except according to the law; There shall not be any crime or sanction unless prescribed by the law; Preventive detention shall not last more than 72 hours and shall not be extended except on the orders of a competent judiciary body and in conformity with the law."

[217] Article 35: "Private property shall be guaranteed and organized by the law." As Ibrahim Hakim, the SADR's former Minister of Foreign Affairs, remarked in 1977: "The Sahara will be a primary commodity producing country, it is necessary to develop these primary resources and it is obligatory to cooperate with the industrialized countries...If the western companies respect Saharan sovereignty, they will be welcome in the Sahara." Hodges, *supra*, at 343.

[218] Article 44: "Aliens that reside legally in the SADR territory shall be free to practice their religions and customs."

[219] Indeed, as early as in its "program of national action" adopted at its second congress, held in 1974, the Polisario listed its goals as the "creation of a republican, national regime, with the effective participation of the masses," the rejection of distinctions based upon tribal affiliation or caste status, the provision of adequate housing and health facilities, the provision of free, compulsory schooling, and the reestablishment of political and social rights for women. The Constitution adopted by the Polisario sets forth these principles once again. During its period of exile in refugee camps in Tindouf, the Polisario have established a system of democratically elected local officials, boasting a number of women members, and a system of universal education where Saharawi students, including women, are educated to the college level and often beyond.

[220] Article 33: "Every citizen who meets all the required legal conditions shall be eligible to vote and be voted for. Article 34: "Every citizen shall have the right to be a candidate for public office according to the conditions stipulated by the law."

[221] This stems, in part, from the position of responsibility women have traditionally enjoyed in Saharawi society as well as other Bedouin societies. For example, Saharawi women have traditionally had equal rights to men in inheritance

played "a decisive role" in the struggle with Spain, smuggling arms and documents, providing intelligence, using their homes as sanctuaries for activists, selling jewelry to finance the struggle, and encouraging their husbands to take up arms.[222] During the war, women often provided logistics support on the front lines. In addition, one of the most infamous combat leaders during the war, participating in many of the more famous battles, was a nurse turned soldier, known as Sidimi. Since the early days of the camps the women have been the driving force behind government institutions, establishing the schools and hospitals, creating the mechanism for food distribution, liaising with external relief agencies, and essentially running the day to day activities of the camps. During the war the grassroots body of the camps, the annual Base Congress, was almost 90 percent women.[223] The overwhelming majority of the committees established to coordinate camp activities were also composed of women. Women have held governorships at the *wilaya* level and diplomatic posts. More recently, the women in the camps have organized a committee called the National Union of Sahrawi Women, which runs the women's school and addresses the political concerns of the women in the camps. This is one of the three "mass organizations" in the camps, the other two being labor and student groups which were also until recently dominated by women.

The refugee camps administered by these women have been acknowledged by relief organizations to be "superbly organized."[224]

As African specialist George Houser once noted:

"I have visited many refugee camps in Africa over the years, but never have I seen a group of people more self-reliant or better organized. Indeed, I found it impossible to think of them as refugees. They have turned to other countries for food and clothing, to be sure, but politically they are independent of outside control. Their camps are not administered by Algerians, the United Nations, or technicians from other countries—the people have organized themselves according to their own way of life. In the camps I had a feeling I was visiting a nation in exile."[225]

To be sure, the government leaders have faced problems trying to drag a population accustomed to centuries old customs and traditions into the modern

---

and divorce and keep their maiden names following marriage. The Saharawi follow a moderate form of Islam in which marriage is monogamous. Violence against women is rare and considered shameful.

222 *See,* S. Zunes & J. Mundy, WESTERN SAHARA: WAR, NATIONALISM & CONFLICT IRRESOLUTION, *supra,* at 133.

223 *Id.* at 134.

224 See Hodges, *supra,* at 234.

225 Cited in S. Zunes and J. Mundy, WESTERN SAHARA: WAR, NATIONALISM & CONFLICT IRRESOLUTION, *supra,* at 112–113.

age. Some of the more elderly residents of the camps continue some of their ancient traditions despite the introduction of modern laws.[226] However, it is clear that the government is trying its best to eliminate any practices that discriminate among population groups or women, and that it has largely succeeded among the younger members of the society.

Despite their success in taming a hostile environment and introducing democratic principles into the society, however, the fact remains that the inhabitants in the camps are refugees—displaced persons without a country. Although the UN has inaugurated a program to enable the refugees to visit family members in Moroccan controlled Western Sahara, it can only accommodate a small fraction of the residents. By far the majority of the residents of the camps have been cut off from their family members on the other side of the berm for more than 40 years. There are two generations of Saharawis in the camps who have never set foot in their homeland, for whom Western Sahara remains a distant dream, a utopian ideal they can only imagine.

Today, the major problem faced by the refugees is not a hostile physical environment, but increasing unrest over the political stalemate at the UN and other events that have quashed their hopes for the future. There is no indication that their determination to create an independent state in Western Sahara has diminished over the years. Far from it—the years of Moroccan occupation has only seemed to solidify their unwillingness to see themselves ruled by a King in Rabat. Likewise, for the most part the Polisario leadership has been able to maintain its support among the camp residents. However, with the abandonment of the referendum process by the international community, the stalemate in negotiations with Morocco, and the recent decision of the Trump administration to recognize Morocco's sovereignty over the territory, the continuation of this support cannot be guaranteed. In mid-2004 a reform movement within Polisario called Khatt al Shahid, which advocated a more militant policy and new leaders, went public.[227] Its influence intensified after the May 2005 intifada and the 2010 uprisings in Laayoune. Activists within the Saharawi community in Western Sahara have

---

[226] A few years ago an Australian film crew created a documentary in which they alleged that slavery was practiced in the camps. This was based largely on the history of a young black women who was taken to the camps by a white woman when she was an infant. The young woman has vehemently denied that she is a "slave," yet it is true that a form of indentured servitude had been practiced in early times by the Saharawis as well as other population groups in Morocco, Mauritania, Mali and elsewhere in the region, and may still be practiced in parts of Mauritania and Mali. Such practices were specifically condemned by the Polisario in their 1974 national program of action. Likewise, certain marriage customs that discriminate against women had been practiced in the past, but are now prohibited under the SADR's laws.

[227] *See,* S. Zunes & J. Mundy, WESTERN SAHARA: WAR, NATIONALISM AND CONFLICT IRRESOLUTION, *supra,* at 122.

become more vocal, and discontent among the young on both sides of the berm has increased.

In 2016, the long-time President of the SADR, and one of its most illustrious war time heros, Mohammed Abdelaziz, died. He was replaced at the helm by another of the long time Polisario leaders, and its first Minister of Defence, Brahim Ghalli. Now that the ceasefire has been repudiated by the Polisario and fighting has recommenced, it is unclear what direction his policies will take.

Today, while Morocco continues to utilize the land and resources of Western Sahara with impunity, and the international community continues to debate the finer points of international policy over the dispute, discontent among the Saharawis has escalated, both among those reduced to second-class citizens in their own country as well as among the original inhabitants of the territory who remain confined in refugee camps in Algeria waiting to exercise the "right to self determination" they were promised by the international community more than forty years ago.

PART II

Legal Issues—
The Question of Sovereignty

MOROCCO'S REFUSAL TO go ahead with a referendum in the territory on the basis of the Settlement Plan raises several legal questions for the international community. Could Morocco legitimately claim sovereignty over Western Sahara in 1975? If not, could the occupation of Western Sahara by Morocco be sanctioned under any theory of international law? Do the Saharawis have a right to self-determination under international law, and if so, what are the contours of this right? Do the Saharawis have a right, under international law, to see to it that the agreement they reached with Morocco for a referendum as part of the ceasefire negotiated by the United Nations is implemented, and if so, how can such a right be enforced? And perhaps just as importantly, what are the practical and political ramifications of the situation in Western Sahara for United States and other policy makers?

(1) The Legal Basis for Morocco's Occupation of Western Sahara

(a) The Doctrine of Territorial Integrity

The entire basis of Morocco's legal claim to Western Sahara rests on the doctrine of territorial integrity, and its claim that Western Sahara was formerly a part of Morocco and should be re-integrated into it. Indeed, the right of existing states to uphold their territorial integrity stands as an important limitation on the right to self-determination of peoples that exist within the state.[1] The importance that

---

[1] L. Seshagiri, *Democratic Disobedience: Reconceiving Self-Determination and Secession at International Law*, 51 Harv. Int'l L.J. 553 (Summer, 2010) pps. 567–577.

the international community attaches to the protection of a state's territorial integrity is laid out in Article 2 of the United Nations Charter, as well as many other texts.[2] The United Nations has declared that "Any attempt aimed at the partial or total disruption of the national unity and the territorial integrity of a country is incompatible with the purposes and principles of the Charter of the United Nations."[3] Accordingly, it can be deduced that there is no unilateral right *per se* for a people within an established and recognized state to secede from that state,[4] and the international legal recognition of a "state" formed by a population that has attempted to secede unilaterally is the exception, not the rule.[5] As was stated in a report of a Special Rapporteur issued by the UN Economic and Social Council in 1980:

> "The express acceptance in [relevant UN resolutions] of the principles of national unity and the territorial integrity of the State implies non-recognition of the right of secession…The right to secession from an existing State member of the United Nations does not exist as such in the instruments or in the practice followed by the Organization, since to seek to invoke it in order to disrupt the national unity and the territorial integrity of a State would be

---

[2] UN Charter Art. 2, para. 4 ('All Members shall refrain in their international relations from the threat or use of force against the territorial integrity or political independence of any state, or in any other manner inconsistent with the Purposes of the United Nations.'); see also, Declaration on Principles of International Law Concerning Friendly Relations and Cooperation Among States in Accordance with the Charter of the United Nations, art. 1, G.A. Res. 2625 (XXV), Annex, UN GAOR, 25th Sess., Supp. No. 28, at 122, UN Doc. A/8028 (Oct. 24 1970) ('The territorial integrity and political independence of the State are inviolable.")("Declaration on Friendly Relations'); Convention on the Rights and Duties of States art. 11, Dec. 26, 1933, 49 Stat. 3097, 165 L.N.T.S. 19 ('The territory of a state is inviolable.') ("Montevideo Convention"); Declaration on the Rights of Indigenous Peoples, G.A. Res. 61/295, Annex, UN Doc. A/Res/61/295 Oct. 2, 2007) ('Nothing in this Declaration may be interpreted as implying for any State, people, group or person any right to engage in any activity or to perform any act contrary to the Charter of the United Nations or construed as authorizing or encouraging any action which would dismember or impair, totally or in part, the territorial integrity or political unity of sovereign and independent States.') ("Indigenous Peoples Declaration").

[3] *See, e.g.,* G.A. Res. 1514(XV) *supra. See also,* Declaration on Friendly Relations, *supra,* ('Nothing in the foregoing paragraphs shall be construed as authorizing or encouraging any action which would dismember or impair, totally or in part, the territorial integrity or political unity of sovereign and independent States conducting themselves in compliance with the principle of equal rights and self-determination of peoples as described above and thus possessed of a government representing the whole people belonging to the territory without distinction as to race, creed or colour.').

[4] C. Warbrick, *States and Recognition in International Law,* INTERNATIONAL LAW, 217 (Malcolm Evans ed., 2nd ed., 2006) at 227 (State practice resists any claim to a right to secession "leading to statehood against the will of the present sovereign.")

[5] J. Crawford, *State Practice And International Law In Relation To Unilateral Secession,* SELF-DETERMINATION IN INTERNATIONAL LAW: QUEBEC AND LESSONS LEARNED, 31 (Anne F. Bayefsky ed., 2000) at 32 ("Outside the colonial context, the United Nations is extremely reluctant to admit a seceding entity to membership against the wishes of the government of the state from which it has purported to secede.")

a misapplication of the principle of self-determination contrary to the purposes of the United Nations Charter."[6]

Although there are certain instances in which a population within an already existing state may have the right to secede under international law,[7] if Western Sahara had been within the internationally recognized boundaries of Morocco in 1975, Morocco would have a strong argument that its rights under the principle of "territorial integrity" are greater than the rights of the inhabitants of the territory under principles of "self-determination," and that the population does not have the right to "secede" unilaterally.

However, Western Sahara was not within the officially recognized borders of Morocco in 1975 when Morocco sent troops to occupy the territory. Indeed, Western Sahara was not even within the internationally recognized borders of the modern Moroccan state when it was created in 1956. Accordingly, the rights of the Saharawis to self-determination cannot be equated with the rights of a subgroup of a recognized state seeking secession against the will of a state asserting its rights of territorial integrity.

Rather, Morocco's claim to the territory rests on an argument that there were ties between the territory and Morocco in the distant past, and the existence of ties between a territory and a state in the *past* is not always sufficient as a matter of law to support a claim of sovereignty by the state over the territory under the principle of territorial integrity after a number of years have passed, with intervening occupations by other states. The excuse of a *past* connection to establish such "territorial integrity" and to justify the annexation of territory against the will of its inhabitants, has been used on previous occasions—the most recent case being Saddam Hussein's excuse for invading Kuwait—and has normally met with the distain of legal scholars and the firm rejection by other governments. As a philosophical principle it suffers from the fact that different governments·can rely upon the principle to justify the annexation of the same territory depending upon

---

6 UN Econ. & Soc. Council [ECOSOC], Sub-Comm. on Prevention of Discrimination & Prot. of Minorities, "The Right to Self-Determination, Implementation of United Nations Resolutions," at 90. UN Doc. E/CN.4/Sub.2/405/ Rev.1 (1980) (prepared by G. Espiell, Special Rapporteur).

7 International law has carved out an exception to the general denial of the right of unilateral secession when a population is "oppressed." The availability of secession when there is evidence of oppression is based on a principle known as the remedial rights theory. *See,* A. Cassese, INTERNATIONAL LAW (2d ed. 2005) at 119 (arguing that right to external self-determination might be appropriate where the central government persistently denies a people political participatory rights, grossly and systematically violates their fundamental human rights, and denies the peaceful settlement of any disputes through the institutions of the central state). The secessionist revolutions that led to the independence of Bangladesh from Pakistan and the formation of new states from the former Yugoslavia (the republics of Slovenia, Croatia, Bosnia and Herzegovina, and Macedonia) and most recently the Republic of South Sudan, are arguably a recognition of the right to external determination of peoples consistently denied the right to effectively participate in their self-governance.

how far back in time scholars are willing to go,[8] and that it is difficult to justify the annexation of a territory over an unwilling population on the basis of what happened two hundred or more years prior. It is a principle that, if accepted by the international community, "would inevitably lead to greater, rather than fewer, conflicts over international boundaries."[9]

For that reason, theories of annexation of territories based on historic ties have usually yielded under principles of international law to the theory that peoples inhabiting a defined territory have a right to determine their own future—the principle of "self-determination."

Of course there have been certain instances in which evidence of historic ties has been used to buttress a claim of sovereignty over a territory. One such instance was the case heavily relied upon by Morocco in its arguments before the International Court of Justice: the case of *The Legal Status of Greenland*.[10] In that case the Court was asked to determine whether Denmark or Norway had the right to claim a swath of land in Greenland that extended to the North Pole. Denmark claimed that because of its historic ties with certain settlements in Greenland, it had the right to claim the territory that constituted the hinterland. The Court agreed. However, at issue in that case was a territory considered *terra nullus* or "no-man's land" where there were no conflicting claims of indigenous peoples, and the question was which of two competing colonial powers should be able to claim it. This was a far cry from the situation presented by Western Sahara, where the court specifically found that the territory was *not* "terra nullus", but rather, inhabited by people who had certain rights under international law. The existence of historic ties to a territory by a colonial power has seldom been

---

[8] For instance, the Algerian justice minister in 1976 observed: "Does Morocco demand the Sahara because some Moroccan traders transited through it to buy gold and slaves in what was then called the 'Soudan'? In this hypothesis, the Sahrawis have the right to demand Morocco and Spain because their ancestors the Almoravids departed from this territory in the eleventh century to spread their authority over the whole region and Andalucia." Bouale Be Hamouda, *La question du Sahara occidental et le droit international* (Algiers, 1976), p. 12; cited by Hodges, *supra*, at 195. Likewise, since prior to 1145 (the date when Sultan Abd el Moumen definitively broke off relations with the Calif of Baghdad) the Calif ruled over Moroccan lands, under Morocco's argument Iraq can legitimately claim Morocco as part of its territory. Indeed, following Morocco's argument to its logical conclusion the states of the Persian Gulf would cease to have the right to exist. Although delimiting national boundaries in tribal areas is difficult, and the boundaries drawn by Western colonialists in Africa and the Middle East can be criticized on many fronts, national boundaries needed to be created if modern day nation states were to emerge, and the creation of a boundary to establish the territory of Western Sahara is no less logical than any other drawn on the map of Africa.

[9] As Professor Thomas M. Franck noted in *The Stealing of the Sahara, supra*, at 698: "This paramountcy of contemporary self-determination over historic claims and the alleviation of ancient wrongs is based on two considerations. First, there is the assumption that any other approach would lead to endless conflicts, as modern states found themselves under pressure to join a general reversionary march backward to a *status quo ante* of uncertain age and validity. Second, it is widely observed that states or even colonies with established boundaries and fixed populations, however unjustly or serendipitously arrived at, soon develop a cohesive logic of their own that should not be lightly overridden."

[10] 1933 P.C.I.J. (ser. A/B) No. 53 at 7.

considered sufficient by the Court to negate the rights of indigenous peoples under international law.

The theory of "integration" has also be used at times to permit the re-integration of lands that had been part of a state in previous times, and at least one author has argued that the right to self-determination for people inhabiting non-self-governing territories, at least in certain circumstances, may be circumscribed by the principle of integration.[11] However, integration has historically been deemed relevant only to tiny territories ethnically and economically parasites of, or deriving from the state that wishes to integrate it,[12] and the principle is not considered by most scholars applicable to larger, more viable territories such as Western Sahara.

Indeed, the International Court of Justice in its Advisory Opinion on Western Sahara noted that:

"The validity of the principle of self-determination, defined as the need to pay regard to the freely expressed will of peoples, is not affected by the fact that in certain cases the General Assembly has dispensed with the requirement of consulting the inhabitants of a given territory. Those instances were based either on the consideration that a certain population did not constitute a "people" entitled to self-determination or on the conviction that consultation was totally unnecessary, in view of special circumstances."[13]

No such "special circumstances" were found to exist with respect to Western Sahara. The Court specifically refused to consider as precedent for the course that should be followed with respect to Western Sahara the fact that the small enclave of Ifni had been retroceded to Morocco without a referendum to ascertain the wishes of its people.[14] In comparing the different ways in which the General

---

[11] See, A. Rigo-Sureda, THE EVOLUTION OF THE RIGHT OF SELF-DETERMINATION: A STUDY OF THE UNITED NATIONS PRACTICE (Leyden, 1973) at 214–20.

[12] An example of the application of this theory might be Hong Kong and its integration with China.

[13] *Advisory Opinion on Western Sahara*, para. 59.

[14] As noted previously, Ifni, a small enclave that was surrounded by Morocco on all sides, was deemed to be one of the "special cases" referred to by the Court in which the "colonial enclave" theory may be invoked. The "colonial enclave" theory declares that legal ties between an enclave and a geographically contiguous entity can exist if, at the onset of colonial occupation, the two territories shared a common political system and a cultural identity. *See*, Laurence Hanaur, in "The Irrelevance of Self-Determination Law to Ethno-National Conflict: A New Look at the Western Sahara Case," 9 Emory Int'l L. Rev. 133 (1995) at 150, fn. 55 ("Hanaur"). The General Assembly had concluded that because of its small and "parasitic" nature, and the circumstances under which it had been ceded initially by Morocco to Spain, Ifni could be retroceded to Morocco without the need for an exercise of self-determination of the indigenous people through a referendum. This principle was also applied to the British colony of Gibraltar and the Portuguese colony of Goa. Some scholars have suggested that this practice violates the principle of self-determination as it has developed and should be discontinued. *See*, Hanauer, *supra*: "no territory should be deprived of its right to choose independence…whatever the circumstances…[A]t the time the people choose their new status…their choice must be unrestricted, and they may choose independence if they prefer, however small and poor their territory may be." Citing the United Nations Institute for Training and Research, "Status And Problems Of Very Small States And Territories," UNITAR Series No. 3, at 15, 19, UN Doc. JC/365/U6 (1969).

Assembly Resolutions from 1966 to 1969 dealt with the two regions, the Court noted that in Resolution 2229 (XXI) the General Assembly requested Spain "to take immediately the necessary steps to accelerate the decolonization of Ifni and to determine with the Government of Morocco, bearing in mind the aspirations of the indigenous population, procedures for the transfer of powers in accordance with the provisions of General Assembly Resolution 1514 (XV)" whereas it requested Spain "to determine at the earliest possible date...the procedures for the holding of a referendum under United Nations auspices with a view to enabling the indigenous population of [Western Sahara] to exercise freely its right to self-determination...." The Court noted that the different policies the General Assembly had applied to the two territories reflected "the difference in nature of the legal status" of the territories, and were noted in each successive Resolution concerning them until Ifni was retroceded to Morocco in 1969. The Court also noted that Morocco had "assented to the holding of a referendum" for Western Sahara. Based upon these considerations, the Court found no justification for applying the precedent of Ifni to the decolonization of Western Sahara.

The *Greenland* and *Western Sahara* cases illustrate how difficult it is for states to gain sovereignty over territory inhabited by an unwilling populace upon a claim of historic ties. Indeed, the emergence of the right to self-determination of peoples in non-self-governing territories has fundamentally altered the concept of sovereignty as it had developed previously. As was noted by Professor Thomas Franck in his separate concurring opinion in the International Court of Justice *Case Concerning Sovereignty over Pulau Ligitan and Pulau Sipadan (Indonesia v. Malaysia) Application by the Philippines for Permission to Intervene,* (Judgment of October 23, 2001):

> "The point of law is quite simple, but ultimately basic to the international rule of law. It is this: historic title, no matter how persuasively claimed on the basis of old legal instruments and exercises of authority, cannot—except in the most extraordinary circumstances—prevail in law over the rights of non-self-governing people to claim independence and establish their sovereignty through the exercise of bona fide self-determination."[15]

Professor Franck went on to elaborate:

> "Under traditional international law, the right to territory was vested exclusively in rulers of States. Lands were the property of

---

[15] at 652.

a sovereign to be defended or conveyed in accordance with the laws relevant to the recognition, exercise, and transfer of sovereign domain. In order to judicially determine a claim to territorial title *erga omnes,* it was necessary to engage with the forms of international conveyancing, tracing historic title through to a critical date or dates to determine which State exercised territorial sovereignty at that point in time. Under modern international law, however, the enquiry must necessarily be broader, particularly in the context of decolonization. In particular, the infusion of the concept of the rights of a "people" into this traditional legal scheme, notably the right of peoples to self-determination, fundamentally alters the significance of historic title to the determination of sovereign title.... Against [the exercise of self-determination] historic claims and feudal pre-colonial titles are mere relics of another international legal era, one that ended with the setting of the sun on the age of colonial imperium."[16]

In conclusion, although there would have been legitimate legal questions over whether the right to self-determination existed for the inhabitants of Western Sahara had Western Sahara been a recognized part of Morocco in 1975,[17] this was not the case. Rather, Western Sahara had for many years been a colony of Spain, and as such deserved the treatment accorded by the international community to other non-self-governing territories. With respect to such non-self-governing territories, the principle that the boundaries established by Western colonial powers should be respected[18] and the population granted the right to determine their

---

[16] at 655–658.

[17] Legal scholars have for the most part rejected theories of sovereignty based upon ethnic and historic claims when they would conflict with already established national borders for very practical reasons. As was noted by S. James Anaya:

"[I]f international law were to fully embrace ethnic autonomy claims on the basis of the historical sovereignty approach, the number of potential challenges to existing state boundaries, along with the likely uncertainties of having to assess competing sovereignty claims over time, could bring the international system into a condition of legal flux and make international law an agent of instability rather than stability."

"The Right to Self-Determination: Historical and Current Development on the Basis of United Nations Instruments" (Aurelie Cristescu, Special Rapporteur), UN Doc. E/CN.4/Sub.2/404/Rev.1 (1981), para. 682.

[18] Chapters XI and XII establish this right for "*territories* whose peoples have not yet attained a full measure of self-government." UN Charter Art. 76(b). Resolution 1514 likewise states: "Any attempt aimed at the partial or total disruption of the national unity and the territorial integrity of a country is incompatible with the purposes and principles of the Charter of the United Nations." G.A. Res. 1514, UN GAOR, 15th Sess., Supp. No. 16, UN Doc. A/4684 (1980) para. 6. Hanaur, *supra,* at 142 suggests that "Territorial requirements functioned as an attempt to outlaw secession of minority groups from established states while ensuring that colonies and other territorially distinct entities would be considered worthy of extra protections and rights in the international system." *See also,* Patrick Thornberry, *Self-Determination, Minorities, Human Rights: A Review of International Instruments,* 38 Int'l & Comp. L.

political future—implemented traditionally by a plebiscite[19]—have been building blocks of public international law for over a half century.[20]

We need not dwell too long on this issue, however, because, as will be seen from the following discussion, Morocco did not exercise sovereignty over the territory of Western Sahara prior to the Spanish rule—a fact confirmed by the decision of the International Court of Justice in 1975.

(b) The Historic Ties between Morocco and the Territory of Western Sahara

Since much of the dispute over Western Sahara centers upon Morocco's claim to historic ties with the territory prior to the period of Spanish colonization, it is important to understand something of the history and culture of the region during that period. As was noted previously, before there were modern day "states" in North Africa the indigenous population of most of the interior of North Africa lived in nomadic or semi-nomadic tribal units that migrated seasonally within loosely defined and often overlapping territories. The geography of the area dictated much of its political history. A natural escarpment extending along most of the present day border between Western Sahara and Morocco, provided a natural barrier, and this barrier, along with the harsh environment of the vast Saharan desert, served to inhibit interaction between the people who inhabited the desert and their northern neighbors for most of their history.

The region of the desert that bordered the Atlantic coast—the area which roughly corresponds to the territory of Western Sahara—was known as the "sahel" and its inhabitants were known as the *ahel es-Sahel*.[21] According to some scholars,

---

Q. 867 (1989) at 872–73; Thomas M. Franck and Paul Hoffman, *The Right of Self-Determination in Very Small Places*, 8 N.Y.U. J. Int'l L. & Pol. 331 (1976) at 370 (paragraph six of Resolution 1514 was specifically designed to apply only to colonies so as to prevent the legalization of internal secession). Despite the well recognized idiosyncrasies of boundaries established by colonial powers both the OAU (now the AU) and the UN have consistently maintained a position that these boundaries should be respected in the decolonization process and in most other circumstances. Professor Franck summarized the position of the United Nations and the AU as follows: "If a territory wishes to join with one or several neighboring states, it should have the right to manifest that preference in the process of decolonization, but it must be the free choice of the majority in that particular colony, and a territory with recognized boundaries may neither be absorbed nor dismembered against the will of its inhabitants." Franck, T., *The Stealing of the Sahara, supra*, at 698.

[19] As Franck has noted after citing precedents in over a dozen cases: "[T]here has also grown up through the vast majority of cases a clear pattern of orderly decolonization through freely conducted elections or plebiscites, often under UN supervision, in which the local population has had the opportunity to choose its own national destiny." Franck, T., *The Stealing of the Sahara, supra*, at 701.

[20] See, for instance, Hanauer, *supra*, at 152 (collectively resolutions of the United Nations establishing norms of self-determination in the context of decolonialization have risen to the status of customary international law); Robert T. Vance, Jr., *Recognition as an Affirmative Step in the Decolonization Process: The Case of Western Sahara*, 7 Yale J. World Pub. Ord. 45 (1980–1981) ("The right of colonial peoples to self-determination is a widely accepted norm of customary international law.").

[21] *Id.* at 8–9.

because of certain cultural and linguistic differences with the Berber tribes to the north and south, the tribes of the *ahel es-Sahel* considered themselves to be a distinct cultural group within the Moorish tribes.[22] However, during this period they did not consider themselves to be a separate *nation*: the concept of a modern day "state" encompassing fixed geographic borders and joining together tribes on a long term basis for common goals was, until the 20th century, unknown.

Those who are familiar with the history of the Arabian peninsula will note certain parallels. As with the Arabian peninsula, the dominant social and political unit was the tribe and, as was the case with the Arabian peninsula, there was superimposed above this tribal framework a layer of dominance by religious figures and figures given some religious, political and legal authority because of Islam. In the case of the Arabian peninsula it was the Caliphs of Baghdad and the Hashemite rulers who traced their ancestry to Mohammed. In the case of North Africa it was the Sultan of the Alawite dynasty in present day Morocco.

The Alawites, who arrived from Arabia sometime in the 13th century, claimed to be descended from the family of Mohammed.[23] When they arrived in the area that constitutes present day Morocco they found a tribal society of mixed Berber and Arab ancestry that had already been converted to Islam and ruled by a succession of leaders claiming religious as well as temporal authority. Unlike the dynasties that had previously ruled Morocco,[24] however, they were formally invited by the people of Fez to come to the capital and take over the throne. The first Alawite ruler, Moulay Rachid, ascended the throne in 1666 and founded a dynasty that was to survive to the present day.[25] The Alawite rulers, like "sultans"

---

[22] The cultural divide between the tribes who spoke Hassania and those who spoke either Berber or Moroccan Arabic was noted as well by the French writer Robert Montague and cited in the materials submitted by Spain to the International Court of Justice in the *Western Sahara Case*. See, Marc Robert Thomas, "Sahara et Communaute," Paris, 1960, extracts pps. 31–34, cited in ICJ Documents, Vol. I, pps. 329–331. The tribal nature of Western Saharan society linked by common linguistic and cultural ties persisted well into the 20th century. The visiting mission of the United Nations sent in 1975 to report on conditions in the territory reported as follows:

> "[The] indigenous population of the Territory is comprised for the most part of persons of Moorish, or Bedouin, race who are united by a common language *hassania* (a form of Arabic), and by strong cultural and traditional ties…[T]he basic social unit, the family, is not thought of as an independent group, but rather as forming a part of a social group (fraction), and family group (subfraction) of a tribe…in most cases extending far beyond the political frontiers of the Territory…This is in conformity with age-old tradition by which the various tribal groups have nomadized over wide-ranging areas without any regard to the political boundaries imposed by colonial regimes…." *See,* The UN Mission Report, *supra,* at 26.

[23] The Alawite dynasty took power from the Saadi dynasty in the mid 17th century. Both claimed descent from Mohammed through Ali and his daughter Fatima.

[24] The Alawites were preceded by the Almohads who themselves were preceded by the Almoravides and the Idrissids. The first Arab invasions of North Africa took place in the 7th century under the Umayed leader Oqba Ben Nafi.

[25] The present King of Morocco, Mohammed VI, is the 18th ruler in the Alawite dynasty. Following the Second World War the title of the ruler of Morocco was changed from "Sultan" to "King."

in other parts of the Moslem world, assumed both the moral and spiritual authority granted to rulers under the Koran.[26]

In the centuries following the establishment of Alawite rule the Sultans became the most prominent religious and political figures in Northwest Africa, and it is clear that the tribes of Western Sahara, which had converted to the Muslim faith when they intermarried with the Beni Hassan, granted the rulers of Morocco some deference as spiritual leaders. There is also evidence that certain of the tribal leaders of Western Sahara for certain periods of time formed political allegiances with the Sultan, at least with respect to common goals.[27] However, as several commentators have noted, Morocco, itself, was not a nation state in the Western sense until the 20th century. Before that it, too, was a "mosaic of tribes" which, according to most historians, was only "loosely ruled by the Sultan's government, the *makhzen*".[28] The regions within present day Morocco which were under the Sultan's direct administration, primarily the plains and the towns, were known as the *bilad el-makhzen*, the "government lands," while the regions within Morocco that were beyond the sultan's control, usually regions of difficult access such as the mountains of the Rif and the three Atlas ranges, were known as the *bilad es-siba*, the "lands of dissidence."[29]

Evidence suggests that during Morocco's pre 20th century history the Sultans were for the most part struggling to consolidate their power over the regions that form present day Morocco, and that intervention in the distant Sahara was for the most part limited to efforts to secure control over the oases that were strategic for the trade caravans across the desert to Morocco from present day Mali and points further south.[30] Moreover, certain commentators have maintained that control

---

[26] The Turkmen chief, Mahmud of Gazna (998–1030) was probably the first to carry the title. Later it was adopted by the Seljuq, the Mamluke and the Ottoman rulers.

[27] As Hodges noted "These nomads may have held the Moroccan sultans in awe, as the most powerful rulers in the Maghreb, or respected their claim to the guardianship of western Islam as *amir al-muminin* (commander of the faithful), a title first taken by the Almohad sultans in the twelfth century. Some nomadic tribes briefly struck up alliances with a Moroccan ruler, by agreeing perhaps to help him achieve his strategic or commercial objectives in the Sahara in return for booty or assistance against tribal enemies. On a few occasions a tribe might even find it wise or opportune to declare its allegiance (*bayaa*) to the sultan, who, in return, might issue a royal decree (*dahir*) naming the tribe's leader as an official *caid*. However, such *dahirs* would never do more than give royal endorsement to independently established leaders; and pledges of allegiance to the sultan were both exceedingly rare and of very little and shortlived practical significance." Hodges, *supra*, at 26.

[28] *Id*. at 25.

[29] *Id*.

[30] This was certainly the claim of Spain in documents it submitted to the International Court of Justice in the *Western Sahara Case*. Spain maintained that there was a "striking absence" of any documentary evidence or other traces of a display of political authority by Morocco with respect to Western Sahara. It rejected the notion that Morocco appointed *caids* in the territory. It claimed, moreover, that Sheikh Ma al-Ainen "exercised his authority...in complete independence of the Sultan" and only aligned himself with the Sultan for their common interest in order to resist French expansion. *See, Advisory Opinion on Western Sahara, supra*, para. 100, p. 38. Spain further alleged "the absence

even over these oases was intermittent at best,[31] and as one writer pointed out, "in the swath of desert encompassing modern day Western Sahara...there were neither significant oases nor settlements of any kind except at Tindouf"[32]—which is in present day Algeria.

Taxation is usually considered an important index of a ruler's authority and historians have noted a distinction during this period between those tribes who were taxed in this period by the Sultan (*bled makhzen*) and those who were not (*bled siba*). Although Morocco, in documents it presented to the International Court of Justice, claimed that the line of demarcation was not geographic,[33] other commentators have suggested that the tribes, or subfractions of tribes, which inhabited Western Sahara belonged almost exclusively to the later category.[34]

Morocco maintained in its case before the International Court of Justice that the tribes of the region of present day Western Sahara paid tribute to the tribes of Morocco proper during this period,[35] and always recognized the Moroccan Sultan as their temporal as well as spiritual leader.[36] However, Spain,[37] as well as a number of historians, have suggested that the Sultan's actual control over the roaming Bedouin tribes of the region was superficial and intermittent, at best. "No attempt was ever made by even the strongest of the Moroccan rulers to administer or tax these tribes, or to halt their incessant intertribal raiding," Hodges noted, "and to have attempted to do so would have been utterly utopian, if only because

of any evidence of the payment of taxes by tribes of Western Sahara" and argued that the Sultan's expeditions of 1882 and 1886 never reached Western Sahara, and denied the unity of the Saharan region with the regions of southern Morocco. *See, Advisory Opinion on Western Sahara, supra,* para. 101, p. 38. These views were ultimately accepted by the Court. *Id,* paras. 103 et seq.

[31] As Hodges noted: "At time, governors and *caids* were appointed by the sultans to administer such strategic areas as the Noun and Touat, and garrisons would be posted there; but there were other periods, often lasting several decades or even a century, when the sultans were too weak to exercise direct control over these remote oasis regions, which accordingly became parts of the *bilad es-siba* like the Atlas and Rif mountains." Hodges, *supra,* at 26.

[32] *Id.,* at 26

[33] ICJ Documents, Vol. III, p. 180. According to these documents, the ties which existed between the tribes and the Moroccan sovereign were not comparable to "European models" but constituted a "pyramidal structure of personal allegiance" perfectly adapted to tribal realities.

[34] Indeed, Spain claimed in documents it submitted to the International Court of Justice in the *Western Sahara Case,* that the Sultan was not even able to impose taxes on the tribes living in the south of present day Morocco. *See, Advisory Opinion on Western Sahara, supra,* para. 101, p. 38.

[35] Morocco cited in the documents it presented to the ICJ a number of instances of intermarriage between members of the southern and northern tribes and periods in which each established dynastic superiority. It also argued that the tribes which inhabited the regions which now constitute Western Sahara and Mauritania paid tribute to the Tekna tribes of Morocco, which in turn had declared their allegiance to the Sultan. *See,* ICJ Documents in the *Western Sahara Case,* Vol. III, pps. 182–184.

[36] According to Morocco, the "profound unity" which existed between the North and the South of Morocco was not affected by the structure of the ancient Moroccan state and its apparent division into the *makhzen* and *siba* regions. With regard to this "Western Sahara always accepted its integration into the area ruled by the Moroccan Sultan [*le cadre etatique cherifien*]." ICJ Documents in the *Western Sahara Case,* Vol. III, p. 177 (*translated from the French*).

[37] *Advisory Opinion on Western Sahara, supra,* paras. 100–101, p. 38.

the nomads were constantly on the move, scattered in small groups over enormous, distant tracts of exceedingly inhospitable territory."[38]

Hodges cites evidence that even Moulay Ismail (1672–1727), the second sultan in the Alawite dynasty who is widely considered to be the Moroccan ruler who played the most prominent role in the Sahara, held little *de facto* power over the tribes of the region. Records indicate that in 1677, after five years of war, he had succeeded in consolidating his power over most of present day Morocco and turned his attention southward. In order to obtain additional recruits for his army and to consolidate his power over the trans-Saharan trade routes he began a series of expeditions through present day Western Sahara into Mauritania where he forged alliances with some of the stronger Beni Hassan tribes in that region. However, according to Hodges, the sultan's interest in the region was largely limited and strategic: he never attempted to control politically or economically the territory south of Morocco and his brief and infrequent contacts with the indigenous population had "almost no impact at all on the region now constituting Western Sahara."[39]

Documents presented to the International Court of Justice suggest that Moulay Ismail's successor, Mohammed Ben Abdallah, admitted that he lacked *de facto* power even in the southern regions of Morocco, north of present day Western Sahara. In the first official document relied upon by Morocco in claiming rights to the Territory—the treaty of 1767 between King Carlos III of Spain and Morocco establishing a Spanish fishing station on the Moroccan coast opposite the Canary Islands—the Sultan warned the inhabitants of the Canaries against any fishing expedition to the coasts of "Oued Noun and beyond" and avoided responsibility for the way they may be treated by the inhabitants of that region, "to whom it is difficult to apply decisions, since they have no fixed residence, travel as they wish and pitch their tents where they choose."[40] The Sultan wrote a letter to the Spanish king informing him that the inhabitants of that region "are neither subordinate to nor fearful of anyone, because they are greatly separated from my dominions and I do not have power over them," and that they "have no fixed abode and move around as it pleases them without submitting to government or any authority."[41]

---

[38] Hodges, *supra*, at 26

[39] *Id.*, at 30

[40] Article 18 of the Treaty of Marrakech of 1767, mentioned by Hodges, *supra*, at 31 (citing the *Advisory Opinion on Western Sahara* at 50). The text referred to above is the English translation of Morocco's French version of the Arabic text. The Spanish version of Article 18 reads: "His Imperial Majesty refrains from expressing an opinion with regard to the trading post which His Catholic Majesty wishes to establish to the south of the Noun River, since he cannot take responsibility for accidents and misfortunes, because his domination (*sus dominios*) does not extend so far...." Hodges, *supra*, at 38, n. 31 (citing the *Advisory Opinion on Western Sahara* at 50).

[41] Hodges, *supra*, at 31, citing the Letter of Moulay Mohamed Ben Abdallah, Sultan of Morocco, to Carlos III, King of Spain, 1 moharrem 1181, in *Legajo 4310, Archivo Historico Nacional de Madrid.*

While succeeding Sultans had sporadic success in exerting dominion over the Bedouin tribes north of the Noun, in present day Morocco, there are indications that none of them succeeded in controlling for any length of time the tribes south of the Noun, in present day Western Sahara. Moulay Hassan, who ruled in the mid 19th century, managed to extend the *makhzen's* administration to the regions of the *bilal es siba* on the fringes of his empire in present day Morocco, but records submitted by Spain to the International Court of Justice during the *Western Sahara Case,* suggest that he was unable to bring the nomads of the desert south of the Noun even nominally under his authority.[42] According to historians he sent agents to Mauritania in an attempt to induce the emirs of Trarza, Adrar, Taagant and Brakna to recognize his authority, but none were willing to do so. Neither did the Reguibat, by then the largest of the Western Sahara tribes, or the main nomadic Tekna tribes to the south of the Noun, the Izarguien, Ait Lahsen and Yagout.[43]

Some Moroccan historians have drawn a distinction between *dominion* and *sovereignty* over Western Sahara, arguing that the Sultan had always had sovereignty (i.e., *de jure* rights) over the territory although not necessary *de facto* dominion.[44] However, other historians have claimed that in the 1799 Treaty of Mequinez, Sultan Moulay Suleiman admitted that he did not even have *de jure* sovereignty over these lands, referring to the peoples who occupied the lands south of the "Noun" river (in present day southern Morocco) as "the inhabitants of those lands" rather than his subjects.[45] Historians draw similar conclusions from Article 12 of the 1856 Anglo-Moroccan Free Trade Agreement and from the Spanish-Moroccan one of 1861.[46]

---

[42] *Advisory Opinion on Western Sahara, supra,* paras. 100–101, p. 38.

[43] Hodges, *supra,* at 25–36. Prior to Hassan's rule various treaties between his predecessor, Moulay Suleiman, who ruled Morocco from 1792 to 1822, and maritime powers such as Spain, Britain and the United States, often contained so-called "shipwreck clauses" obligating the Sultan to help save and protect to the best of his ability, sailors shipwrecked along the coast of present day southern Morocco and Western Sahara. However, the Sultan recognized in these Treaties that he did not "exercise his domination" over the region of Western Sahara and could only implement such clauses by negotiating the release of such seamen upon the payment of a ransom. *See,* Hodges, *supra,* at 31.

[44] *See,* Rachid Lazrak, *Le contentieux Territorial entre le Maroc et l'Espagne,* Dar el Kitab, Casablanca, 1974, at 39 ff., cited in Jose Ignacio Alguero Cuervo, *The Ancient History of Western Sahara and the Spanish Colonisation of the Territory,* INTERNATIONAL LAW AND THE QUESTION OF WESTERN SAHARA, *supra,* at 26, fn. 1. This was also one of the arguments presented by Morocco in the 1975 Advisory Opinion procedure before the International Court of Justice. *See, Advisory Opinion on Western Sahara, supra,* at 12 ff.

[45] *See,* Jose Ignacio Alguero Cuervo, *The Ancient History of Western Sahara and the Spanish Colonisation of the Territory,* INTERNATIONAL LAW AND THE QUESTION OF WESTERN SAHARA, *supra,* at 26, fn. 24. It should be noted, however, that Morocco claimed in its submissions to the International Court of Justice that these words do not comport with the Arabic text.

[46] Indeed, the only treaty that would tend to support Morocco's claim is the Anglo-Moroccan Agreement of March 1885, which implied British recognition of the Sultan's authority over the stretch of coast between the Draa River and Cape Bojador. However, some historians have suggested that the only reason the British recognized this authority was to have someone to claim compensation from in the event British companies were prevented from trading along this coast.

From these various historical accounts the most that can be deduced is that when the Spanish colonized Western Sahara in the late 19[47]th century, they found a nomadic society based on tribal loyalty and tribal rivalry, in which the concept of unity into a "state" in the Western sense was lacking. The political ties among the indigenous tribes were superficial and intermittent. The political ties between these individual tribes and the Sultan of Morocco were even more superficial, intermittent and largely ceremonial, and the political ties between these tribes as a *group* and the Sultan were nonexistent.

Although the proponents of the "Greater Morocco" theory have pointed, legitimately, to a number of intertwining relationships between some of the inhabitants of Western Sahara and succeeding Moroccan governments throughout the past five hundred years,[48] and there can be no doubt of the Sultan's importance as a religious figure during this period, it is fair to say that the evidence as a whole does not suggest the existence of a consistent relationship of ruler and subject over important temporal areas at any time during this period.

This, at least, was the conclusion of the International Court of Justice in 1975 when the issue was put before it in the *Western Sahara Case*.[49]

---

[47] Despite the existence of earlier contacts between Spain and the territory which reached as far back as the 15th century, Spain did not engage in significant acts of colonial power over the territory until the 20th century, and, after much debate over the issue by the parties, the International Court of Justice chose 1884, the date of the Conference of Berlin, as the date that began the period of Spain's colonization of Western Sahara. *See, Advisory Opinion on Western Sahara, supra,* at 38 para. 77.

[48] *See,* for instance, the Oral Testimony of M. Benjelloun before the ICJ, in the *Western Sahara Case*, Vol. IV, pps. 193–216 (1974), in which he gives a detailed account of numerous historic relationships between the tribes of the territory and the tribes which inhabit present day Morocco. Moroccan historians also legitimately point to the involvement of many prominent members of Western Saharan tribes in the struggle for the liberation of Morocco from the French and the liberation of "Spanish Sahara" from the Spanish. Among the more prominent of these is Sheikh Ma el-Ainin, a Sahrawi spiritual leader of the late 19th century whose son fomented a rebellion against both France and Spain that lasted until his followers were defeated in 1910. There is evidence that at some point, in order to rid the territory of Western influences, Sheikh Ma el-Ainin pledged his allegiance to the Sultan of Morocco. Also, during Morocco's struggle for independence from France in the 20th century a number of prominent Saharawis— including members of the Polisario—took part. Many of the Polisario leaders were, in fact, educated in Morocco and some were born there. However, considering the lack of educational facilities in Western Sahara it is understandable that the majority of educated Saharawis in 1974 would have been educated elsewhere. Also, besides the fact that all of the relationships forged in the late 19th and early 20th centuries occurred *after* the time of Spanish colonization, it is unclear whether they constituted a recognition of *sovereignty* or merely alliances to achieve a common goal. In any event, one can conclude that the allegiances that existed in the early 20th century underwent a transformation as the prospect of independence grew greater, as exhibited by the sentiment against Moroccan sovereignty expressed by large segments of the population during the visit of the UN Mission in 1975.

[49] After hearing arguments on both sides of the question, the court declared:

"The materials and information presented to the Court show the existence, at the time of Spanish colonization, of legal ties of allegiance between the Sultan of Morocco and some of the tribes living in the territory of Western Sahara.... On the other hand, the Court's conclusion is that the materials and information presented to it do not establish any tie of territorial sovereignty between the territory of Western Sahara and the Kingdom of Morocco.... Thus the Court has not found legal ties of such a nature as might affect the application of resolution 1514(XV) in the decolonization of Western Sahara and, in particular, of the principle of self determination

(c) The Western Sahara Case

Because there have been so many attempts by pundits and others to distort the findings of the International Court of Justice during the years since it addressed the issue of sovereignty over Western Sahara,[50] it is imperative to set the record straight by a detailed examination of its decision.

It is important, at the outset, to note that the Court's decision in the Western Sahara case established for the first time a standard by which claims of territorial sovereignty based on prior contacts should be weighed against the competing rights of self-determination. Before evaluating Morocco's claims in the Advisory Opinion it issued in 1975, the Court first put the question of past ties into context. It noted that the case involved an issue of decolonization and recognized at the outset the right of self-determination as the principle right at stake in the decolonization process.[51] For that reason it stipulated that only ties of a formal, traditional political and legal nature between the Moroccan state and the colony could overcome the application of the principle of self-determination. It also noted that the question of "legal ties"[52] must be examined in the context of a territory in which the indigenous population exhibited a tribal and nomadic social and political organization, and followed nomadic routes which necessarily caused them to pass through areas of adjacent states.[53]

It was within this context that the Court evaluated Morocco's arguments.

Morocco's legal claim to Western Sahara was based upon the allegation that the Western powers had divided the Moroccan state into separate colonies, one of which was Western Sahara.[54] It argued that it had been a special kind of state,

---

through the free and genuine expression of the will of the peoples of the Territory...." *Advisory Opinion on Western Sahara, supra,* para. 162, p. 60.

[50] For instance, as noted previously, the day after the decision was published, King Hassan II in a radio broadcast declared that the Court had found in favor of Morocco's claims and this false assertion has been repeated throughout the years by various Moroccan officials and legal scholars who quote those portions of the decision which admitted that certain ties existed between the Sultan and some leaders of some tribes in the territory for some periods and for some purposes, fail to mention the penultimate conclusion of the Court that no ties sufficient to establish sovereignty existed.

[51] *Advisory Opinion on Western Sahara, supra,* at 12, 32. The ICJ, when asked by the General Assembly in Resolution 3292 to determine the legal ties between Morocco and Mauritania and Western Sahara, construed the words "legal ties" in light of the purpose of Resolution 3292(XXIX) and the policy that should be adopted with respect to the decolonization of Western Sahara.

[52] The Court dealt with the definition of "legal ties", saying that it

"must be understood as referring to such 'legal ties' as may affect the policy to be followed in the decolonization of Western Sahara. In this connection the Court cannot accept the view that the legal ties the General Assembly had in mind in framing Question II were limited to ties established directly with the territory and without reference to the people who may be found in it. Such an interpretation would unduly restrict the scope of the question, since legal ties are normally established in relation to people." *Advisory Opinion on Western Sahara, supra,* para. 85.

[53] *Advisory Opinion on Western Sahara, supra,* para. 88.

[54] Morocco contended that the decolonization of Western Sahara required reintegration into Morocco on the theory that pre-colonial Morocco had been divided by the Western powers and that it was only seeking the recognition

called *sherifian*, in which the allegiance of tribes rather than territorial acquisition formed the basis of an alliance.[55] It produced two types of evidence of such allegiance: alleged internal displays of the Sultan's authority over Western Saharan tribes[56] as well as the alleged recognition of Morocco's sovereignty in international treaties of the period.[57]

Morocco claimed an "immemorial possession" of the territory based not on an isolated act of occupation, but on the public display of sovereignty, uninterrupted and uncontested, for centuries.[58] In support of this claim, Morocco referred to a series of events throughout history, that it claimed were sufficient to establish sovereignty under the test established by the Permanent Court of International Justice case of *Legal Status of Eastern Greenland*.[59]

These events included certain royal decrees appointing *caids* to head allegedly Saharan tribes;[60] the alleged declarations of allegiance by Saharawi leaders, most

---

of its legitimate territorial boundaries in accordance with paragraph 6 of Resolution 1514(XV) and Resolution 2625(XXV). *See*, the UN Mission Report, *supra*. In general, it argued that Western Sahara has always been linked to the interior of Morocco by common ethnological, cultural and religious ties, and that the Sakiet El Hamra was artificially separated from the Moroccan territory of the Noun by colonization." *Advisory Opinion on Western Sahara, supra*, para. 99. Morocco based its claim upon the argument of an alleged "immemorial possession" of the territory and that it had exercised "uninterrupted authority" over the region in the period immediately preceding its colonization following the precedent established by Denmark in *The Legal Status of Eastern Greenland* case.

55   Morocco's argument drew a distinction between Western concepts of territorial sovereignty and the looser forms of relationships characteristic of Islamic states. *See*, Roger S. Clark, *Western Sahara and the United Nations Norms on Self-Determination and Aggression*, INTERNATIONAL LAW AND THE QUESTION OF WESTERN SAHARA, *supra*, at 50.

56   In the words of the Court: "The principal indications of 'internal' display of authority invoked by Morocco consist of evidence alleged to show the allegiance of Saharan *caids* to the Sultan, including *dahirs* and other documents concerning the appointment of *caids*, the alleged imposition of Koranic and other taxes, and what were referred to as 'military decisions' said to constitute acts of resistance to foreign penetration of the territory. In particular, the allegiance is claimed of the confederation of Tekna tribes, together with its allies, one part of which was stated to be established in the Noun and another part to lead a nomadic life the route of which traversed areas of Western Sahara: through Tekna *caids*, Morocco claims, the Sultan's authority and influence were exercised on the nomad tribes pasturing in Western Sahara. Moreover, Morocco alleges that, after the marabout Ma ul-'Aineen established himself in Smara in the Sakiet El Hamra in the late 1890's much of the territory came under the direct authority of this sheikh, and that he himself was the personal representative of the Sultan. Emphasis is also placed by Morocco on evidence of two visits of Sultan Hassan I in person to the southern area of the Souss in 1882 and 1886 to maintain and strengthen his authority in the southern part of his realm, and on the dispatch of arms by the Sultan to Ma ul-'Aineen and others in the south to reinforce their resistance to foreign penetration."

57   In addition to evidence of allegiance (*bay'a*) by certain tribal leaders, the appointment of *caids*, the imposition of Koranic and other taxes, acts of military resistance to foreign penetration of the territory, and certain alleged religious and cultural ties between the inhabitants of the region and the Sultan, Morocco also cited certain so-called "shipwreck" treaties between the Sultan of Morocco and Western states, as well as bilateral treaties of the late nineteenth and early twentieth centuries whereby Great Britain, Spain, France and Germany were alleged to have recognized that Moroccan sovereignty extended as far south as Cape Bojador or the boundary of the Rio de Oro. *Advisory Opinion on Western Sahara, supra*, para. 99.

58   *Advisory Opinion on Western Sahara, supra*, para. 90.

59   P.C.I.J., Series A/B, No. 53 *supra*.

60   Morocco particularly relied upon the allegiance of certain Teckna tribes which allegedly traversed Westen Sahara as well as southern Morocco. Through these Teckna *caids*, Morocco claimed, the Sultan's authority and influence were

particularly Sheikh Ma el-Ainin, to various sultans;[61] and Moroccan expeditions under Sultan Hassan I in 1882 and 1886 into the Noun region of southern Morocco.[62] Particular stress was placed by Morocco on Moulay Hassan's expedition to the southern region of Morocco in 1882 and 1886, when some Tekna chiefs were appointed, and on the relationship between Sheikh Ma el-Ainin and the Sultan in the 1890s.

The Court agreed that Morocco in the pre-colonial period had characteristics of a "Sherifian State"and that such a state had special characteristics: "Its special character consisted in the fact that it was founded on the common religious bond of Islam existing among the peoples and on the allegiance of various tribes to the Sultan, through their *caids* or sheikhs, rather than on the notion of territory." However it concluded that "Such an allegiance...if it is to afford indications of the ruler's sovereignty, must clearly be real and manifested in acts evidencing acceptance of his political authority. Otherwise, there will be no genuine display or exercise of State authority. It follows that the special character of the Moroccan State...do[es] not dispense the Court from appreciating whether at the relevant time Moroccan sovereignty was effectively exercised or displayed in Western Sahara"[63]

The Court went on to explain that "what must be of decisive importance...is not indirect inferences drawn from events in past history but evidence directly relating to effective display of authority in Western Sahara at the time of its colonization by Spain and in the period immediately preceding that time."[64] It considered the

---

exercised on the nomad tribes pasturing in Western Sahara. *Advisory Opinion on Western Sahara, supra,* para. 99. However, as noted previously, the Court was persuaded by evidence that the Moroccan Sultan in the 1800s lacked authority over all but a few tribes within present day Morocco, agreeing with Spain that the Moroccan "state" in the 1800s consisted partly of the *bled makhzen* (areas actually subject to the Sultan), and partly of the *bled siba* (areas in which *de facto* the tribes were not submissive to the Sultan). Morocco argued that this fact merely described two types of relationship between the Moroccan local authorities and the central power, not a territorial separation, and should not be considered relevant in determining the Sultan's authority over the tribes of Western Sahara. However, the Court noted evidence produced by Spain that the *bled siba* "was not administered by the *makhzen*; it did not contribute contingents to the Sherifian army; no taxes were collected there by the *makhzen*; the government of the people was in the hands of *caids* appointed by the tribes, and their powers were derived more from the acquiescence of the tribes than from any delegation of authority by the Sultan," and that "even if these local powers did not totally reject any connection with the Sherifian State, in reality they became *de facto* independent power...historical evidence shows the territory between the Souss and the Dra'a to have been in a state of permanent insubordination and part of the *bled siba*; and that this implies that there was no effective and continuous display of State functions even in those areas to the north of Western Sahara." *Advisory Opinion on Western Sahara, supra,* para. 96.

[61] As noted previously, Morocco relied to a great extent on the relationship which existed between Ma el Ainin, and the Moroccan Sultan, claiming that once the tribal leader established himself in Smara, Western Sahara, in the late 1890s, much of this territory came under the direct authority of this sheikh, and that he became the personal representative of the Sultan. *Advisory Opinion on Western Sahara, supra,* para. 99.

[62] Sultan Hassan I allegedly visited the southern area of the Souss to maintain and strengthen his authority and to reinforce the local inhabitants' resistance to foreign penetration. *Advisory Opinion on Western Sahara, supra,* para. 99

[63] *Advisory Opinion on Western Sahara, supra,* para. 95.

[64] *Id.* para. 93.

events cited by Morocco to be "far-flung, spasmodic and often transitory."[65] It also found many of these alleged events to be unsupported by evidence.[66] It concluded, for instance, that the royal decrees appointing *caids* only related to tribes inhabiting areas within present day Morocco and did not constitute evidence of the Sultan's authority over the tribes of Western Sahara. Nor did it find evidence of the levying of Moroccan taxes in the territory convincing. It deemed the material presented as to the activities of Ma el Ainin insufficient to constitute a display of the Sultan's authority in Western Sahara. As to the expeditions of 1882 and 1886, the Court found "...they did not reach even as far as the Dra'a, [in present day Morocco] still less Western Sahara..."[67]

Although the Court acknowledged certain cultural and religious ties between some[68] of the disparate Western Saharan tribes and the Sultan, it did not deem these ties and the vague oaths of allegiance between these tribes and the Sultan a sufficient basis for an assertion of Moroccan sovereignty over the territory as a

---

[65] *Id.,* para. 91.

[66] As noted previously, many of these alleged facts were disputed by Spain. Spain argued (1) that the appointment of *caids* was purely formal, only confirming established chiefs, and that such appointments did not relate to indigenous tribes of Western Sahara but only to tribes indigenous to southern Morocco; (2) that Ma el Ainin was never the "personal representative" of the Sultan, but merely concluded an alliance on equal terms with the latter for the purpose of resisting French expansion from the south; (3) that the Sultan's expeditions had gone no further south than Tiznit and Goulimine in present day Morocco; (4) that the migratory, nomadic tribes of Western Sahara had not submitted to Moroccan authority; and especially, (5) that Western Saharan tribes had not paid taxes to the Moroccan authorities. *Advisory Opinion on Western Sahara, supra,* paras. 100, 101.

[67] In the words of the Court:

> "The material before the Court appears to support the view that almost all the dahirs and other acts concerning caids relate to areas situated within present-day Morocco itself and do not in themselves provide evidence of effective display of Moroccan authority in Western Sahara. Nor can the information furnished by Morocco be said to provide convincing evidence of the imposition or levying of Moroccan taxes with respect to the territory. As to Sheikh Ma ul-Ainin, the complexities of his career may leave doubts as to the precise nature of his relations with the Sultan, and different interpretations have been put upon them. The material before the Court, taken as a whole, does not suffice to convince it that the activities of this sheikh should be considered as having constituted a display of the Sultan's authority in Western Sahara at the time of its colonization.
>
> Furthermore, the information before the Court appears to confirm that the expeditions of Sultan Hassan I to the south in 1882 and 1886 both had objects specifically directed to the Souss and the Noun and, in fact, did not go beyond the Noun; so that they did not reach even as far as the Dra'a, still less Western Sahara.... Again, although Morocco asserts that the Regheibat tribe always recognized the suzerainty of the Tekna confederation, and through them that of the Sultan himself, this assertion has not been supported by any convincing evidence. Moreover, both Spain and Mauritania insist that this tribe of marabout warriors was wholly independent. *Advisory Opinion on Western Sahara, supra,* para. 104.

[68] The Court was very clear that it had concluded that there had been ties between Morocco and only *some* of the tribes of Western Sahara, repeating this conclusion at several points in its Opinion. *See, for instance,* para. 107: ("[T]he material...does not show that Morocco displayed effective and exclusive State activity in Western Sahara. It does, however, provide indications that a legal tie of allegiance had existed at the relevant period between the Sultan and some, but only some, of the nomadic peoples of the territory."), and para. 118: ("Examination of the provisions [of treaties] discussed above shows, therefore,...that they cannot be considered as implying international recognition of the Sultan's territorial sovereignty in Western Sahara...they are to be understood as concerned with the display of the Sultan's authority or influence in Western Sahara only in terms of ties of allegiance or of personal influence in respect of some of the nomadic tribes of the territory.").

whole. In other words, the formal legal ties between the Sultan and the inhabitants as a whole were wanting.[69]

The Court concluded by stating that "the paucity of evidence of actual display of authority unambiguously relating to Western Sahara renders it difficult to consider the Moroccan claim as on all fours with that of Denmark in the *Eastern Greenland* case.[70]

In short, the vague oaths of allegiance to the Sultan and/or certain Moroccan tribes of *some* leaders of *some* Sahrawi tribes during *some* periods of time for *some* purposes and the lack of control exhibited by the Sultan over the government and the everyday lives of the people of the territory did not establish the "continued display of authority" or "effective occupation" that had established title to a territory in other cases.[71]

The Court summarized its conclusions by stating:

> "Thus, even taking into account the specific structure of the Sherifian State, the material so far examined does not establish any tie of territorial sovereignty between Western Sahara and that State. It does not show that Morocco displayed effective and exclusive State activity in Western Sahara."

Next, Morocco pointed to various treaties between it and foreign states as evidence of international acts that established the international community's recognition of Moroccan sovereignty over the territory. These included eighteenth and nineteenth century treaties with major European maritime powers,[72] the Anglo-Moroccan agreement of 1895 concerning a trading concession in "Terfaya," and an exchange of letters in 1911 between France and Germany allegedly recognizing the sovereignty of Morocco over certain portions of Western Sahara.[73]

The Court found this evidence similarly unconvincing. The Court did not

---

[69] As note previously, the Court agreed that a "legal tie of allegiance" existed between the Sultan and some of the Saharawi tribes. *Advisory Opinion on Western Sahaara, supra,* paras. 38, 107,118. However, it found that the ties that were proven to have existed did not establish any tie of *territorial* sovereignty between Western Sahara and the two states. *Id.* at 68 (emphasis added). The Court also found that the Sultan's religious status did not represent an exercise of territorial sovereignty. *Id.,* para. 103. With respect to the analogy with the *Eastern Greenland* case, the Court remarked that "the paucity of evidence of actual display of authority unambiguously relating to Western Sahara renders it difficult to consider the Moroccan claim as on all fours with that of Denmark in the Eastern Greenland case." *Id.,* at 43. As a result, the Court declared that the evidence "does not establish any tie of territorial sovereignty between Western Sahara and [Morocco]. It does not show that Morocco displayed effective and exclusive State activity in Western Sahara." *Id.,* at 49.

[70] *Advisory Opinion on Western Sahara, supra,* para. 92.

[71] See *Legal Status of Greenland (Denmark v. Norway), supra,* and Hanauer, *supra,* at 162 fn. 96.

[72] These included a treaty with Spain in 1767, and so-called "shipwreck" treaties in 1836, 1856 and 1861 with the United States, Great Britain and Spain, respectively, concerning the rescue and safety of shipwrecked mariners.

[73] *Advisory Opinion on Western Sahara, supra,* para. 108

consider the so-called "shipwreck" treaties between Morocco and foreign states evidence of the international community's recognition of Moroccan sovereignty over the area; nor did it find that the 1895 Anglo-Moroccan agreement evidenced the implied international recognition of the Sultan's territorial sovereignty over Western Sahara by Great Britain.[74] As to the 1911 exchange of letters between France and Germany, the Court found only that they "...recognize or reserve for one or both parties a 'sphere of influence' as understood in the practice of the time."[75]

Accordingly, the Court found that "Examination of the various elements adduced by Morocco in the present proceedings does not...appear to the Court to establish the international recognition by other States of Moroccan territorial sovereignty in Western Sahara...."[76]

In the words of the Court:

> "The materials and information presented to the Court show the existence, at the time of Spanish colonization, of legal ties of allegiance between the Sultan of Morocco and some of the tribes living in the territory of Western Sahara.... On the other hand, the Court's conclusion is that the materials and information presented to it do not establish any tie of territorial sovereignty between the territory of Western Sahara and the Kingdom of Morocco.... Thus the Court has not found legal ties of such a nature as might affect the application of resolution 1514(XV) in the decolonization of Western Sahara and, in particular, of the principle of self determination through the free and genuine expression of the will of the peoples of the Territory...."

Advisory Opinion on Western Sahara, supra, para. 162.

In conclusion, according to the International Court of Justice Morocco was not able to demonstrate ties between the population of Western Sahara *as a whole* and *over a continuous period* and *in a significant fashion* to the Moroccan Sultan. Nor was it able to demonstrate the recognition of Moroccan sovereignty by the international community. As a result, under the criteria it adopted for examining claims of sovereignty based upon historic ties,[77] the Court found Morocco's claims legally insufficient.

---

[74] *Id.,* paras. 108–123.

[75] *Id.,* para 126.

[76] *Id.,* para. 128.

[77] Morocco did not establish the "continued display of authority" or "effective occupation" that had established title to a territory in other cases. *See, Legal Status of Greenland (Denmark v. Norway),* P.C.I.J. (ser. A/B) No. 53 (Ap.5),

(d) The Legitimacy of Morocco's Occupation of Western Sahara in 1975

As is noted above, both the evidence adduced by historians and that which was presented by Morocco to the International Court of Justice fail to support Morocco's claim that Moroccan sultans exercised sovereignty over the tribes of Western Sahara prior to the Spanish colonial rule. Moreover, it is questionable whether such "historic ties" could form a legal basis for a claim to the territory contrary to the wishes of its inhabitants even if they had been established.

In addition, even assuming that Morocco could assert a legal claim to the territory, it is questionable whether the means chosen by Morocco to enforce its claim could be sanctioned under international law: Morocco occupied Western Sahara in 1975 not by peaceful means, but by force and contrary to the will of its inhabitants and the international community.[78] Numerous legal scholars have come to the conclusion that this was a violation of norms of international law.[79] Indeed, according to some legal scholars, the occupation of Western Sahara by Morocco by military means since 1975 should be considered an illegal act of aggression, as that term is defined in pertinent United Nations resolutions[80] and the United Nations Charter.[81]

Nor can the agreement of Spain, Morocco and Mauritania in the Madrid Accords, under which Spain acquiesced in the occupation of the territory by the

---

supra. See also Hanauer, *supra,* at 162 fn. 96.

[78] It should be noted that Morocco's legal claim to sovereignty over the territory based upon historic ties had, by the time of the Green March and the outbreak of war, already been dismissed by the International Court of Justice.

[79] For instance, Roger S. Clark, *Western Sahara and the United Nations Norms on Self-Determination and Aggression, supra,* at 49 ("The Moroccan invasions were an obvious breach of the United Nations principles on self-determination.").

[80] The Moroccan invasion is arguably a breach of the United Nations Charter provisions prohibiting the use of force in Article 2, paragraph 4, and the provisions of Chapter VII concerning threats to the peace, breaches of the peace and acts of aggression. In addition, it would appear to qualify as an act of aggression under Article 3, Paragraph (a) of the UNGA Res. 3314 (XXIX), which defines an act of aggression as "The invasion or attack by the armed forces of a State of the territory of another State, or any military occupation, however temporary, resulting from such invasion or attack, or any annexation by the use of force of the territory of another State or part thereof." For a discussion of this issue see Roger S. Clark, *Western Sahara and the United Nations Norms on Self-Determination and Aggression,* in INTERNATIONAL LAW AND THE QUESTION OF WESTERN SAHARA, *supra,* at 54–55; *see also,* Stephanie Koury, *The European Community and Member States' Duty of Non-Recognition Under the EC-Morocco Association Agreement: State Responsibility and Customary International Law,* in INTERNATIONAL LAW AND THE QUESTION OF WESTERN SAHARA, *supra,* at 175 ("Morocco's invasion of the Western Sahara in 1975 constitutes an act of aggression on two grounds. The first is the use of force by a state in a manner inconsistent with the UN Charter. The second is the explicit prohibition of the annexation of territory by force in order to acquire the territory of another state or part thereof.").

[81] As was noted by J. Mundy in *The Legal Status of Western Sahara and the Laws of War and Occupation, Grupo de Estudios Estrategicos (GEES),* June 26, 2007, pps. 2–3: "Morocco's flagrant disregard of Security Council Resolution 380, its armed invasion, and its use of thousands of civilians to coerce Spain to negotiate, all amounted to a severe violation of the UN Charter's most fundamental constraints against the use of force in international affairs. These violations of *jus ad bellum* are unambiguous when we consider Article Two of the UN Charter."

other two states, be considered a "treaty" capable of transferring sovereignty over the territory to Morocco and justifying its use of force to occupy it. This is for the simple reason that Spain had no sovereign rights to transfer: it was merely an "administering power." It has long been held that a non-self governing territory has a separate status from its administering power.[82] Indeed, Western Sahara continues to be considered a "non-self governing territory" subject to de-colonization by the United Nations.

The Madrid Accords did not even transfer the status of "administering power" to Morocco and Mauritania. Under accepted United Nations practice Spain could only transfer administrative rule over the territory to its inhabitants or the United Nations, not to another state. Accordingly, the Madrid Accords did not confer the status of administering power to Morocco, nor has Morocco ever been designated an administering power over Western Sahara by the United Nations, a fact reflected in an advisory opinion of the United Nation's Legal Advisor issued in 2002.[83] Indeed, the present King of Morocco has repeatedly denied both the status of the territory as a "non-self-governing-territory" and the idea that Morocco has the status of an "administering power." In a speech to the nation on November 6, 2014, the 39th anniversary of the Green March, he clearly stated his position: "We say 'No' to the attempt to change the nature of this regional conflict and to present it as a decolonization issue. Morocco is in its Sahara [sic] and never was an occupying power or an administrative power. In fact, it exercises its sovereignty over its territory."[84]

In conclusion, there is no international legal principle that would support the right of Morocco to occupy by force or claim sovereignty over the territory of Western Sahara in 1975.

Nothing has happened since 1975 to change that situation.[85] The fact

---

[82] Declaration of Principles of International Law Concerning Friendly Relations and Co-operation Among States in Accordance with the Charter of the United Nations, G.A. Res. 2625, U.N.GAOR, 25th Sess., Supp. No. 28, at 121, UN Doc. A/8028 (1970). As was noted in General Assembly Resolution 2625: "[t]he territory of a colony…has, under the Charter, a status separate and distinct from the territory of the State administering it; such separate and distinct status under the Charter shall exist until the people of the colony…have exercised their right of self-determination in accordance with the Charter, and particularly its purposes and principles." G.A. Res. 2625, UN GAOR, 25th Sess., Supp. No. 28, UN Doc. A/8028 (1970), at 24. See, Advisory Opinion on Western Sahara, supra, (separate opinion of Judge de Castro), see also, Vance, supra, at 59, fn. 81.

[83] Letter dated 29 January 2002 from the Under Secretary General for Legal Affairs, the Legal Counsel, addressed to the President of the Security Council, UN Doc. S/2002/161, February 12, 2002, discussed infra in the section concerning natural resources.

[84] moroccoworldnews.com

[85] It should be noted, in that regard, that proponents of Morocco's legal rights have at times cited the Madrid Accords as a "treaty" which conferred Moroccan sovereignty over Western Sahara. However, as noted above, Spain itself did not possess "sovereignty" over Western Sahara when it entered into these accords. It was merely an "administering power" over the territory, which was recognized by all parties as being a "non-self governing" colony. Accordingly, Spain could not confer such sovereignty on Morocco or any other state.

that Morocco has occupied the territory for more than forty years does not, by itself, affect its status under law. Indeed, there have been instances of longer occupations—such as Indonesia's occupation of East Timor—in which the people of a non-self governing territory have successfully invoked their right to self-determination against claims of sovereignty on the part of the occupier. Only if the occupation meets the requirements of "effective control" might an occupation of long standing confer upon an occupier a different legal status. The principle of "effective control" suggests that a state may acquire title to territory belonging to another state through its consistent, flagrant and unopposed exercise of dominion over the territory for a sufficient period of time. It essentially incorporates elements of the common law doctrine of "prescription."[86]

The principle of effective control was discussed extensively by the Supreme Court of Canada in the *Reference on Secession of Quebec*. The Court noted that "an illegal act may eventually acquire legal status, if, as a matter of empirical fact, it is recognized on the international plane." The Court went on to state that the law has recognized "through a combination of acquiescence and prescription, an illegal act may at some later point be accorded some form of legal status."[87] Accordingly, the illegal annexation of a territory or part of a territory by a state may, after a long period of acceptance by the international community and acquiescence by the involved population,[88] permit the state to acquire sovereign rights over the territory.

However, Morocco's occupation of Western Sahara has not been peaceful and unopposed; it has been violently opposed by the involved population. Moreover, it resulted from the use of force which is condemned by the Charter of the United Nations and several General Assembly resolutions further negating its legitimacy. Morocco has never requested or been accorded by the United Nations the status of an "administering power" over the territory[89]—a status which would be inconsistent

---

[86] The International Court of Justice has addressed claims of effective control in a number of cases. *See*, for instance, *Minquiers and Ecrehos*, I.C.J Reports (1953) analyzing the competing claims of France and England to certain Channel islands; *Right of Passage over Indian Territory*, I.C.J Reports (1960), analyzing the claim of Portugal to sovereignty over certain villages surrounded by Indian territory; *Frontier Dispute*, I.C.J Reports (1986); *Land, Island and Maritime Frontier Dispute*, I.C.J Reports (1992); *Territorial Dispute*, I.C.J Reports (1994); *Kasikili/Sedudu Island*, I.C.J Reports (1999); *Maritime Delimitation and Territorial Questions between Qatar and Bahrain*, I.C.J Reports (2001); *Land and Maritime Boundary between Cameroon and Nigeria*, I.C.J Reports (2002); and *Sovereignty over Pulau Litigan and Pulau Sipadan*, I.C.J Reports (2002).

[87] Reference re: Secession of Quebec, [1998] 2 S.C.R. 217 para. 140–146.

[88] The term "peaceful" means more than the mere absence of violence. In the *Chamizal* arbitration between the United States and Mexico in 1911, the United States claimed title to a disputed tract of land on the Mexican border, claiming that it had "undisturbed, uninterrupted and unchallenged" possession since 1848. The arbitrators rejected the claim noting that there had been diplomatic protests during that time. *See, The Chamizal Arbitration*, RI.A.A. (1911) at 309, 328.

[89] The clearest pronouncement that Morocco has not been conferred the status of administering power by the UN was contained in the opinion of Hans Corell, Undersecretary General for Legal Affairs of the United Nations on 29 January 2002, concerning the right of Morocco to enter into certain oil exploration contracts. See discussion *infra* in the section discussing natural resources.

with a claim of sovereignty. Arguably then, its rights under international law, rather than being those of a sovereign, may be no greater than those of an "occupying power", under which it would enjoy only limited rights, if any,[90] over the peoples and resources of the territory.

(2) The Rights of the Saharawis to Self-Determination

By contrast, it is evident that the indigenous inhabitants of the territory—the Saharawis—today enjoy a right under international law to self-determination. It is clear that Western Sahara falls within the category of "nations" who enjoy this right under the United Nations Charter[91] and the many General Assembly resolutions that attempt to define self-determination—in particular resolution 1514, the "Declaration on the granting of independence to colonial countries and peoples",—as well as the two UN human rights covenants (the International Covenant on Civil and Political Rights[92] and the International Covenant on Economic, Social and Cultural Rights[93]), both of which are sources of binding positive law according to Article 38(1)(a) of the statute of the International Court of Justice. Moreover, as noted previously, the UN General Assembly[94] and the UN Security Council[95] have explicitly recognized the right of the people of Western Sahara to self-determination in a consistent series of resolutions.

---

90 Indeed, as an *illegal* occupying power, it may have no legal rights at all to the peoples and resources.

91 It has been argued that the Charter only establishes the right to self-determination for entities capable of signing the Charter, i.e., "states." However, according to Aurelie Cristescu, Special Rapporteur, the Coordination Committee of the UN Secretariat has stated that "the word 'nation'…is broad and general enough to include colonies…." See, United Nations, The Right to Self-Determination: Historical and Current Development on the Basis of United Nations Instruments, UN Doc. E/CN.4/Sub.2/404/Rev. 1 (1981).

92 International Covenant on Civil and Political Rights, adopted 16 Dec. 1966, entered into force March 23, 1976, 999 U.N.T.S. 171. This Covenant was ratified by Morocco on August 3, 1973. It was also ratified by the United States on September 8, 1992.

93 International Covenant on Economic, Social and Cultural Rights, adopted December 16, 1966, entered into force January 3, 1976, 993 U.N.T.S. 3. This Covenant was ratified by Morocco on August 3, 1973. It was also ratified by the United States on October 6, 1977.

94 *See, for instance*, G.A. Resolutions 2072 (1965); 2229 (1966); 2354 (1967); 2428 (1968); 2591 (1969); 2711 (1970); 2983 (1972); 3162 (1973); 3292 (1974); 3458 (1975); 45 (1976); 22 (1977); 31 A & B (1978); 37 (1979); 19 (1980); 46 (1981); 28 (1982, 40 (1983); 40 (1984); 50 (1985); 16 (1986); 78 (1987); 33 (1988); 88 (1989); 21 (1990); 67 (1991); 25 (1992); 49 (1993); 44 (1994); 36 (1995); 143 (1996); 75 (1997); 64 (1998); 87 (1999); 141 (2000); 69 (2001); 135 (2002); 109 (2003); 131 (2004); 144 (2005), 415 (2006); 116 (2008), 101 (2010).

95 See, for example, Security Council Resolutions 650 (1990), 690 (1991), 1131 (1997), 1122 (1997), and 1495 (2003). In its first resolution on the issue of Western Sahara, in 1975, the Security Council reaffirmed the terms of G.A. Res. 1514(XV) (December 14, 1960), which expressed the principle of self-determination for the people of non-self-governing territories. S/Res/377(1975) In all of its subsequent resolutions, including its most recent resolution in 2020, the Security Council reaffirmed its commitment to the right to self-determination of the people of the Territory. See, also, S/Res/379, 380 (1975); S/Res/621 (1988); S/Res/658 (1990); S/Res/690, 725 (1991); S/Res/809 (1993); S/Res/907 (1994); S/Res/973, 995, 1002, 1017, 1033 (1995); S/Res/1042, 1056, 1084 (1996); S/RES/1108, 1131, 1133 (1997); S/Res/1148, 1163, 1185, 1198, 1204, 1215 (1998); S/Res/1224, 1228, 1232, 1235, 1238, 1263, 1282 (1999); S/Res/1292, 1301, 1309, 1324 (2000); S/Res/1342, 1349, 1359, 1380 (2001); S/Res/1394, 1406, 1429

The International Court of Justice clearly affirmed this right in its Advisory Opinion.[96] The importance of the Court's opinion in the case of Western Sahara on the development of the principle of self-determination extends far beyond the facts of that case. Some scholars consider this Advisory Opinion to be "authority for key textbook lessons on the status, scope and content of the right under international law,"[97] defining not only the *scope* of the right,[98] but also the permissible ways in which it may be *exercised*,[99] It is clear from the Court's opinion that Western Sahara was within the group of former colonies to whom the right definitively applied, that Morocco did not possess any superseding territorial rights, and that the only way in which this right could be exercised is through the freely expressed will of the people of Western Sahara.

Even though there are differences of opinion over how a right *erga omnes* may be established under international law, some scholars have concluded that General Assembly resolutions and advisory opinions of the International Court of Justice, when taken together, may establish such a right.[100] Justice Dillard adopted this principle, and applied it in his decision supporting the application of the

---

(2002); S/Res/1463, 1499, 1485, 1495, 1513 (2003); S/Res/1523, 1541, 1570 (2004); S/Res/1598, 1634 (2005); S/Res/1675, 1720 (2006); S/Res/1754, 1783 (2007); S/Res/1813 (2008); S/Res/1871 (2009); S/Res/1920 (2010).

[96] Although both the decision of the International Court of Justice and the various resolutions of the Security Council and the General Assembly speak in terms of the rights of the *people* of Western Sahara, it is clear from the context in which this term is used that the intent was to establish a right for the indigenous population of the territory—the Saharawis—a majority of whom are currently refugees in camps in Algeria, and not for the numerous settlers from Morocco and elsewhere who have settled in the territory during the period of Moroccan occupation.

[97] *See*, the discussion of Catriona Drew in *The Meaning of Self-Determination: 'The Stealing of the Sahara' Redux?*, in INTERNATIONAL LAW AND THE QUESTION OF WESTERN SAHARA, *supra*, at 90–91.

[98] From this opinion legal scholars have drawn the conclusion that the customary principle of self-determination that emerged in the 1960s was a right belonging to colonial and not to all peoples. E.g. A. Cassese, SELF DETERMINATION OF PEOPLES: A LEGAL REAPPRAISAL, Cambridge University Press, 1995, at 88; H. Hannum, AUTONOMY, SOVEREIGNTY, AND SELF-DETERMINATION: THE ACCOMMODATION OF CONFLICTING RIGHTS, University of Pennsylvania, rev.ed. (1996) at 41; C. Drew, *The Meaning of Self-Determination: 'The Stealing of the Sahara' Redux?*, in INTERNATIONAL LAW AND THE QUESTION OF WESTERN SAHARA, *supra*, at 90.

[99] The Court interpreted the 1960 Colonial Declaration as "confirming" and "emphasizing" that the application of the right of self-determination requires a free and genuine expression of the will of the peoples concerned. Its essential feature was free choice, that the right confers a right, not to a particular outcome, but to a particular process—one that entails the freely expressed will of peoples. *See*, C. Drew, *The Meaning of Self-Determination: 'The Stealing of the Sahara' Redux?*, *supra*, at 91; A. Cassese, *supra*, at 89.

[100] As was noted by Laurence S. Hanauer:

"Individual General Assembly resolutions and I.C.J. advisory opinions are not binding; Article 10 of the Charter gives the General Assembly the power to make recommendations only, and while these recommendations may carry moral force, they do not, individually create legal obligations. Collectively, however, in combination with the Charter and human rights covenants, and after years of evolving state practice, they have developed a set of norms of self-determination that have achieved the status of customary international law, defined by Article 38(1)(b) of the I.C.J. Statute as a "general practice accepted as law." As a result, the I.C.J. in 1971 declared in its advisory opinion on Namibia that Resolutions 1514, 1541, 2625, and others, representing "the subsequent development of international law in regard to non-self-governing territories, as enshrined in the Charter of the United Nations, made the principle of self-determination applicable to all of them."

principle of self-determination to Western Sahara, when he stated in his separate opinion:

> "...the cumulative impact of many resolutions when similar in content, voted for by overwhelming majorities and frequently repeated over a period of time may give rise to a general *opinio juris* and thus constitute a norm of customary international law.... [T] his is the precise situation manifested by the long list of resolutions which, following in the wake of resolution 1514 (XV), have proclaimed the principle of self-determination to be an operative right in the decolonization of non-self-governing territories."[101]

Justice Dillard's separate opinion was echoed by the majority of the Court in *Legal Consequences of the Construction of a Wall in the Occupied Palestinian Territories* (2004). In the words of the Court:

> "As to the principle of self-determination of peoples...Article 1 common to the International Covenant on Economic, Social and Cultural Rights and the International Covenant on Civil and Political Rights reaffirms the right of all Peoples to self-determination, and lays upon the States parties the obligation to promote the realization of that right and to respect it, in conformity with the provisions of the United Nations Charter. The Court recalls its previous case law, which emphasized that current developments in 'international law in regard to non-self-governing territories, as enshrined in the Charter of the United Nations, made the principle of self-determination applicable to all [such territories]', and that the right of peoples to self-determination is today a right *erga omnes*."[102]

The Irrelevance of Self-Determination Law to Ethno-National Conflict: A New Look at the Western Sahara Case, supra, at 152 *quoting The Legal Consequences for States for the Continued Presence of South Africa in Namibia (South West Africa) Notwithstanding Security Council Resolution 276* (1970), 1971 I.C.J. 4 (June 21), at 31. *See also*, M. Brus, *The Legality of Exploring and Exploiting Mineral Resources in Western Sahara*, in INTERNATIONAL LAW AND THE QUESTION OF WESTERN SAHARA, *supra*, at 214 ("Modern international law...seems to support the fact that resolutions can have normative value and may be regarded as of importance in constituting customary international law.") referring to a statement of the International Court of Justice in its advisory opinion on the legality of the use or threat of use of nuclear weapons, *Legality of the Threat or Use of Nuclear Weapons*, ICJ Reports 1996, para. 73.

101 *Advisory Opinion on Western Sahara, supra,* at 121 (separate opinion of Dillard, J).

102 Advisory Opinion, *Legal Consequences of the Construction of a Wall in the Occupied Palestinian Territories,* (2004) at 8. This opinion echoed the conclusions of the Court in the *East Timor (Portugal v. Australia) Judgment,* ICJ Reports 1995, p. 102, para. 29, wherein in response to Australia's claim that states were under no international law obligation to promote self-determination in territories over which they exercised no control, the Court replied that "Portugal's

Even scholars who do not accept this argument generally agree that rights under international law can be established through state practice; that is the implementation of a principle by a sufficient number of states in a sufficient number of contexts over a period of time—particularly when supported by resolutions implemented by the Security Council.[103] According to these criteria the right of non-self-governing colonies to exercise self-determination in determining their future government would appear to be firmly enshrined in principles of international law, for it has been a principle that has been adopted and applied by the international community—including the United States and other members of the Security Council—in a variety of contexts throughout the past eighty years.[104]

Accordingly, every principle of international law historically adopted by the international community supports the Saharawis' right to self-determination.

Of course, self-determination can manifest itself in a number of different ways. United Nations Resolutions 1541(XV) and 2625 (XXV) described the ways in which the colonial status of a territory may be terminated by the territory reaching a "full measure of self government." This could occur, in terms of the Resolution, by emergence as a sovereign independent state, by free association with an independent state or by integration with an independent state, or, indeed, by "the emergence into any other political status freely determined by a people."[105] Accordingly, there exists an option of integration with another state.

However, there exist guidelines to ensure that the choice to integrate with another state is genuine and on a basis of equality, and results from the "freely expressed wishes of the Territory's peoples acting with full knowledge of the change in their status, their wishes having been expressed through informed and democratic processes, impartially conducted and based on adult suffrage."[106] Likewise, there is

---

assertion that the right of peoples to self-determination, as it has evolved from the Charter and from United Nations practice, has an *erga omnes* character, is irreproachable. The principle of self-determination…is one of the essential principles of contemporary international law."

[103] *See*, for instance, Thomas de Saint Maurice, *Sahara Occidental 2001: Prelude d'un Fiasco Annonce* Actualite et Droit International, February 2002, at 2–3, citing the decision of the ICJ in the case of *East Timor (Portugal v. Australia)*, June 30, 1995, par. 29. *See also*, UN Special Rapporteur of the Subcommittee on Prevention of Discrimination & Protection of Minorities, "The Right to Self-Determination: Implementation of United Nations Resolutions," 12 UN Doc. E/CN.4/Sub.2/405/Rev.1.UN Sales No. E.79.XIV.5 (1980)(prepared by Hector Gros Espiell) *cited in* "The Legal Issues Involved in the Western Sahara Dispute: The Principal of Self-Determination and the Legal Claims of Morocco," UN Committee, Bar Association of the City of New York, June 2012 ("NYCBar Self-Determination Report") at 28 fn 96. ("[N]o one can challenge the fact that, in light of contemporary international realities, the principle of self-determination necessarily possesses the character of *jus cogens*.")

[104] The most recent example is East Timor, which gained its independence through a plebiscite in 1999.

[105] G.A. Res. 2625 (XXV), 25 UN GAOR, Supp. (No. 28) at 121, IN Doc. A/8028, 1971.

[106] G.A. Res. 1541, Principles VIII and IX. Principle IX declares that "Integration should have come about in the following circumstances:…(b) The integration should be the result of the freely expressed wishes of the territory's peoples acting with full knowledge of the change in their status, their wishes having been expressed through informed and democratic processes, impartially conducted and based on universal adult suffrage. The United Nations could,

a requirement that the integrating territory should have attained "an advanced stage of self-government" so that its peoples would have the capacity to make a responsible choice. Although there have been occasions in which such self-determination has been assessed through means other than a plebiscite, these situations have been rare, and the results largely criticized,[107] and the contexts in which they have arisen would not appear to apply to Western Sahara. The International Court of Justice declared as much in the *Western Sahara Case* when after noting "special circumstances" in which the principle of self-determination might not be applied through the consultation of the inhabitants of the territory in question, it did not deem the case of Western Sahara to present such circumstances.[108] In any event, the principle of self-determination would require that the option of independence be available,[109] and would not appear to include a "political solution" imposed upon the Saharawis by an occupying power, the United Nations, or the United States.[110]

---

when it deems it necessary, supervise these processes." General Assembly Resolution 2625 (XXV), the "Declaration on Principles of International Law concerning Friendly Relations and Co-operation among States in accordance with the Charter of the United Nations" mentions other possibilities besides independence, association or integration. But in doing so it reiterates the basic need to take account of the wishes of the people concerned: "The establishment of a sovereign and independent State, the free association or integration with an independent State or the emergence into any other political status *freely determined by a people* constitute modes of implementing the right of self-determination by that people." (emphasis added)

[107] One of the exceptions to the rule was the case of West Irian. Formerly the Dutch New Guinea, it was claimed by Indonesia shortly after Indonesia gained its independence in 1945. However, it remained under Dutch control despite several Indonesian armed incursions. Acceding to pressure from the United States, the Netherlands and Indonesia signed the "New York Agreement" in 1962 under which the Netherlands agreed to allow the territory to be administered by Indonesia, after a temporary transfer of authority to the United Nations. Under the terms of the Agreement Indonesia was required to make arrangements by 1969 for the inhabitants of the region to choose whether or not to be incorporated into Indonesia. However, rather than conduct a plebiscite, the agreement of the inhabitants of the region to join Indonesia was supposedly obtained through an "Act of Free Choice," voted by Regional Councils whose members were effectively selected by Indonesia, and many critics have charged that it did not constitute a valid act of self-determination of the people. *See,* Viktor Kaisiepo *The Case of West Papua's Sovereignty: The Exclusion of West Paupa's Indigenous Peoples From the Process of Determining their Destination,* INTERNATIONAL LAW AND THE QUESTION OF WESTERN SAHARA, *supra,* at 147–161; John Saltford, THE UNITED NATIONS AND THE INDONESIAN TAKEOVER OF WEST PAPUA, 1962–1969: THE ANATOMY OF BETRAYAL (Routledge Curzon, London, 2003).

[108] As discussed previously, the Court in the *Western Sahara* case noted that "The validity of the principle of self-determination, defined as the need to pay regard to the freely expressed will of peoples, is not affected by the fact that in certain cases the General Assembly has dispensed with the requirement of consulting the inhabitants of a given territory. Those instances were based either on the consideration that a certain population did not constitute a 'people' entitled to self-determination or on the conviction that a consultation was totally unnecessary, in view of special circumstances." *Advisory Opinion on Western Sahara, supra,* at 33. Commentators have suggested that Ifni, a former colony of Spain that was retroceded to Morocco in 1969 might fall into this category, noting that Ifni was a "clear cut acquisition" from Morocco during the colonial period pursuant to "what we might now characterize as an unequal treaty". *See,* Roger S. Clark, *Western Sahara and the United Nations Norms on Self-Determination and Aggression,* INTERNATIONAL LAW AND THE QUESTION OF WESTERN SAHARA, *supra,* at 50–51.

[109] As the Secretary General acknowledged: "It is difficult to envision a political solution that, as required by Security Council resolution 1429(2002) provides for self-determination but that nevertheless precludes the possibility of independence as one of several ballot questions." Report of the Secretary-General on the Situation Concerning Western Sahara, UN Doc. S/2003/565, May 23, 2003, para. 52.

[110] As one scholar noted: "…identifying colonialism as the legal basis for self-determination is significant because it places the Western Sahara entitlement at the very top of a normative hierarchy…[T]his precludes any argument

The above principles define the right to self-determination as applied to the rights of a colonial territory. However, since Western Sahara is one of the last remaining "colonies" that would be subject to these rights—which developed in the context of the Western imperialism of the 19th century—an argument has been advanced that the issue should be re-examined light of the right to self-determination as it has recently developed and been applied in different contexts.[111] Another argument has been raised that the supervening occupation of the territory by Morocco may have eroded this right.

Neither argument has a legal justification. Morocco's occupation of Western Sahara has not affected the legal status of the territory. As noted previously, the UN General Assembly's resolution about non-self-governing territories[112] declared that the territory of a non-self-governing territory has a status "distinct from the territory of the State administering it," and that such separate and distinct status "shall exist until the people of the Non-Self-Governing Territory have exercised their right of self-determination." In a Legal Opinion addressed to the President of the Security Council in 2002, discussed more fully in the section on use of natural resources, *infra,* the Under-Secretary-General for Legal Affairs, Hans Corell, affirmed that Spain's transfer of *de facto* authority to Morocco and Mauritania in 1975 "did not affect the international status of Western Sahara as a Non-Self-Governing Territory," and that it retains that status today.[113]

As has been noted previously, the supervening occupation of Morocco for a number of years has not affected the status of the territory under international law. Indeed, as recently as 1999 the application of the principle of self determination led to the independence of another former colony, East Timor, under strikingly similar circumstances. In the East Timor case, faced with East Timor's *de facto* transition from Portuguese colony to Indonesian province, and despite many years of occupation, the International Court of Justice reaffirmed the fact that "East Timor remains a non-self-governing territory and the people has the right

---

that the right of self-determination can be satisfied by an offer of autonomy that excludes the option of independent statehood or that the applicable law is so confused or indeterminate that it provides no meaningful guidance as to the content of the Western Saharan self-determination entitlement." C. Drew, *The Meaning of Self-Determination: 'The Stealing of the Sahara' Redux?,* INTERNATIONAL LAW AND THE QUESTION OF WESTERN SAHARA, *supra,* at 94.

[111] As Catriona Drew observed, like East Timor, the Western Sahara case is one of decolonization in an otherwise predominantly secessionist era, when the right to self-determination has largely developed in the context of groups within a recognized state who wish to secede. *See,* C. Drew, *The Meaning of Self-Determination: "The Stealing of the Sahara" Redux?, supra,* at 93.

[112] G.A. Res. 1541 (XV).

[113] Letter dated 29 January 2002 from the Under Secretary General for Legal Affairs, the Legal Counsel, addressed to the President of the Security Council, UN Doc. S/2002/161, February 12, 2002, ("Corell Opinion") *supra.* For a more recent consideration of Western Sahara as a non-self-governing territory, see Special Committee on Decolonization 4th Meeting (AM), GA/COL/3159, June 6, 2007, paras. 6 and 8.

to self-determination."[114] And as was noted in the previous section, the doctrine of "effective occupation" does not apply.

The fact that President Trump has declared that the United States recognizes Morocco's sovereignty over Western Sahara, even if continued as a policy under the incoming Biden administration, does not by itself change its status under international law. Indeed, by far the majority of states have decried that position as have the majority of legal scholars.

Accordingly, there is no valid reason for departing from the principles of self-determination applied to colonies in the case of Western Sahara. Yet, even assuming *arguendo* that the more stringent legal norms suggested in the context of the struggles for independence of peoples within an already existing state are deemed legitimate and applied to the Western Sahara situation,[115] the position of the Saharawis still appears compelling. Indeed, it is hard to justify the application of the principle of self-determination to permit the independence of Kosovo, a small nation carved out of former Yugoslavia, and not Western Sahara.

It has been suggested that at least in certain contexts—such as Kosovo—a people wishing to avail themselves of the right to self-determination should be required to "earn" it. This theory has been advanced by the Independent Commission on Kosovo[116] as well as those advocating the "Roadmap" for the independence of Palestine.[117] Earned sovereignty is described as entailing "the conditional and progressive devolution of sovereign powers and authority from a state to a substate entity under international supervision"[118] and comprises three core elements (shared sovereignty, institution building, and a determination of final status),[119] and three optional elements (phased sovereignty, conditional

---

[114] *Case concerning East Timor (Portugal v. Australia)*, ICJ Reports, 1995, paras. 31 and 37.

[115] It has been suggested, for instance, that the right to self-determination should not permit the creation of a number of "micro" states, with limited resources, out of already existing states.

[116] Independent Commission on Kosovo, The Kosovo Report: Conflict, International Response, Lessons Learned, 2000, available at *http://www.kosovocommission.org/reports*. The approach was further elaborated in Independent Commission on Kosovo, The Follow-Up of the Kosovo Report: Why Conditional Independence? 2001, *supra*. See, also C. Drew, *The Meaning of Self-Determination: 'The Stealing of the Sahara' Redux?*, INTERNATIONAL LAW AND THE QUESTION OF WESTERN SAHARA, *supra*, at 96; P. Williams, *Earned Sovereignty: The Road to Resolving the Conflict over Kosovo's Final Status*, 31 Denver Journal of International Law and Policy, 2002–2003, pps. 387–425.

[117] *See*, "A Performance-Based Roadmap to a Permanent Two-State Solution to the Israeli-Palestinian Conflict", available at http://www.un.org/media/roadmap122002.html.

[118] P. Williams and F. Pecci, *Earned Sovereignty: Bridging the Gap Between Sovereignty and Self-Determination*, 40 Stanford Journal of International Law, 2004 at 349; *see also*, C. Drew, *The Meaning of Self-Determination: 'The Stealing of the Sahara' Redux?*, INTERNATIONAL LAW AND THE QUESTION OF WESTERN SAHARA, *supra*, at 96.

[119] P. Williams, M. Scharf and J. Hooper, *Resolving Sovereignty Based Conflicts: The Emerging Approach of Earned Sovereignty*, 31 Denver Journal of International Law and Policy, 2002–2003, *supra*, pps. 349–350.

sovereignty, and constrained sovereignty). "Conditional sovereignty" usually refers to the requirement that sovereignty be conditioned on the territory meeting certain benchmarks, such as "protecting human and minority rights, halting terrorism, developing democratic institutions, instituting the rule of law and promoting regional stability."[120]

These criteria are intended to place conditions on groups wishing to gain independence in the post colonial era which would ensure that the interests of the larger international community—for instance, to refrain from supporting groups that encourage terrorism or would establish totalitarian regimes—are served should the international community support such independence. However, there are no interests of the larger international community that would be served by forcing the Saharawis to accept shared sovereignty with Morocco as a prelude to possible independence, or "supervised" sovereignty after independence. Morocco has already rejected a version of the "earned sovereignty" approach by rejecting the Baker Plan, and as long as it refuses to agree to any plan that could ultimately result in independence for the territory its position renders moot any plan that guarantees true self-determination for the Saharawis.

With respect to the "conditional sovereignty" criteria, the Saharawis would appear to pass the test. As will be discussed more fully later,[121] not only have the Polisario demonstrated their commitment to democratic and non discriminatory principles in the government of their refugee camps, they have prepared a "blueprint" for the government institutions they would establish upon independence that reaffirms their dedication to such principles. Concerning the issue of terrorism it should be noted that apart from unsubstantiated and self-serving accusations by Morocco, no evidence has been produced that the Polisario are somehow linked to terrorist groups or have engaged in terrorist acts, and the Polisario have firmly disavowed Islamic extremists and their actions.

Finally, there is no legal basis under which the Saharawis may be forced to "share" their right to self-determination with others who do not possess this right. As was noted in the report on the legal issues involved in the Western Sahara dispute published by the Association of the Bar of the City of New York in 2012,[122]

---

[120] As was noted by Catriona Drew "…under the Roadmap, progress towards the creation of an independent Palestinian state depends on the Palestinians meeting a host of conditions relating to the cessation of violence and terrorism, constitutional reform, restructuring of the security services, elections and so forth…More elaborately, in Kosovo, the United Nations 'Standards before Status' (and later 'Standards for Kosovo') laid down detailed benchmarks relating to: democratic institutions; the rule of law; freedom of movement; sustainable returns and the rights of communities; the economy; property rights; dialogue with Belgrade; and the Kosovo protection corps." *See*, C. Drew, *The Meaning of Self-Determination: 'The Stealing of the Sahara' Redux?, supra,* at 98.

[121] *See,* the discussions of this issue in the sections dealing with the way forward and political issues, *infra.*

[122] NYCBar Self-Determination Report, *supra,* at 40.

"There are innumerable instances in which citizens of a colonial power or other foreigners have resided in colonies during the period of colonial rule and thereafter until self-determination has been rightfully exercised. In almost all instances of de-colonization through a UN approved referendum or other process, the people entitled to vote on their future have been limited to those who have been considered the indigenous inhabitants of the territory. Indeed, it would be inimical to the principle of self-determination of the peoples of colonies to permit people brought into the colony by the colonial powers to participate in the exercise of this right. It would be even more inimical to the principle of self-determination of the peoples of colonies to grant the right to people brought into the colony by a power occupying the colony illegally by force. Accordingly, although there may be difficulties in describing the criteria applicable to an indigenous group permitted to exercise the right to self-determination, or in ascertaining whether a particular individual actually belongs to such a group, there is usually no question that the right should be limited to legitimate members of the indigenous group unless they, themselves, wish to confer this right upon others."[123]

The definition of "peoples" who would be entitled to exercise the right to self-determination in the Western Sahara context has already been established both by the parties and the United Nations.[124] The 1991 Settlement Plan defined those eligible to vote in the referendum as all those Saharawis, eighteen years or over, who were counted in a 1974 census of the population taken by the Spanish authorities.[125] Later these criteria, by agreement of the parties, were expanded to include not only individuals on the Spanish census who were 18 years or older (Category 1), but also persons who could prove that they were living in the territory as members of a Saharan tribe at the time of the 1974 census but were not counted (Category II), persons who were members of the immediate family of individuals in Categories I or II (Category III), persons born of a Saharan father born in the territory (Category IV), and persons who were members of a Saharan tribe and who resided in the Territory for six consecutive years or intermittently for 12 years

---

[123] This was also the conclusion of Jaume Saura Estapa, Professor of International Law, Barcelona, Spain ("…only the [indigenous] people can be asked about its future, and not the inhabitants brought in by the colonizing (or occupying) power. The UN has devoted a huge effort to ascertaining the actual composition of the Saharawi people…. It must be reaffirmed that only the individuals identified by MINURSO constitute the Saharawi people and that they are thus the only ones to be legitimately asked about the issue of their political future.") J. Estapa, *Western Sahara: A Solution for the Conflict on the Basis of Full Respect for International Law*, in INTERNATIONAL LAW AND THE QUESTION OF WESTERN SAHARA, *supra*, at 323.

[124] The United Nations made it clear early on that the "peoples" entitled to exercise the right to self-determination for Western Sahara would be the indigenous inhabitants of the region. *See*, for instance, the resolutions of the General Assembly, G.A. Res. 2229 (1966), G.A. Res. 3458-A (1975) and G.A. Res. 3458-B (1975).

[125] Report of the Secretary-General on the Situation Concerning Western Sahara, UN Doc. S/21360, 18 June 1990, Part I: The Settlement Plan, para. 24.

prior to the Spanish census (Category V). Although the criteria for eligibility were expanded, they still strove to include only Saharawis with ties to the territory on the list, and not Moroccan settlers. It was on this basis that MINURSO created the provisional voters' list that was published in 1999. It is true that in a bow to Moroccan interests, James Baker proposed expanding this list to include Moroccan settlers. However, his proposals were never accepted by the parties, and under international law principles any expansion of the list to include such individuals would need to be acceptable to those whose rights would be affected.

In conclusion, as was noted by the Association of the Bar of the City of New York in a seminal report on the legal issues involved in the dispute over Western Sahara, international legal principles strongly support the right of the Saharawis to exercise self-determination in the choice of whether they wish to be an independent nation or form an alliance with another country, and in the latter case, to determine what type of alliance and with whom.[126]

(3) The Right to a Referendum and Enforcement of the Settlement Plan

(a) Under International Law

The right to self-determination under international law exists because the international community has conferred that right upon inhabitants of former colonies. But do these inhabitants have a right to a *referendum* as a means to exercise this right?

Unfortunately, case law is unclear as to the means by which such a right may be exercised. As was noted by the Association of the Bar of the City of New York,[127] the General Assembly Resolutions on the subject of self-determination provide little guidance on the precise method by which the people's freely determined choice of political status is to be made known. The International Court of Justice has noted both in the *Advisory Opinion on Western Sahara* and other decisions that the law requires "the need to *consult* the wishes of the people of the territory as to their political future,"[128] (emphasis added) and that the principle of self-determination

---

[126] As was stated in the NYCBar Self-Determination Report, *supra*: "[T]the peoples of the disputed territory have a right to exercise self-determination in a free and fair manner...there is a credible legal argument...that complete independence as a separate sovereign state should remain a viable option without any interference from a third party...the peoples of such Non-Self-Governing Territories do not forfeit the opportunity to choose the independence option preferred by Resolution 1514 because of intervening circumstances imposed unilaterally by the administering authority or occupying state." at 66.

[127] NYCBar Self-Determination Report, *supra*, at 67–68.

[128] *Advisory Opinion on Western Sahara, supra*, para. 64.

meant "the need to pay regard to the freely expressed will of peoples."[129] The Court noted that in General Assembly Resolution 2229 (XXI), and in subsequent Resolutions dealing specifically with Western Sahara, the General Assembly had selected a referendum conducted under UN auspices as the mode of consultation it deemed to be the most appropriate method for ascertaining the freely expressed will of the peoples. However, the Court did not take a position on whether a referendum was legally required as opposed to other possible methods of consultation.

However, there is strong precedent for the holding of referendums or plebiscites on the issue of self-determination, at least in the colonial context,[130] and the International Court of Justice's Advisory Opinion concerning Western Sahara affirmed that the means employed to grant self-determination must be the "result of the freely expressed wish of the territory's peoples acting with full knowledge of the change in their status, their wishes having been expressed through informed and democratic processes, impartially conducted and based on universal adult suffrage."[131] In other words, the means employed to assert a peoples' self-determination must be through a fairly conducted, democratic process, with participation by all concerned. It is difficult to see how this could be accomplished other than through some sort of referendum.

Some supporters of Morocco's position have pointed to circumstances in which the United Nations has decided the issue of sovereignty over a territory without a referendum or plebiscite, and have argued that this demonstrates that the right of self-determination may be exercised through negotiations.[132] However,

---

[129]   *Id*, para 59.

[130]   Hanauer, *supra*, at 154–155; Franck, T, *The Stealing of the Sahara*, *supra*, at 699–701 ("[T]here has grown up through the vast majority of cases a clear pattern of orderly decolonization through freely conducted elections or plebiscites, often under UN supervision, in which the local population has had the opportunity to choose its own national destiny.") In his analysis, Franck found a pattern and practice in the UN as far back as 1954, in which the UN supervised plebiscites or elections for UN Trust Territories and, after implementation of the Special Committee in 1961, for ordinary colonies. The most recent example of the resort to a referendum to resolve a conflict over issues of sovereignty was the Comprehensive Peace Agreement ("CPA") on Sudan, signed in 2005, under which, after a certain period of time, the people of South Sudan could choose between perpetuating a power-sharing agreement or opting for full independence; with the Abyei people deciding in a separate referendum whether to join the north or the south.

[131]   G.A. Res. 1541(XV), cited with approval by the International Court of Justice in the *Advisory Opinion on Western Sahara*, *supra*, paras. 32–33; see also para. 115 n.5 (separate opinion of Dillard, H.).

[132]   Examples often cited are the Cook Islands and Niue, Aceh (an autonomous territory within Indonesia), New Caledonia (a colony of France) and Bougainville (an autonomous territory within Papua New Guinea). In Cook Islands and Niue, autonomy in association with New Zealand was achieved through some sort of popular consent but without a formal referendum. But these regions are independent in many ways, including their ability to negotiate treaties and conduct their own foreign policy. In Aceh, a negotiated compromise led to an incremental devolution of power. However the inhabitants of Aceh only agreed to end a 29 year war of independence after the tsunami of 2004 left most of them destitute. In New Caledonia and Bougainville, a devolution of power was also agreed through negotiations. But there *was* a referendum held in New Caledonia in 1987, in which the majority of the inhabitants voted to remain a colony of France (albeit with some autonomy), and France agreed to allow the inhabitants another two referendums in which to choose independence. A second referendum was held on November 4, 2018 and a

these examples have, for the most part, concerned the small territories subject to the principle of "integration," or territories that were not considered non-self-governing territories, or territories considered "terra nullius."[133] A situation in which something other than a fair referendum was used to determine sovereignty over a territory—West Irian—has been widely condemned as a black spot on the reputation of the United Nations. Ironically, as part of its autonomy proposal, Morocco has suggested that after the parties agree to the proposal it be submitted to the "concerned people" for approval in a referendum! Apparently Morocco believes that it *is* possible to conduct a referendum—as long as the option of independence is not on the table!

(b) Under Contract or Treaty Principles

Apart from this right to a fair and democratic process under general principles of international law, there may be a separate right the Saharawis enjoy in the context of this dispute to have the *referendum* and terms of the *Settlement Plan* and the *Houston Accords* enforced under contract or treaty principles and the norms applied to the consensual settlement of disputes among states and subgroups of states by arbitration or mediation. Quite simply, it is incontestable that the referendum process and the Settlement Plan were agreed by the parties as a means to end an armed conflict. Even though there was no signed agreement, until the *Houston Accords,* the parties' agreement to support the Plan "in principle" and subsequent acquiescence in the terms of the Plan as set forth by the Secretary-General and a technical commission of Polisario and Moroccan representatives in July of 1989,[134]

---

third took place on October 4, 2020, with 84% of the population participating. In both of these the people chose to remain a colony of France. In Bougainville, the cite of the largest conflict in Oceania since WWII, in which an estimated 15,000 people died, a ceasefire was negotiated between the New Guinea government and two rebel factions in 1997 in which greater powers were given the local population. As part of the peace settlement a referendum on independence was agreed; it took place in 2019 and the people overwhelmingly chose independence. Negotiations are currently underway to discuss the implementation of the vote. Accordingly, each one of these situations posed characteristics not present in Western Sahara, several of them included a referendum, and most of them provide a poor model for the exercise of the self-determination of the Saharawi people.

[133] As was noted in the NYCBar Self-Determination Report, there exist three principal types of cases: (1) *Cases arising outside the colonial context* (for example, Chechnya, Corsica, the Basque Country, Kosovo, etc.), where the concept of self-determination in the sense of secession does not apply at all, given the lack of a colonial nexus, (2) *Challenges to the territorial definition of former colonial entities* (for example, Sri Lanka, Philippines, Burma, India in relation to tribal peoples), where a former colony exercised the right to self-determination, but ethnic movements emerging within the newly independent state sought separation, and (3) *Challenges to the implementation of colonial self-determination* (for example, Eritrea, Somaliland, Kashmir, perhaps Southern Sudan and the Comoros and Mayotte), where it is argued that the doctrine of *uti possidetis juris* was wrongly applied at the point of decolonization, or that an entity was wrongfully incorporated into the newly independent state at that moment. See NYCBar Self-Determination Report, *supra,* at 71, fn 223.

[134] The UN Secretariat established a technical commission to work out the "terms, ways and means of carrying out the peace proposals" that had been agreed to "in principle" in 1988. This technical commission first met on July 12, 1989, and included representatives from Polisario and Morocco. While the proposals were being hammered out,

and implementation of its terms by both parties until 2000, carry all the earmarks of an implicit acceptance under normal contract law principles.

Even if it could be argued that neither party accepted wholeheartedly the terms of the Settlement Plan when it was first submitted to the UN Security Council,[135] the written acceptance by both parties of the *Houston Accords* negotiated by James Baker, which essentially incorporated the terms of the Settlement Plan by reference, constitutes additional evidence of a legally enforceable agreement. As such these agreements possess the attributes of an armistice or treaty between the parties, administered by the United Nations and the AU, and just as with respect to any other armistice or treaty, they should not be able to be abrogated by one party without legal consequences.

Indeed, it is difficult to believe that a situation can exist in which a belligerent state party can agree to the terms of a plan to settle a dispute with another belligerent party under the auspices of the United Nations and then, after a period of over fifteen years of expense and effort on the part of the United Nations to put that plan into effect, simply refuse to go ahead with it because the decisions made by the United Nations—in total conformity with and in order to carry out the terms of its mandate—do not cater to its position, without suffering any repercussions under international law.[136]

Likewise, even assuming, *arguendo*, that Morocco had a legal right to claim and occupy Western Sahara in 1975, any rights it might have had at that time under international law to annex the territory outright were arguably compromised by its subsequent agreement with the Polisario, the United Nations and the AU in 1991 to cease hostilities and have the issue submitted to the indigenous inhabitants

two issues surfaced as the most contentious: the number of Moroccan troops to be withdrawn, and the process of voter identification for the referendum. Work and discussion at the technical level proceeded over the course of the year, supervised by UN Secretary-General Perez de Cuellar. The Secretary General finally unveiled his settlement proposals—revised in accordance with the agreement of this technical commission—to the Security Council on June 13, 1990. The plan detailed the role of the UN special representative, the arrangements for a cease-fire, the guidelines for the referendum (including voter identification procedures), the exchange of political prisoners and POWs, and the return of the refugees to the territory.

[135] There is evidence that both parties had expressed reservations to some of the provisions. King Hassan sent a personal letter to the Secretary General enumerating Morocco's reservations, specifically the issues of voter enfranchisement and the fact that "independence" was an option. The Polisario demanded a total Moroccan withdrawal so that Western Sahara could be placed under UN trusteeship and that the territory be sealed off to prevent an influx of settlers from Morocco. The final version of the Settlement Plan acquiesced in neither of these demands. However, later, at Morocco's request, the criteria for eligible voters was expanded in a manner it deemed satisfactory.

[136] As one commentator put it, "[w]hile states have a wide choice of disputes settlement means as indicated in Article 33 of the Charter, once they have exercised their option and a solution has been arrived at through a peaceful means so selected, the parties to a dispute are required to comply with it. It is not open to any of them to avoid compliance by arguing that the solution was not in conformity with the principles of justice." V.S. Mani, *The Role of Law and Legal Considerations in the Functioning of the United Nations*, in COLLECTIVE SECURITY LAW, (Nigel White ed.) (Routledge, 2003) at 80.

for determination by referendum under the auspices of the United Nations and the AU.

Looking back on that compromise, there are indications that Morocco's decision was a strategic one, aimed at shoring up its power base in the territory and in the diplomatic community and pursuing policies to ensure that if a referendum ever did take place, it would be on terms that would ensure Morocco's victory.[137] Having failed to influence in its favor the list of voters eligible to participate in the referendum, Morocco's only possible course of action was to renounce the referendum entirely. Nevertheless, its implicit agreement to a referendum and the terms of the Settlement Plan, and agreement to the *Houston Accords* negotiated by James Baker, is arguably not without legal consequences.

If the principles of international law normally applied to the settlement of state conflicts through arbitration were applied to this situation, there would clearly be such consequences. Indeed, there is a long history of states resolving disputes with each other on such sensitive issues as the delineation of borders through a mutually agreed arbitrator or mediator. Just as in the case of commercial disputes, there are

---

[137] Remarks by Driss Basri, the former Moroccan Minister of the Interior in charge of the Western Sahara portfolio, whose power was only exceeded by that of the King, in a 2003 interview with the Moroccan weekly *Al-Ayam* suggests this. When asked why Morocco agreed to share Western Sahara with Mauritania in the Madrid Accords, he responded that it was a tactical move to forestall independence and that "Sahara had to return to Morocco whether it liked it or not." When asked whether he was in favor of Morocco's agreement in 1991 to hold a referendum he replied "No, I was for the referendum only in a tactical way," and that the King in response to the same question had remarked "Do you think we are devoid of common sense? We would not embark in a referendum if we are not sure we would win it." *Al-Ayam*, 29 May—4 June, 2003. Indeed, throughout the history of the dispute both the present King and his father consistently made public statements indicating that they had no intention of permitting the option of independence, while at the same time officially supporting the idea of a referendum. When the special mission of the UN visited Morocco in 1975 the King informed it that Morocco would not accept the inclusion of independence among the options to be put to the Western Saharans in a referendum. The only acceptable question was: "Do you want to remain under the authority of Spain or to rejoin Morocco?" UN Mission Report, *supra*, at 85. In 1981, at the same time as King Hassan II was announcing his official "acceptance" of the referendum proposed by the OAU—with "independence" as an option—he announced in a broadcast to the Moroccan people that "The recovery of our Sahara is well and truly accomplished...This Sahara is ours. We are not prepared to give it up, and though we are in favor of any agreement that can put an end to the conflict, we cannot allow any such agreement to be made at the expense of an integral part of our national territory." *Le Monde*, March 5, 1980. On June 24 of the same year he pledged on TV that "we will not renounce a single grain of this Moroccan Sahara for which so many of us have sacrificed our blood and which has cost us so much money." *Le Monde*, June 26, 1981. When he returned to Morocco after the OAU summit he made it clear that he saw the referendum "as an act of confirmation" through which the "Moroccan citizens of the Sahara" would be able to affirm their allegiance to Morocco. As far as the Polisario were concerned, he refused even to acknowledge their existence as a party to the dispute, declaring that "For me, the parties interested by the Saharan affair remain Morocco, Algeria and Mauritania, to the exclusion of Polisario, which has never existed for the African community." *Le Monde*, July 4, 1981; *The Guardian* (London), July 4, 1981. The position of the King did not waver throughout the subsequent years. During the period in which MINURSO was attempting to register potential voters—when the UN was prohibited from communicating directly with the Sahrawi population in the territory and all information about the referendum was controlled by the Moroccans—Moroccan literature on the subject made no mention of the option of "independence," instead referring to the referendum only as a means to "affirm" the territory's annexation with Morocco. The Moroccan government persists to this day in deeming the conflict one between Morocco and Algeria and attempting to cast the Polisario as mere "Algerian puppets."

decisions of the International Court of Justice holding that once a state has agreed to the settlement of a dispute in such a manner, it cannot casually abdicate its responsibilities to proceed or to respect the decision of the arbitrator.

In 1950, for instance, the International Court of Justice in the *Interpretation of Peace Treaties with Bulgaria, Hungary and Romania* Advisory Opinion (First Phase) addressed the contentions of the governments of Bulgaria, Hungary and Romania, that they were not obligated to submit to arbitration by commissions set up by the United Nations, issues concerning whether they were upholding their human rights obligations under peace treaties they had entered into with certain allied and associated powers after the Second World War which called for the arbitration of disputes through such commissions. The governments denied the existence of treaty violations and refused to cooperate with the setting up of the commissions. The United Nations General Assembly requested an Advisory Opinion of the Court. The Court held that a dispute referable to arbitration by such a commission existed under the terms of the treaties and that the refusal of a party to appoint an arbitrator was a breach of its treaty obligations and a breach of its international responsibilities.[138] In the *Interpretation of Peace Treaties with Bulgaria, Hungary and Romania* Advisory Opinion (Second Phase), the Court was asked to determine whether the Secretary General of the United Nations was empowered to appoint an arbitrator to represent one of the parties if that party refused to abide by its treaty obligations requiring it to nominate an arbitrator. Although the Court decided that the Secretary General was not empowered to constitute an arbitral panel in a manner inconsistent with the treaty provisions, it noted, in *dicta*, that once an arbitral panel was properly constituted it would be empowered to make a valid award despite the withdrawal of an arbitrator or the lack of cooperation of a party.[139]

Similarly, the Court in the *Ambatielos Case (Greece v. United Kingdom)* Merits: Obligation to Arbitrate, May 19, 1953)[140] found that the United Kingdom was under an obligation to submit to arbitration disagreements with Greece over the validity of claims made on behalf of private persons based on a 1886 commercial treaty between the countries. According to the Declaration of 1926 both governments had agreed to submit to arbitration a certain category of disputes, including those under the 1886 treaty, and the Court found that once the parties had agreed to submit these disputes to arbitration they could not refuse to abide by the selected process.

---

[138] ICJ Reports (1950), p.77.

[139] *Id.*, at 229.

[140] ICJ Reports (1953), p. 10, 23.

In the *Applicability of the Obligation to Arbitrate Under Section 21 of the United Nations Headquarters Agreement of 26 June 1947*, April 26, 1988, the Court in its Advisory Opinion also upheld the validity of an arbitration clause and found that a dispute existed between the United States and the United Nations under the Headquarters Agreement which the United States was under an obligation to submit to arbitration.

As noted above in the case involving Bulgaria, Hungary and Romania, the Court had held that once validly constituted, an arbitral tribunal may continue and issue a valid award even without the participation of one of the parties or one of the arbitrators, or when some of the elements of the agreed process could not be accomplished.

Indeed, as S.M. Schwebel, in *International Arbitration: Three Salient Problems* (Grotius, Cambridge, 1987) remarked:

> "[I]t is difficult to credit the contention that, once the parties have entered into a treaty to arbitrate…which they implement by the establishment of an arbitral tribunal, designed to hear and resolve a particular dispute, and that tribunal receives and studies pleadings or actually hears part or all of a case which the parties present to it at the considerable cost to themselves, one party lawfully may render all this nugatory by the expedient of withdrawing its arbitrator."[141]

Once an award has been made by a properly constituted tribunal, it carries the force of law. Wallace-Bruce, in enumerating the principles governing the international arbitration process, lists the binding nature of tribunals and the finality of their decisions and comes to the conclusion that unless the agreement explicitly states otherwise, the *effectiveness* principle of international law demands that an arbitral award be both binding and final. The International Court of Justice has concurred. In the *Case Concerning the Arbitral Award of 31 July 1989 (Guinea-Bissau v. Senegal)* (1991)[142] the Court found that an arbitral award delineating common maritime boundaries between the countries in accordance with an arbitration agreement was valid and validly made, rejecting the contrary argument of Guinea-Bissau, and accordingly held that both parties had an obligation to enforce it. The Court noted that:

---

[141] Page 159. Judge Schwebel discusses various cases in which a state party has been required by the International Court of Justice to submit to an agreed method of resolving a dispute with another state. *See also,* S.M. Schwebel, Luke Sobota, Ryan Manton, INTERNATIONAL ARBITRATION: THREE SALIENT PROBLEMS, 2nd Ed. (Grotius, Cambridge, 2020).

[142] ICJ Reports (1991), p. 53

"[W]hen States sign an arbitration agreement, they are concluding an agreement with a very specific object and purpose: to entrust an arbitration tribunal with the task of settling a dispute in accordance with the terms agreed by the parties, who define in the agreement the jurisdiction of the tribunal and determine its limits."[143]

The Court further stated that the arbitrators have broad power to interpret their jurisdiction under an arbitration agreement, citing:

"...a rule consistently accepted by general international law in the matter of international arbitration...that, in the absence of any agreement to the contrary, an international tribunal has the right to decide as to its own jurisdiction and has the power to interpret for this purpose the instruments which govern that jurisdiction."[144]

In the *Case Concerning the Arbitral Award Made by the King of Spain on 23 December 1906*, the Court in 1960 also held not only that the parties had an obligation to implement a validly made arbitration award, but also that the arbitrators had broad power to interpret their own jurisdiction. In contesting the award rendered by the King, the issue raised by Nicaragua was whether the process by which the King had been appointed sole arbitrator was consistent with the terms of the arbitration agreement and whether such an appointment could be made and an award issued after the treaty whose provisions were at issue had expired.

The Court found that:

"In the opinion of the Court it was within the power of the arbitrators to interpret and apply the articles in question in order to discharge their function..."[145]

The Court further cited as relevant the facts that Nicaragua had raised no question in the arbitral proceedings before the King with regard either to the validity of his designation as arbitrator, or his jurisdiction as such, and that Nicaragua had fully participated in the arbitral proceedings before the King.

The decision of the Court can be easily supported by the principle of estoppel. As Ian Brownlie once observed, "A considerable weight of authority supports the

---

[143] ICJ Reports (1991), p.72, citing the *Delimitation o the Maritime Boundary in the Gulf of Maine Area, Judgement,* (ICJ Reports, 1984, p.266, para. 23).

[144] ICJ Reports (1991), pps. 68–69, citing *Nottebohm, Preliminary Objection, Judgement* (ICJ Reports, 1953, p. 119).

[145] ICJ Reports (1960), p. 206

view that estoppel is a general principle of international law, resting on principles of good faith and consistency."[146] He goes on to state: "Examples of judicial application of the broader version of the principle [of estoppel] are the Arbitral Award by the King of Spain[147] and the Temple case.[148] In the former case Nicaragua challenged the validity of the award on several grounds: the Court held the award valid and stated that it was no longer open to Nicaragua, who by express declaration and by conduct, had recognized the award as valid, to challenge its validity. In the Temple case Thailand sought to avoid a frontier agreement on the ground of error. In this case also the Court held that Thailand was precluded by her conduct from asserting that she did not accept the treaty...In the Jurisdiction Phase of the Nicaragua case the International Court held that the 'constant acquiescence' of Nicaragua in the various public statements...to the effect that Nicaragua was bound by its 1929 Declaration 'constitute a valid mode of manifestation of its intent to recognize the compulsory jurisdiction of the Court under Article 36, paragraph 2, of the statute...'"[149]

When put into the context of an international arbitration agreement an argument can clearly be made that Morocco is under a duty to abide by the terms of the Settlement Plan and the results of any referendum conducted by the United Nations pursuant to the Settlement Plan.

The Settlement Plan and the *Houston Accords* contain all the essential elements of an arbitration agreement: they contains a clear delineation of the issues which must be resolved and the process by which they must be resolved, and a clear conferral of authority to the United Nations to resolve such issues. Both these issues and the scope of authority of the decision maker on such issues are sufficiently defined in the Settlement Plan to permit enforcement; the fact that the process by which these issues are resolved would require further refinement by the decision maker is no obstacle to enforcement—indeed, such a situation is the norm in international arbitrations. Accordingly, it can be argued that the United Nations enjoys the authority to fashion the procedures to settle those issues in accordance with the Settlement Plan without obtaining the consensus of both parties at every step and over every issue.

If resort to general legal principles does not lead to this conclusion, than a careful examination of the creation of the Settlement Plan certainly would. Indeed,

---

[146] *See,* Brownlie's PRINCIPLES OF PUBLIC INTERNATIONAL LAW, *supra,* at 420.

[147] ICJ Reports (1960), *supra,* p. 213.

[148] ICJ Reports (1962), p. 32.

[149] *See,* Brownlie's PRINCIPLES OF PUBLIC INTERNATIONAL LAW, *supra,* at 606, citing ICJ Reports (1984), p. 411.

it would appear from the earliest documents outlining the terms of the Settlement Plan that agreement of the parties over every issue involving its enforcement was not what the parties—or the United Nations—initially intended. In the first Report of the Secretary General outlining the provisions of the Settlement Plan, S/1990/21360 (June 18, 1990) under the heading "Mandate and Functions of the Special Representative of the Secretary General," the Secretary General indicated that during the period of transition and until the proclamation of the results of the referendum, the Special Representative would have sole and exclusive authority to resolve all questions concerning the referendum, its organization and its control.[150] If there was any doubt that the parties had conferred "sole" and "exclusive" authority upon the United Nations to fashion the procedures by which the referendum would be conducted it was quickly removed in the following Report of the Secretary General, S/1991/22464 (19 April 1991), in which he noted:

> "The two parties, namely the Kingdom of Morocco and the Frente POLISARIO, recognize in the settlement proposals that sole and exclusive responsibility for the organization and conduct of the referendum is vested in the United Nations. Accordingly, I will issue regulations governing the organization and conduct of the referendum that will essentially embody the relevant provisions of the settlement proposals agreed to by the parties. My Special Representative, acting under my authority and, as necessary, on instructions from and in consultation with me, will have sole and exclusive responsibility over all matters with regard to the organization and conduct of the referendum. He will be authorized to issue rules and instructions consistent with the regulations issued by me...."

If there is no need to obtain the consensus of the parties over every issue relating to the organization of the referendum, one of the major problems cited by the Secretary General in resolving this dispute evaporates. Moreover, if such were the case, there would be no need to obtain a Security Council resolution specifically conferring authority upon the United Nations to fashion rules for implementing the Settlement Plan without the consensus of the parties over the details of such implementation: that authority was already conferred by the parties when they agreed to the Settlement Plan.

Indeed, if the rules developed in the context of international arbitration were

---

[150] UN Doc. S/1990/21360 at 2.

applied to the present circumstances the fact that the United Nations Security Council assumed a role in the dispute under Chapter 6 of the United Nations Charter,[151] (which permits the mediation of disputes at the behest of the concerned parties), instead of Chapter 7,[152] (which authorizes the Security Council to take measures to preserve the peace without regard to the wishes of the concerned parties), would not prohibit the Security Council from enforcing an agreement of the parties reached through its mediation.

The fact that the United Nations failed to interpret its mandate so as to assert authority over the conduct of the referendum and instead permitted the parties to control every aspect of its organization was a major tactical error that virtually ensured that its mission could not be carried out. The fact that it later permitted Morocco to withdraw from the referendum process and breach its agreement with the Saharawis, the AU and the UN with impunity is unconscionable.

---

[151] Chapter 6 of the UN Charter, involving the "Pacific Settlement of Disputes" calls upon member states to resolve through negotiation or other peaceful means any dispute which is likely to endanger the maintenance of international peace and directs the Security Council to call upon the parties to settle such disputes by such means. It also empowers any member to bring any dispute to the attention of the Security Council, and in such cases for the Security Council to recommend appropriate procedures.

[152] Chapter 7 of the UN Charter, involving "Action With Respect to Threats to the Peace, Breaches of the Peace, and Acts of Aggression" empowers the Security Council to take appropriate action to maintain peace regardless of the approval of the belligerents.

PART III

Legal Issues—The Right to Resources

SUBSUMED IN THE right to self-determination is the right of a people to permanent sovereignty over their natural resources.[1] However, ever since its occupation of the territory, Morocco has freely used the resources of Western Sahara, including its phosphates, fisheries, agricultural products, sand, and most recently wind power, without the consent of the native inhabitants and essentially for its own benefit. And Morocco has noted its intention to utilize any oil or precious minerals that might be discovered within its borders. This raises a question: does Morocco have a right under international law to utilize these resources, and if so, under what conditions?

(1) The Rights of An Administering Power

(a) The 2002 Advisory Opinion of the UN Undersecretary for Legal Affairs

In 2002, the Undersecretary of the United Nations for Legal Affairs, Hans Corell, attempted to address these questions.

As was noted previously, in October of 2001 the Moroccan "Office National de Recherchés et d'Exploitations Petrolieres" (ONAREP) concluded two contracts for oil-reconnaissance and evaluation activities in areas of off-shore Western Sahara,

---

[1] "Declaration of Permanent Sovereignty over Natural Resources," G.A. Res 1803 (XVI) (December 14, 1962); Article 1(2) of the International Covenant on Civil and Political Rights (1976) and Article 1(2) of the International Covenant on Economic, Social and Cultural Rights (1976), United Nations Council for Namibia, "Decree No. 1 for the Protection of Natural Resources of Namibia," adopted in G.A. Res. 3295 (December 13, 1974), and G.A. Res. 57/132 (February 25, 2003). For a discussion of this right, see C. Drew, *The East Timor Story: International Law on Trial*, 12 European Journal of International Law, 2001, at 651–684, and Stephanie Koury, *The European Community and Member States' Duty of Non-Recognition under the EC-Morocco Association Agreement: State Responsibility and Customary International Law*, INTERNATIONAL LAW AND THE QUESTION OF WESTERN SAHARA, *supra*, at 170–172.

one with a subsidiary of the United States oil-company Kerr McGee (Kerr McGee du Maroc, Ltd.) and the other with a subsidiary of the French oil company TotalFinaElf (TotalFinaElf E&P Maroc). Concluded for an initial period of 12 months, both contracts contained standard options for the relinquishment of the rights under the contract or its continuation, including an option for future oil contracts in the respective areas.

In November of 2001, at the urging of the Polisario, the President of the Security Council addressed a letter to the United Nations Undersecretary for Legal Affairs, Hans Corell, requesting his opinion on "the legality in the context of international law, including relevant resolutions of the Security Council and the General Assembly of the United Nations, and agreements concerning Western Sahara," of these contracts.

In an opinion issued on January 29, 2002 in response to this request ("the Corell Opinion"),[2] Corell first analyzed the legal position of Morocco in Western Sahara. He determined that the Madrid Accords "did not transfer sovereignty over the territory, nor did it confer upon any of the signatories the status of an administering Power—a status which Spain alone could not have unilaterally transferred," and that the transfer of administrative authority to Morocco and Mauritania in 1975 "did not affect the international status of Western Sahara as a Non-Self-Governing Territory." He noted furthermore that "Morocco…is not listed as the administering Power of the territory in the United Nations list of Non-Self-Governing Territories…."[3]

Nonetheless, despite his conclusion that Morocco had never been designated the "administering power" of the territory, for the purpose of answering the question posed by the President of the Security Council, Corell examined the historic rights and obligations of administering powers—reasoning that these would be the most expansive rights Morocco could claim, and that if Morocco's activities were impermissible under the rights accorded to administering powers there would be no need to discuss Morocco's actual status.

He noted that the rights of "administering powers" are limited; that they have the obligation "to ensure that all economic activities in the Non-Self-Governing Territories under their administration do not adversely affect the interests of the peoples of such territories, but are instead directed to assist them in the exercise of their right to self-determination."[4] He noted as well the resolutions

---

[2] Letter dated January 29, 2002, from Undersecretary of the United Nations for Legal Affairs Hans Corell to the President of the Security Council, S/2002/161 (February 12, 2002), *supra,* ("the Corell Opinion")

[3] Corell Opinion at 2.

[4] Citing G.A. Res. 35/118 (December 11, 1980); 52/78 (December 10,1997); 54/91 (December 6, 1999); 55/147 (December 8, 2000); and 56/74 (December 10, 2001).

declaring that "the exploitation and plundering of the marine and other natural resources of colonial and Non-Self-Governing Territories by foreign economic interests, in violation of the relevant resolutions of the United Nations, is a threat to the integrity and prosperity of these Territories," and that "any administering Power that deprives the colonial peoples of Non-Self-Governing Territories of the exercise of their legitimate rights over their natural resources...violates the solemn obligations it has assumed under the Charter of the United Nations."[5]

He then referred to instances in the past in which mineral exploitation by administering powers had been questioned. After concluding that the case law of the International Court of Justice was inconclusive on the extent to which administering powers may utilize natural resources during their period of occupation in the two cases in which that issue had been presented,[6] he then referred to the practice of States, and noted that such precedent was also inconclusive: in the case of Namibia, the exploitation of uranium and other natural resources by South Africa was condemned,[7] whereas in the case of East Timor an arrangement with Australia for the exploitation of oil and natural gas deposits was approved on the basis that representatives of the East Timorese people had actively participated in the arrangement.[8]

Despite the inconclusive nature of State practice concerning this issue,

---

[5] Citing G.A. Res. 48/46 (December 10, 1992) and 49/40 (December 9, 1994).

[6] In the Case of East Timor, Portugal argued that in negotiating with Indonesia an agreement on the exploration and exploitation of the continental shelf in the area of the Timor Gap, Australia had failed to respect the right of the people of East Timor to permanent sovereignty over its natural wealth and resources, and the powers and rights of Portugal as the administering Power of East Timor. In the absence of Indonesia's participation in the proceedings, however, the ICJ concluded that it lacked jurisdiction to decide the issue. In the Nauru Phosphate Case, Nauru claimed the rehabilitation of certain phosphate lands worked out before independence in the period of the Trusteeship administered by Australia, New Zealand and the United Kingdom. Nauru argued that the principle of permanent sovereignty over natural resources was breached in circumstances in which a major resource was depleted on grossly inequitable terms and its extraction involved the physical reduction of the land. Following the Judgment on the Preliminary Objections, the parties reached a settlement and a Judgment on the merits was no longer required.

[7] Corell noted that the exploitation of uranium and other natural resources in Namibia by South Africa and a number of Western multinational corporations was considered illegal under Decree No. 1 for the Protection of the Natural Resources of Namibia, enacted in 1974 by the United Nations Council for Namibia, and was condemned by the General Assembly (G.A. Res. 36/51 of November 24, 1981, and 39/42 of December 5,1984). He suggested, however, that the case of Namibia "must be seen in the light of Security Council resolution 278 (1970) of 30 January 1970, which declared that the continued presence of South Africa in Namibia was illegal and that consequently all acts taken by the Government of South Africa were illegal and invalid."

[8] Corell suggested that the case of East Timor under the United Nations Transitional Administration in East Timor (UNTAET) was "unique" in that it involved the decisions of a UN body, not an "administering power." By the time UNTAET was established in October 1999, the Timor Gap Treaty was fully operational and concessions had been granted in the Zone of Cooperation by Indonesia and Australia. In order to ensure the continuity of the practical arrangements under this Treaty, UNTAET concluded an Exchange of Letters with Australia for the continued operation of the terms of the Treaty. Two years later, in anticipation of independence, UNTAET negotiated with Australia a draft "Timor Sea Arrangement" which was to replace the Treaty. On both occasions, according to the Legal Counsel, UNTAET "consulted fully" with representatives of the East Timorese people, who "participated actively" in the negotiations.

Corell nevertheless distilled certain legal principles in common: where resource exploitation activities are conducted for the benefit of the peoples of non-self-governing territories, on their behalf, and in consultation with their representatives, "they are considered compatible with the Charter obligations of the administering Power, and in conformity with the General Assembly resolutions and the principle of 'permanent sovereignty over natural resources' enshrined therein."[9] On the other hand, when such activities are conducted in disregard of the needs and interests of the people of that territory, they are illegal. Although he determined that the specific contracts between Morocco and the oil companies referred to him were not in themselves illegal, since they did not entail exploitation or the physical removal of the mineral resources, he noted that "if further exploration and exploitation activities were to proceed in disregard of the interests and wishes of the people of Western Sahara, they would be in violation of the international law principles applicable to mineral resource activities in Non-Self-Governing Territories."[10]

The conclusion of the Legal Counsel was reaffirmed by the General Assembly in a number of resolutions, most recently General Assembly Resolution 61/123 of December 14, 2006 in which *inter alia*, the General Assembly stated that it:

> "1. *Reaffirms* the right of peoples of Non-Self-Governing Territories to self determination…as well as their right to the enjoyment of their natural resources and their right to dispose of those resources in their best interest;
>
> 2. *Affirms* the value of foreign economic investment undertaken in collaboration with the peoples of the Non-Self-Governing Territories and in accordance with their wishes…."

According to the Under Secretary General for Legal Affairs of the United Nations and the General Assembly, therefore, Morocco has no right to enter into any contracts for the exploitation of the natural resources of Western Sahara unless it can demonstrate that such exploitation is being done in accordance with the interests and wishes of the people of Western Sahara and inure to their benefit, and not primarily to the benefit of Morocco, and any such contracts would be considered illegal and unenforceable under international law.

---

[9] Corell Opinion at 7.

[10] Corell Opinion at 8.

(b) Morocco's Response

Following the Corell Opinion, Morocco only slightly modified its activities. In an attempt to convince the international community that it was exploiting the resources of the territory for the benefit of the local community and with their consent, it revived a previously disbanded consultative group, CORCAS, made up of pro-Moroccan Saharawis, who "approved" its decisions, following which it invested in local infrastructure projects.

Meanwhile, its utilization of the resources of the territory continued unabated.

(i) Oil Exploration/Exploitation

As noted previously, in October 2001, the Moroccan state oil company, ONHYM, entered into agreements with subsidiaries of Kerr-McGee and TotalFinaElf, to engage in pre-exploration activities in the oil reserves off the coast of Western Sahara. The agreement with Kerr-McGee's subsidiary would have allowed the company to explore approximately 110,000 square kilometers of deep water off the coast of Western Sahara, while the agreement with TotalFinaElf's subsidiary was for exploration of a 115,000 square kilometer area off the coast of the Dakhla region.

Following the release of the Corell Opinion, both Kerr-McGee[11] and Total S.A. (successor to TotalFinaElf) continued to engage in research and evaluation work in the territory. However, both companies eventually abandoned exploration activities in the region at least in part due to negative publicity.[12] The withdrawal of Kerr-McGee in particular came after the Norwegian Government's Petroleum Fund, one of the largest investment funds in the world, liquidated its $52 million investment in the company on the basis of the conclusion of the Fund's Council on Ethics that "based on the rationale behind the general rules of international law in this area...the economic activities off shore Western Sahara can be considered unethical."[13]

---

[11] Kerr McGee du Maroc Ltd. entered into a reconnaissance permit with ONHYM for the Boujdour area offshore from the portion of Western Sahara currently occupied by Morocco. The permit was renewed on several occasions and the contract was valid through 2006. See C. Wilson, *Foreign Companies Plundering Western Sahara Resources: Who is Involved and What is Being Done to Stop This?*, INTERNATIONAL LAW AND THE QUESTION OF WESTERN SAHARA, *supra*, at 254. In its 2006 SEC filing, the parent company listed the Boujdour block as being part of Moroccan territory and within its exploration plans.

[12] See, e.g., *Kerr-McGee Folds*, Le Journal Hebdomadaire, January 12, 2005; SADR Petroleum Authority, Press Release dated May 3, 2006 (http://www.sadroilandgas.com/pdfs/kerr_mcgee_withdrawl.pdf); *No oil off Sahara*, Afrol News, November 29, 2004 (http://www.afrol.com/articles/14879).

[13] The Petroleum Fund's Council on Ethics, "Recommendation on exclusion from the Government Petroleum Fund's investment universe of the company Kerr-McGee Corporation," Oslo, April 11, 2005, at 6. The Fund's Council on Ethics determined, *inter alia*, that Kerr-McGee's activities in Western Sahara constituted an unacceptable risk for contributing to other particularly serious violations of fundamental ethical norms.

However, Total's interest resurfaced in 2011 with its acquisition of a license for the biggest block, and the withdrawal of these companies did not deter others from entering the market. By October of 2010, according to ONHYM, Morocco's state owned petroleum company, it had at least four corporate partners engaged in exploratory activities in regions that include Western Saharan territory: Kosmos,[14] San Leon Energy,[15] Longreach Oil & Gas,[16] and DVM International.[17]

Then, in October 2013, Cairn Energy, a Scottish company, entered into a joint venture agreement with Kosmos to explore the Boujdour sector.

Total announced in December 2015 that it would not prolong its reconnaissance contract as first test results were not propitious. However, San Leon and Kosmos, as of the end of 2016, still held one or two licenses in Western Sahara, and although in its 2015 Annual Report Cairn stated that the Boujdour license was in the process of being relinquished, it also stated that the joint venture is looking to enter into a new exploration license in the area.[18]

According to data collected by the NGO Western Sahara Resource Watch,[19] as of the end of 2016, the firms conducting activities connected to the extraction of oil and gas in Western Sahara, either directly or through subsidiaries, included San Leon, Kosmos, Cairn, Glencore PLC, New Age (African Global Energy, Ltd.), Teredo Oils, Ltd., PetroMaroc Corp./Longreach Oil and Gas, Ltd., and XPlorer Plc. Most of the foreign companies have since left the market, but both San Leon, Kosmos and Cairn have left the door open to future involvements.

Although the initial activities of these firms were only "exploratory," they clearly envisaged exploitation. In December of 2014, Kosmos was responsible for the first off-shore drilling operations in Western Sahara with the rig "Atwood Achiever." In 2015 San Leon drilled the first on-shore well in Western Sahara.

And Morocco has given no indication that it will cease oil exploration activities. In April of 2019, Gesto Energy, a Portuguese company, announced on its website that it had been selected by the government of Morocco to "identify and study

---

[14] In 2004, U.S.-based Kosmos Energy and its affiliate Kosmos Energy Offshore Morocco ("Kosmos") purchased a 30% interest in the Boujdour sub-basin from ONHYM. In 2006, Kosmos entered into a Petroleum Agreement with ONHYM granting it a 75% interest in the Boujdour sub-basin.

[15] In 2008, the Irish energy firm, San Leon Energy Plc, through its subsidiary, San Leon Morocco Ltd, ("San Leon") entered into 8-year licenses with ONHYM regarding the Zag Basin and Tarfaya Onshore basins.

[16] In 2008 and 2009, U.K.-based Longreach Oil & Gas Ventures Ltd. entered into licenses with ONHYM relating to the exploration of the Zag Basin and Tarfaya Onshore block.

[17] In February 2010, Australian-based DVM International, Ltd. acquired a 75% working interest and operatorship in the Tarfaya Offshore Block.

[18] Cairn's Annual Report, 2015, p. 33, cited in Western Sahara Resource Watch, April 18, 2016.

[19] Western Sahara Resource Watch is an organization established in Brussels in 2005, dedicated to monitoring Morocco's use of the resources of Western Sahara, informing the public, and lobbying to stop the trade in products from the territory. It publishes information on the internet at wsrw.org.

areas with geothermal potential in the provinces of south of Morocco in an area of more than 140,000 km2, corresponding to Moroccan Sahara," and signed a contract for the project with ONHYM. In December, 2019, Gesto reported that its team had collected samples of water and gas during November in "southern Morocco." Despite being asked to do so, Gesto has refused to hand over the collected data to the Saharawi authorities and the United Nations.[20]

None of these companies obtained the permission of the Polisario, the representatives of the Saharawi people recognized as such by the United Nations, for any of their activities, and they have sparked a public outcry and the withdrawal of support from some of their major financial backers. For instance, Norway's sovereign wealth fund has excluded several of these firms from its portfolio because of their activities in Western Sahara,[21] and other funds and investors have taken similar measures against them and the other firms which have benefitted from Morocco's use of the territory's resources. This has dissuaded some companies from entering the market; however, others have remained.

It should be noted that oil and gas are non-renewable commodities, and once they are depleted, they cannot be replaced. If Morocco succeeds in extracting oil and gas from Western Sahara without the permission of the Saharawis, and without the revenue from such extraction inuring principally to their benefit, the rights of the indigenous population of the territory under international law will be severely compromised.

(ii) Phosphate Extraction

One of the principal export commodities of Western Sahara is high-grade phosphate ore. Phosphate ore, like oil and gas, is a finite commodity, which once depleted, cannot be renewed. Morocco has depleted the Western Sahara phosphate reserves for over 40 years, selling phosphates emanating from Western Sahara on the international market. By 2020 the top strata of phosphates—the highest quality—had already been depleted.[22] The Boucraa mine has now become a wholly owned subsidiary of Morocco's state owned mining company, Office Cherifien de Phosphates ("OCP"), which has marketed its produce as its own.

---

[20] *See,* Western Sahara Resource Watch, April 8, 2020.

[21] *See also,* Recommendation of February 8, 2016 to exclude Kosmos Energy Ltd. And Cairn Energy Plc.; Recommendation of December 21, 2015 to exclude San Leon Energy Plc; Recommendation of September 28, 2014 to exclude Inhophos Holdings, Inc.; Recommendations in 2010 and 2011 on the exclusion of the companies FMC Corporation and Potash Corporation of Saskatchewan; Recommendation of May 15, 2009 on the exclusion of the company Elbit Systems Ltd.

[22] Western Sahara Resource Watch report, "P for Plunder 2020: Morocco's Exports of Phosphates from Occupied Western Sahara," February, 2020, at 3.

In 2006 it was reported that vessels carried phosphates from the harbor of Laayoune directly to fertilizer processors in Florida and Louisiana,[23] Colombia, Mexico, Venezuela, Australia, New Zealand and a number of companies in Eastern Europe, Asia and Western Europe.[24] Although some importers have since then dropped out of the market (due largely to pressure from their investors and adverse publicity), it was estimated that vessels carrying phosphates originating in Western Sahara in 2019 still supplied importers in China, New Zealand, India and, most recently, Brazil.[25]

According to Western Sahara Resources Watch, two Canadian companies, Agrium and PotashCorp., were behind two-thirds of all imports of phosphates from Western Sahara in 2015.[26] Potash imported phosphates from Western Sahara for over two decades, and was the single largest importer of Boucraa's output in 2015. In 2015 the company purchased 474,000 tonnes, more than twice as much as in the previous year, in eight shipments, with an estimated value of $56.5 million.[27] In that year Agrium, another Canadian firm, imported nearly as much—442,000 tonnes. Another large importer over the past seven years was Lifosa, whose parent company is the Russian fertilizer manufacturer Euro Chem.

On January 1, 2018 Potash merged with Agrium to form a new company, Nutrien. From 2013 to the end of 2018, Potash/Agrium/Nutrien accounted for approximately 50% of the phosphate rock mined in Western Sahara.

Due to concerns that the importers of phosphates from Western Sahara are violating international human rights standards, a number of sovereign wealth funds ceased their investments in those companies. In 2015 the Swedish government divested its assets in Agrium and its pension fund removed PotashCorp and Incitec Pivot, another importer, from its portfolio. The Norwegian insurance company KLP also divested its holdings in Agrium, and the government's pension fund in 2015 canceled its investments in Mexican importer Innophos Holdings. The pension fund of Luxembourg removed all importers of phosphates from Western Sahara from its portfolio, and the pension fund of the Netherlands ceased investing in OCP SA.

These measures produced results. Innophos ceased imports of products from Western Sahara after 2014; Incitec after 2016. On February 16, 2016, due to

[23] The companies in Florida and Louisiana were subsidiaries of PotashCorp, a Canadian company.

[24] C. Wilson, *Foreign Companies Plundering Western Sahara Resources: Who is Involved and What is Being Done to Stop This?*, INTERNATIONAL LAW AND THE QUESTION OF WESTERN SAHARA, *supra*, at 270–271.

[25] Western Sahara Resource report "P for Plunder 2020: Morocco's Exports of Phosphates from Occupied Western Sahara," at 19.

[26] *See*, Western Sahara Resource Watch report,"P for Plunder 2015," April 8, 2016, which traced all shipments of phosphate rock from Western Sahara in 2015.

[27] *Id*. at 15.

adverse publicity, Euro Chem announced its decision to end its importation of products from Western Sahara. Nutrien discontinued purchasing Western Sahara phosphates directly at the end of 2018. However, it owns a significant percent of the stock of another company, Sinofert Holdings, Ltd., whose major stockholder is the government of China, and which entered the market in 2018.[28]

Western Sahara Resource Watch reported in 2020 that Moroccan exports of phosphates from Western Sahara in 2019 dropped to the lowest level since 2012, accounting for 1.03 million tonnes, valued at $90 million, down from 1.9 million tonnes, worth $164 million in 2018.[29]

However, although some companies have left the market, four new importers have emerged. Besides Sinofert Holdings, these include Paradip from India, which started imports in 2016, Coromandel, also from India, which took a shipment in January of 2019, and most recently an unknown company in Brazil. Together with Ballance Agri-Nutrients and Ravensdown, both from New Zealand, they represent the companies currently in the market.[30]

In 2019, the government of New Zealand urged the two Kiwi companies to refrain from importing phosphate from Western Sahara, and protestors have staged a number of marches protesting the imports.[31] However, so far the companies have not complied.

It would appear, therefore, that despite the fact that the exportation of phosphates from Western Sahara by Morocco clearly violates principles of international law, the trade in this product will continue until and unless the international community finally holds Morocco accountable.

(iii) Wind Power/Renewable Energy

On December 15, 2015, Western Sahara Resource Watch reported that Siemen's Wind Power, a subsidiary of German company Siemens, and Enel Green Power, an Italian firm, had won a tender to construct two wind farms in Western Sahara as part of a wind farm project in collaboration with a Moroccan company Nareva.[32] Nareva is a subsidiary of SNI Holding, a company owned by the Moroccan royal family.[33] As of 2020, 22 windmills are already in operation. Construction of the

---

[28] Western Sahara Resource Watch, January 27, 2019.

[29] Western Sahara Resource Watch report, "P for Plunder 2020: Morocco's Exports of Phosphates from Occupied Western Sahara," February 2020.

[30] *Id.*, at 11. According to reports there were possibly two other unknown companies in Brazil and China.

[31] Western Sahara Resource Watch, May 9, 2020.

[32] Western Sahara Resource Watch, December 15, 2015.

[33] *Id.* According to Western Sahara Resource Watch, the King owns 74% of the company.

remainder is expected to take place in the coming year. These wind farms are part of a government plan to obtain over 50% of Morocco's energy from renewable sources by 2030, the government announced at COP21.[34]

A new report by WSRW details how as part of this plan Morocco expects to build over 1000 megawatts of renewable energy plants in Western Sahara.[35]

According to OCP, Morocco's state-owned phosphate company, 95% of the energy now used to power the exportation of phosphates from the Boucraa mines is provided by the 22 wind farms built by Siemens.[36] Much of the remaining energy produced by these wind farms and the ones planned for the future in the territory is expected to be exported to Europe. On November 16, 2016, Spain, Portugal, France and Germany signed a joint declaration with Morocco for future cooperation on renewable energy as a prelude to the purchase of clean energy from Morocco in the foreseeable future.

Much of this clean energy will come not from Morocco, but from Western Sahara.

(iv) Fisheries and Agricultural Products

Besides phosphates the most lucrative, and controversial, trade in products from Western Sahara involves fisheries.

The waters off the coast of Western Sahara contain some of the best fishery resources in Africa—resources which are in high demand by residents of European nations. It is not surprising, then, that during the past thirty years the European Union, and its predecessors the EEC and EC, have been parties to several trade agreements with Morocco that involve fishery and agricultural products resources, all of which either explicitly or implicitly permitted their application to territories over which Morocco exercised not only sovereignty but also "jurisdiction," or which failed to limit explicitly the territorial application of their scope. In all of these cases the European officials who negotiated these agreements knew or should have known that they would be applied by Morocco to goods from the territory of Western Sahara. It is within the context of these trade agreements that the right of Morocco to exploit the resources of the territory has been most hotly debated.

In 1988 and again in 1992, when the EEC negotiated its first fisheries sector agreements with Morocco,[37] its stated purpose was to provide "fishing opportunities

---

[34]   Western Sahara Resource Watch, December 15, 2015.

[35]   *See,* Western Sahara Resource Watch report, "Powering the Plunder," November 2, 2016.

[36]   *See,* Western Sahara Resource Watch report, "P for Plunder 2020: Morocco's Exports of Phosphates from Occupied Western Sahara," February, 2020 at 11.

[37]   Prior to this, as part of the agreement under which Spain and Portugal became members of the EEC, the EEC in 1985 assumed responsibility for some of their existing fisheries agreements with Morocco. *See,* OJL 302, November 15, 1985, page 128; OJ L 232, August 19, 1987, page 18–19; OJ L 346, December 10, 1987, page 35. *See also,* "Report

for fishermen of the enlarged Community in the waters over which Morocco has sovereignty *or jurisdiction*."[38] (italics supplied).

This was followed by a new fisheries agreement in 1995. By its terms, the scope of the agreement covered waters "of which the Kingdom of Morocco has sovereignty *or jurisdiction*" (Article 1).[39]

In 2006 the European Union negotiated another EU-Moroccan fisheries agreement, the Fisheries Partnership Agreement ("FPA")[40] which set forth a scheme in which the government of Morocco received direct financial contributions from the European Union in exchange for issuing fishing licenses for European Union vessels. Again, there was no effort to limit the scope of the agreement to those waters over which Morocco exercised sovereignty. Article 2 provided that the "Moroccan fishing zone" governed by the agreement "means the waters falling within the sovereignty *or jurisdiction* of the Kingdom of Morocco." The text of the FPA did not describe the boundary of the maritime areas covered in the agreement.[41]

There was no delineation of the southern border of Morocco's "jurisdiction" in any of these agreements. However, there was evidence that the parties clearly understood that these agreements would be applied to the waters off the coast of Western Sahara. For instance, the list of ports and fishing companies accepted under the 2006 agreement, which were devised for the prior 1995 EC-Morocco fisheries agreement, included companies operating out of ports in Western Sahara, including Dakhla, Boujdour, and Laayoune,[42] and there was evidence of fishing

---

on Legal Issues Involved in the Western Sahara Dispute: Use of Natural Resources," Committee on the United Nations, Bar Association of the City of New York, April 2011 ("NYCBar Resources Report") at 16.

[38] OJ L 99, April 16, 1988, pages 45, 47, 61; OJ L 181, July 12, 1988, pages 1–17; OJ L 218, August 1, 1992, pages 137–138; OJ L 407, December 31, 1992, pages 3–14. Both of these agreements augmented the Moroccan treasury. The protocol to the 1988 agreement provided for the EEC to make a number of financial contributions to Morocco, including direct disbursements to its Ministry of Maritime Fishing and Merchant Navy. Articles 2 and 6 of the 1992 agreement provided for financial disbursements to build up Moroccan scientific research, and develop Morocco's human resources and training facilities for the maritime industry. *See* OJ L 407, December 31, 1992, pages 3–14, *cited in* NYCBar Resources Report at 16–17.

[39] It also contained direct references to benefits and direct financial contributions to Morocco. OJ L 306, December 19, 1995, pages 7–43. For example, Article 3 provided that the parties shall undertake the sustainable development of Morocco's fisheries sector, including "development of port infrastructure and the improvement of conditions for the reception of fishing fleets in Moroccan ports."Article 4 provided for a financial contribution to the vocational training of seamen." *See,* NYCBar Resources Report at 16–17.

[40] *See,* http://eur-lex.europa.eu/LexUriServ/LexUriServ.do?uri=OJ:L:2006:141:0004:0037:EN:PDF. OJ L 141, May 29, 2006, page 4 *et seq.*, adopted pursuant to Council Regulation (EC) No. 764/2006 (OJ L 141, May 29, 2006, at 1), *cited in* NYCBar Resources Report at 17.

[41] *See* Legal Opinion of the European Parliament Legal Service, SJ-0085/06, dated February 20, 2006, paragraph 45, at 9; San Martin, Pablo, "EU-Morocco Fisheries Agreement: The Unforeseen Consequences of a Very Dangerous Turn," Colaboraciones del Grupo de Estudios Estrategicos (GEES), no. 1013 (http://www.gees.org/articulos/ eu_morocco_fisheries_agreement_the_unforeseen_consequences_of_a_very_dangerous_turn_2601, accessed May 16, 2010), *cited in* NYCBar Resources Report at 18.

[42] Annex B to European Community Decision 95/30/EC, amended EU 08/07/2005.

by European Union and Moroccan vessels in Western Saharan waters while these agreements were in force.[43] Moreover, there were no requirements under this or any of the previous agreements that any portion of the funds contributed by the European Union would be used for the benefit of the people of Western Sahara. Rather, Morocco was given "full discretion" regarding the use of the funds.[44]

Following the conclusion of the FPA in 2006, the European Parliament asked its Legal Service to provide an opinion on the question of whether that agreement would be compatible with the principles of international law.[45] In an unpublished opinion circulated in 2006,[46] the Legal Service referred to the criteria outlined in the Corell Opinion and, proceeding under the assumption that Morocco was the *de facto* "administrator" of Western Sahara, noted: (1) that Western Sahara had a special status under international law: the status of a Non-Self-Governing Territory under Article 73 of the United Nations Charter, and (2) that according to the principles of international law applicable to a territory of that status, Western Sahara "enjoys the right to the natural resources of the territory, in the sense that economic activities concerning those resources shall not be carried out in disregard of the interests and wishes of the local population."[47] It then concluded that the question depended upon whether the Moroccans disregarded their obligations to the Saharawis under such principles and suggesting that if they did, the Community could "suspend" the operation of the agreement.[48] Meanwhile, a series of written Parliamentary questions and answers with the Committee on Fisheries during the period confirmed that according to data reported under the FPA, catches were taking place in areas off the coast of Western Sahara.[49]

This was the first of several opinions of the European Union Legal Service that concluded that the trade agreements between the EU and Morocco may be violating international law. On July 13, 2009 the Legal Service issued a second legal opinion containing an analysis of whether the implementation of the FPA to

---

[43] According to the U.S. Central Intelligence Agency, besides permitting European vessels to fish in the territorial waters of Morocco, they were also permitted to fish in the waters off the coast of Western Sahara. *See*, "CIA World Factbook 2010—Western Sahara," (https://www.cia.gov/library/publications/the-world-factbook/geos/wi.html) *cited in* NYCBar Resources Report at 17.

[44] OJ L 141, pages 6 and 9.

[45] Doc. SJ-0085/06, D(2006)7352, February 2006.

[46] *See* Legal Opinion of the European Parliament Legal Service, SJ-0085/06, dated February 20, 2006, paragraph 45, at 9 (available by unofficial copy at http://www.arso.org/LegalopinionUE200206.pdf); see also the report, dated May 4, 2006, of the European Parliament Committee on Fisheries, A6-0163/2006.

[47] *Id.* para. 37.

[48] M. Brus, *The Legality of Exploring and Exploiting Mineral Resources in Western Sahara*, INTERNATIONAL LAW AND THE QUESTION OF WESTERN SAHARA, *supra*, at 213.

[49] *See*, written questions E-1073/08 of March 4, 2008, E-4295/08 of July 25, 2008, and E-0717/10 of February 16, 2010, and the written answers thereto by Commissioner Borg, *cited in* the NYCBar Resources Report at 20.

date was in compliance with international law, and recommended that EU officials conduct an assessment of how the FPA was being administered by Morocco.[50]

The assessment suggested by the Legal Service was never carried out.[51] Rather, the Commission suggested that it was Morocco's responsibility to ensure compliance with the rights of the people of Western Sahara under international law.[52] This suggestion was not adopted by the members of Parliament, however, who refused to extend the FPA beyond February of 2012.[53]

The failure of the European Parliament to extend the EU-Moroccan Fisheries Agreement spurred negotiations to draft a new agreement. In December of 2013, the European Union and Morocco announced a "new" fisheries Protocol to the FPA. However, this new Protocol did not cure the defects in the old agreement. It included no precise delimitation of the scope of its application.[54] It simply referred to a Moroccan "fishing zone, " which included "waters in which the Kingdom of Morocco exercises its jurisdiction as regards fishing," and provided that vessels may be licensed to fish in waters south of 29 degrees latitude. It can again be inferred that the parties envisaged applying the agreement to the waters off the Western Sahara coast: while failing to explicitly exclude Western Saharan waters from this zone, it explicitly excluded Cape Spartel.

Moreover, the Legal Service, in an opinion it issued on November 4, 2013, warned the Commission once again that "[Morocco] has in the past, namely in its relations with the EU, implemented the fisheries protocols as authorizing access to fish resources 'in these areas' [i.e., off the coast of Western Sahara]."[55] It declared that EU-flagged vessels "[appear to] have fished in the waters off Western Sahara,"[56] noting that "this can be deducted from the data provided by

---

[50] Associated Press (Brussels), "EU assembly report questions Morocco fishing deal," February 23, 2010 (http://finance.yahoo.com/EU-assembly-report-questions-apf-3855611862.html?x=0&.v=1); *see also* the written Parliamentary question to the Commission on Fisheries, confirming the content of the legal opinion (E-1758/10, dated March 22, 2010). An unofficial copy of this Legal Services opinion, (SJ-1269/09) issued on July 13, 2009, can be accessed at *http://www.wsrw.org/index.php?parse_news=single&cat=105&art=1346, cited in* the NYCBar Resources Report at 20.

[51] Rather, discussions at the time in Parliament highlighted the fact that European Union officials had been unable to obtain information from Morocco about the socioeconomic effects of the fishing activities and the industry support provided by the European Union under the terms of the agreement. *See* written questions E-1758/10 of March 22, 2010, E-2633/10 of April 20, 2010, and E-5723/10 of July 22, 2010, and the written answers thereto by Commissioner Damanaki, *cited in* the NYCBar Resources Report at 20.

[52] *See* written answer E-2633/10.

[53] *See* "Fisheries: EU initials extension of the fisheries protocol with Morocco," European Parliament Press Release, dated February 28, 2011, available at http://ec.europa.eu/fisheries/news_and_events/press_releases/2011/20110228/index_en.htm#.

[54] It is described only as a Protocol which grants vessels of the European Union fishing opportunities "in waters in which the Kingdom of Morocco exercises its jurisdiction as regards fishing."

[55] Legal Service Opinion, SJ-0665/13, November 4, 2013.

[56] Legal Service Opinion, SJ-1269/09, July 13, 2009, para. 5.

the Member States to the Commission pursuant to their obligations established by Community legislation on 'control,'" and that "it has also been explicitly acknowledged in several Commission declarations."[57]

It noted that "compliance with international law requires that economic activities related to the natural resources of a Non-Self-Governing Territory are carried out for the benefit of the people of such Territory and in accordance to their wishes." It then found that "it is not demonstrated that the EC financial contribution is used for the benefit of the people of Western Sahara," pointing out that the actions undertaken by Morocco "essentially aim at improving the infrastructure of the ports of Western Sahara and that this is not necessarily equal to benefiting the people of Western Sahara insofar as they are not mentioned in the programming documents and it is not known whether and to what extent they are able to take advantage of such improvements."[58]

The Legal Service further noted that it had not found any indication that the Saharawis were benefitting from the financial contributions under the agreement[59]—a requirement under international law—and concluded: "In the event that it could not be demonstrated that the FPA was implemented in conformity with the principles of international law concerning the rights of the Saharawi people over their natural resource, principles the Community is bound to respect, the Community should refrain from allowing vessels to fish in the waters off Western Sahara by requesting fishing licences only for fishing zones that are situated in the waters off Morocco."[60]

The fisheries agreement was not the only European Union-Moroccan agreement to suffer from the same inadequacies. In 2011, in the midst of the turmoil over the FPA, the European Commission began negotiations with Morocco on an accord concerning the liberalization of trade in certain agricultural products, including

---

[57]   *Id.* para. 15. On October 8, 2013, in response to questions of the Chair of the Committee on Fisheries the Legal Service admitted that previous protocols were implemented so as to permit European Union vessels to fish in those zones. *See* Legal Service Opinion, SJ-0665/13, November 4, 2013.

[58]   Legal Service Opinion, SJ-0269/09, July 13, 2009.

[59]   As was noted by the NYCBar Resources Report, *supra*, at 22: "[The report of the Legal Service] concluded that it could not be demonstrated that the financial contributions under the FPA are being used for the benefit of the people of Western Sahara because the sectoral fisheries policy's matrix of objectives and results did not contain 'specific actions explicitly foreseen with a view to benefit the population of Western Sahara;' nor were actions foreseen to target Western Sahara ports such as Laayoune, Dakhla, and Boujdour sufficient, because those ports were 'undisputed' to be in territory controlled by Morocco and the demography of those regions had been substantially modified due to Moroccan settlement and lack of integration of the Saharawi population." (quoting the Legal Service Opinion, SJ-0269/09, July 13, 2009, *supra*, paras. 25–29).

[60]   It also recommended that the Joint Committee attempt to find an amicable settlement which would fully respect the rights of the Saharawi people under international law, but that if such an amicable settlement could not be found, the Community should either suspend the agreement in conformity with Article 15 and Article 9 of the Protocol, or apply the agreement in such a way that EU flagged vessels are excluded from the exploitation of the waters of Western Sahara.

fish, which would modify Protocols 1, 2, and 3, and their annexes to the Euro-Mediterranean Association Agreement with Morocco that had entered into force in 2000.[61] The proposed Agricultural Accord contained some of the same deficiencies that applied to the fisheries agreement and, like the fisheries agreement, was negotiated without the consent or participation of any legitimate representatives of the Saharawis. Prior to the conclusion of these negotiations, the European Union Legal Service advised the authorities to clarify whether and how the proposed Accord would be applied to the territory of Western Sahara, and how it would benefit the local people of Western Sahara, before concluding the proposed Accord.

At the same time the Association of the Bar of the City of New York undertook an extensive investigation of the legal aspects of Morocco's use of the resources of the territory ("NYCBar Resources Report").

After noting the history of the negotiations of the various European Union—Morocco trade agreements, as well as the evidence deduced by the European Union Legal Service, the NYCBar Resources Report concluded that:

"Certain of Morocco's commercial fishing activities in waters off the coast of Western Sahara may be in violation of the State's obligations under international law. In particular, the EU-Morocco FPA currently in force grants Morocco complete discretion with respect to the use of funds paid by the EU to Morocco in part as compensation for access to territorial waters including those adjacent to Western Sahara. The Committee is unable to ascertain any information regarding Morocco's use of sums received under the FPA; indeed, the European Commission has also been unable to obtain this information. The Committee is of the opinion that retention by Morocco of any portion of those sums relating to fishing activities in Western Sahara's territorial waters, or disbursement of such funds without consideration for the interests of Western Sahara or the Sahrawi people, would violate international law. Further, to the extent commercial fishing activities are currently taking place in Western Saharan waters, such activities must be done in consultation with the Sahrawi population and any benefits from the activities must flow to the Sahrawi people."[62]

A number of other scholars also suggested that unless the FPA clarified that the agreement only applied to those waters over which Morocco enjoys *de jure* sovereign rights, and not to any waters which are merely under its "jurisdiction," the agreement should be deemed contrary to international law.[63]

---

[61]   2000/204/EC,ECSC; 2000/205/EC.

[62]   NYCBar Resources Report at 28.

[63]   *See,* for instance, V. Chapaux, *The Question of the European Community-Morocco Fisheries Agreement,* in INTERNATIONAL LAW AND THE QUESTION OF WESTERN SAHARA, *supra,* at 235.

The European Union ignored the advice of the Legal Service, the Association of the Bar of the City of New York, and other legal scholars.

In September, 2012, the Agricultural Accord was finalized. It went into effect on October 1, 2012. Moreover, on March 1, 2013, the European Union and Morocco launched negotiations to enact a Deep and Comprehensive Free Trade Agreement which would include a broad range of tangible products and intangible services, including fishery products.

In December of 2013 the European Parliament voted in favor of the new FPA, and it went into effect in July 2014.

These two events—the finalization of the Agricultural Accord in 2012 and the enactment of the new FPA in 2014—resulted in a series of legal actions before the courts of Europe that have had a serious impact on the development of jurisprudence concerning the use of the territory's resources.

(c) Cases Before the European Courts: Agricultural Accord

(i) Decisions of the Courts

In the midst of the ongoing negotiations between the European Union and Morocco concerning an expanded trade agreement, and the EU's refusal to abide by the advice of its Legal Service to investigate whether or not Morocco's use of the resources of the territory was consistent with international law, representatives of the Saharawis decided to take legal action. On November 19, 2012, the Polisario filed suit in the General Court of the European Union (CJEU) to have the decision of the Council and the Agricultural Accord annulled.[64]

The Legal Service of the Council and the Commission challenged the petition to have the Accord annulled on both jurisdictional and substantive grounds. However, on December 10, 2015, the General Court in Luxembourg (CJEU), issued a judgment granting the petition of the Polisario and annulling the contested decision in so far as the Accord would apply to the territory of Western Sahara. In partially annulling the Accord, the Court held, *inter alia,* that the Council had failed to fulfill its obligation, prior to the conclusion of that agreement, to examine whether there was any evidence of the exploitation of the resources of that part of the territory controlled by Morocco which was liable to adversely affect its inhabitants and their fundamental rights.

In April of 2016, both the Council and the Commission appealed this decision before the European Court of Justice (ECJ) in Brussels, and five European countries intervened in support of these appeals.[65]

---

64 Case T-512/12 Front Polisario v. Council, (2012/497/UE).

65 Case C-104/16 Council v. Front Polisario.

However, it was the Advisory Opinion delivered to the Court by Advocate General Melchior Wathelet[66] also supporting, in part, these appeals, that proved to have the greatest influence on the decision of the Court.

Advocate General Wathelet disagreed with both the reasoning and the conclusion of the General Court on several key points. His major disagreement concerned its findings with respect to the scope of the contested agreement, in particular its finding that there had been an implicit agreement by the parties to apply it to the territory of Western Sahara. In his view the fact that Article 94 of the agreement restricted its scope to the 'territory' of Morocco meant that did not apply to Western Sahara, since the latter had not been recognized by the EU, the UN, or any government as being under the sovereignty of Morocco, and hence it could not legally be considered part of the 'territory' of Morocco.[67] To the contrary, he noted that Western Sahara is a non-self-governing territory subject to the United Nations' rules on de-colonization, and that under international law it has a status distinct from Morocco, even if Morocco could be considered its *de facto* "Administering Power"[68]—a statement to which the Council agreed. He then declared that under 'state practice' the extension of the terms of a treaty by an Administering Power of a non-self-governing territory to that territory must be stated in the terms of the treaty,[69] and concluded that since the parties did not expressly include such an extension in the contested agreement, the scope of the agreement did not extend to Western Sahara.[70] He rejected in passing the Council's argument that the EU could apply the agreement to Western Sahara without recognizing that it was part of the territory of Morocco or subject to its sovereignty,[71] and then reasoned that since the EU did not recognize Morocco's sovereignty over the territory, in negotiating the agreement the EU could not have intended that it be deemed applicable to it.[72] For these reasons he argued that the agreement should not be annulled,[73] and that the Polisario lacked standing to raise its claims.[74]

---

[66] Advisory Opinion of the Advocate General in Case C-104/16, delivered on September 13, 2016 ("Wathelet Opinion"), Document 62016CC0104, which can be found at eur-lex.europa.eu.

[67] Wathelet Opinion, paras. 68, 82

[68] *Id.,* paras. 71–75

[69] *Id.,* para. 79

[70] *Id.,* para. 80

[71] *Id.,* para. 83

[72] *Id.,* para. 86

[73] *Id.,* para. 114

[74] He also rejected the argument that the agreement should nevertheless be considered applicable to Western Sahara because a long-standing practice of applying the agreement, and its predecessors, to the territory *de facto* demonstrated the parties' acceptance of a modification of its express terms. He distinguished the rules of *estoppel* (para. 95) (which

On December 21, 2016 the Court rendered its decision on the appeals, basically following the Advocate General's line of reasoning.

The Court first analyzed the international law principles applicable to the interpretation of treaties. It noted that Article 29 of the Vienna Convention on Treaties, entitled 'Territorial scope of treaties', provides that "Unless a different intention appears from the treaty or is otherwise established, a treaty is biding upon each party in respect of its entire territory." It interpreted the terms "entire territory" to mean that the treaty should apply only to a state's internationally recognized territory and not territory under a state's "jurisdiction," and that any extension of the terms of a treaty to other lands must be expressed in the treaty. It noted that Article 31 of the Convention, entitled 'General rule of interpretation,' provides, in part, that "There shall be taken into consideration...(b) any subsequent practice... which establishes the agreement of he parties regarding its interpretation," but disagreed with the argument that the *de facto* application of the agreement to products originating in Western Sahara for a number of years constituted a "tacit acceptance" of the application of the agreement to the territory by the parties.[75] In fact, it affirmed the *erga omnes* nature of the right to self-determination by the peoples of a non-self-governing territory, affirmed the fact that Western Sahara was such a non-self-governing territory, and concluded that it would be against international law for the agreement to apply to Western Sahara without the consent of its "people", the Saharawis,[76] which was not given.[77] Accordingly, it concluded that the European Union could not have intended that the agreement be applied to the territory and, therefore, that there was no "subsequent practice" of the sort that would modify the express terms of the agreement to include Western Sahara. Finally, the Court referred to Article 34 of the Convention, entitled 'General rule regarding third States,' which provides that "A treaty does not create either obligations or rights for a third State without its consent," and held that the agreement could not be applied to a "third party"—in this case the people of Western Sahara—without their consent.[78]

---

might permit a *modification* of the express terms of a treaty on the basis of party conduct), from the rules of treaty *interpretation* set forth in Article 31(3)(b) of the Vienna Convention (which provides that subsequent practice may be taken into consideration when interpreting the terms of a treaty), and considered the evidence produced in the case "insufficient" to prove such a long-standing practice within the meaning of the Convention. Moreover, he stated that for 'subsequent practice' to exist within the meaning of Article 31(3)(b) of the Convention, there must be an 'indisputable concordance' between the positions of the parties such as to establish the meaning of a treaty provision, and since it had been established that the EU and Morocco had different views on the interpretation of the relevant terms of the contested agreement, there was no such concurrence (para.100).

[75] Case C-104/16 Council v. Front Polisario, Court Opinion, paras. 85, 99, 108.

[76] *Id.*, para. 91.

[77] *Id.*, paras. 107, 123, 124

[78] *Id.*, para. 100

Since the Court found that the agreement did not apply to the territory of Western Sahara, it found that the Polisario lacked standing to contest it, and overturned the decision of the General Court that it should be annulled.

(ii) Analysis

Certain important legal principles can be gleaned from the decision of the Court of Justice on the Agricultural Accord.

First, the Court clearly affirmed a fact that should be apparent to any student of international law but which has been ignored repeatedly by Morocco—that Western Sahara retains the status of a non-self-governing territory under international law whose people have a right to self-determination, and is not part of the internationally recognized "territory" of Morocco.

Equally as important, the Court acknowledged that this right to self-determination is of an *erga omnes* character which must be respected by the European Union and its member states as well as all members of the United Nations.

Furthermore, the Court noted that under international law, regardless of whether or not Morocco is considered to enjoy the rights of an "administering power" over Western Sahara, the territory has a separate and distinct status from Morocco and must be considered a "third party" under the law of treaties and, accordingly, that it would be contrary to international law principles for the European Union to agree to a treaty with Morocco which would apply to the territory of Western Sahara without the consent of the people of Western Sahara.[79]

And as to the definition of the "people of Western Sahara," the court noted that they must be considered the *indigenous* people of the territory, i.e., the Saharawis.[80]

Finally, the Court refused to accept the argument that the Polisario should lack standing to represent the interests of the Saharawis on economic issues before the courts of the European Union, instead noting their acceptance by the United Nations as the representatives of the people of Western Sahara,[81] and only dismissing their claim on the basis that they had no standing to challenge an agreement between the European Union and Morocco that did not concern the territory of Western Sahara.

---

[79] *Id.,* para. 108.

[80] The Court, referring to the proclamations of the UN General Assembly and the International Court of Justice, stated: "[T]he UN General Assembly in its various resolutions on Western Sahara repeatedly expressed its concern in respect of 'enabling the indigenous population of the Territory to exercise freely its rights to self-determination' as the ICJ noted in paras. 62, 64, and 68 of its Advisory Opinion on Western Sahara." Case C-104/16 Council v. Front Polisario, Court Opinion, para. 91.

[81] Case C-104/16 Council v. Front Polisario, Court Opinion, para. 105.

However, in other ways the Court's decision left many questions unanswered. The Court, as well as the Advocate General, made the point that to the extent that a trade agreement by its terms is applicable only to products emanating from the "territory" of Morocco, defined as the territory over which Morocco's sovereignty is recognized under international law, it should be considered valid under the principles laid down by the Corell Opinion. But the Court in part relied on its finding that if the parties had intended its application to extend to territory over which Morocco exerted *jurisdiction* as well as sovereignty, or defined the territorial boundaries in a different way and clearly stated as much in the agreement, a different interpretation of the scope of the treaty, and hence its legality, might result. The FPA negotiated in 2013 contained just such language,[82] and in 2013 the EU agreed with Morocco that EU fishing vessels—mostly Spanish—would get access to waters off the coast of Western Sahara under its terms.

And the decisions of both European courts conveniently ignored some important issues, such as the relationship between investment in the territory and the inability of the Saharawis to achieve their rights through a United Nations political process. The ICJ in *Legal Consequences for States in the Continued Presence of South Africa in Namibia* drew a relationship between a state's utilization of the resources of a territory and the prolongation of its occupation of the territory. It was for this precise reason that the Court admonished the international community to refrain from entering into agreements with South Africa that would enhance its economic incentives to remain in Namibia. There can be no doubt that occupying a territory becomes more attractive if an occupying state is allowed to use the resources of the territory for its own benefit. Today, Morocco insists on exercising all the prerogatives of a sovereign towards Western Sahara, including using the resources of the territory for its own economic gain. If the international community permits Morocco to do this there is little incentive for Morocco to negotiate an end to its conflict with the Saharawis. It is a matter of record that Morocco unilaterally withdrew from its agreement to permit a referendum to end the conflict in 2003, and that since that time direct talks between the parties have failed to show any promise in resolving the conflict. During this period, however, Morocco has intensified its economic activities in Western Sahara and reaped billions of dollars from the use of the territory's resources. The fact that states should prohibit such investments was duly recognized by the United Nations.[83]

---

[82] It grants vessels of the European Union fishing opportunities "in waters in which the Kingdom of Morocco exercises its jurisdiction as regards fishing."

[83] The Charter of Economic Rights and Duties of States provides in paragraph 16.2 "No State has the right to promote or encourage investments that may constitute an obstacle to the liberation of a territory occupied by force." *See*, G.A. Res. 3281 (December 12, 1974).

In addition, the courts glossed over the facts on the ground. It is clear that the Agricultural Accord had never been applied only to products emanating from Moroccan territory. It had always been applied equally (in fact, some would say primarily) to products emanating from Western Sahara. This fact was later admitted by the Council in its decision concerning the negotiation of amendments to the protocols of the EU-Morocco Association Partnership Agreement in 2019,[84] which will be discussed later. The Advocate General's suggestion that the evidence of this situation produced before the General Court was 'insufficient' to establish a long-standing practice, even if true (and I suggest that it was *not*) is *irrelevant* for the simple fact that the existence of such a long-standing practice was *admitted* at the time the case was decided by both the European Council,[85] the European Commission,[86] and the Polisario,[87] confirmed by the General Court, and re-confirmed by the European Court of Justice in Brussels.[88]

(d) Cases Before the UK and European Courts: Fisheries Partnership Agreement (FPA)

In March of 2014, the Polisario brought suit in the General Court of the European Union Court of Justice (CJEU)[89] against the European Council to request the annulment of its decision concluding the new Fisheries Partnership Agreement (FPA) and Protocol with Morocco, raising essentially the same issues it had raised in the earlier suit concerning the Agricultural Accord.

While this case was pending, in 2015 a British NGO, Western Sahara Campaign United Kingdom (WSCUK), filed an action in an English High Court alleging that products originating in Western Sahara were being imported into the United Kingdom under the EU-Morocco Association Partnership Agreement contrary to international law, and that the Revenue and Customs Service would be acting unlawfully by giving preferential tariffs to products allegedly originating in Morocco but actually originating from Western Sahara. In addition, they argued that the FPA should be annulled as contrary to international law, and that the Department for Environment, Food and Rural Affairs should be prevented from granting fishing quotas under its terms to British fishing vessels in waters off the coast of Western Sahara. In October of 2015 an English court referred the case

---

[84] Council decision 2019/217 on January 28, 2019, which can be found at eur.lex.europa.eu.

[85] Case C-104/16 Council v. Front Polisario, Court Opinion, paras. 67, 87.

[86] *Id.,* paras. 65, 87.

[87] *Id.,* para. 87.

[88] *Id.,* paras. 118, 121.

[89] Case T-180/14, Front Polisario v. Council, March, 2014.

to the European Union's courts, stating with regard to both the fisheries and the agricultural agreements that "there is an arguable case of a manifest error by the [European] Commission in understanding and applying international law relevant to these agreements."

In 2017 the European Union Court of Justice (CJEU) decided to rule on the suit referred to it by the English court first. The Advocate General, on January 10, 2018, published his Opinion on that case.[90]

The Advocate General first reiterated the principles announced by the Court in the Agricultural Accords case, then went on to say: "the solution envisaged by the Council and the Commission in order to render the application of the [FPA] consistent with the judgment of 21 December 2016…would be to extend its scope by agreement in the form of an exchange of letters between the European Union and the Kingdom of Morocco so that Western Sahara would be expressly covered…. I am not persuaded by that line of argument. If the application to Western Sahara of an international agreement concluded with the Kingdom of Morocco, the territorial scope of which does not expressly include that territory, would be incompatible with the right of the people of that territory to self-determination, than an international agreement which, like the Fisheries Agreement and the 2013 Protocol, is applicable to the territory of Western Sahara and the adjacent waters and authorises the exploitation by the European Union of the fishery resources of Western Sahara would a fortiori also be incompatible with that right."[91]

He went on to discuss the international law aspects of the proposed Agreement, and after concluding that Morocco's assertion of sovereignty over the territory was the result of a breach of the right of the people of Western Sahara to self-determination,[92] in which the FPA played a part, he stated:

"Since the assertion of Moroccan sovereignty over Western Sahara is the result of a breach of the right of the people of that territory to self-determination… the European Union has failed to fulfil its obligation not to recognise the illegal situation resulting from [that breach] and also not to render aid or assistance in maintaining that situation. For that reason…the Fisheries Agreement and the 2013 Protocol are incompatible with [the statutes governing the European Union] which impose on the European Union the obligation that its external action is to protect human rights and strictly respect international law.[93]

---

[90] Advocate General's Opinion on Case C 266/16, delivered on January 10, 2018, "Wathelet Opinion 2", Document 62016CC1266, which can be found at eur-lex.europa.eu.

[91] Wathelet Opinion 2, paras. 144–145.

[92] Id., paras. 147, 186.

[93] Id., para. 212.

He went on to criticize the mechanism for payments under the FPA. He noted that in accordance with Article 3(4) of the Protocol the bulk of EU payments to Morocco—EUR 40 million—is to be paid to the Treasurer-General of the Kingdom into an account opened with the Public Treasury, and that according to Article 3(5) and 6(1) the Moroccan authorities would have full discretion regarding its use.[94] Only the EUR 14 million set aside for the sectoral fisheries policy in Morocco would be subject to a mechanism for monitoring and control by the EU in collaboration with the Moroccan authorities.[95]

He found this arrangement inadequate to safeguard the interests of the people of Western Sahara:

"In the first place, the 2013 Protocol does not contain any commitment on the part of the Kingdom of Morocco to use the financial contribution paid by the Union for the benefit of the people of Western Sahara in proportion to the quantities of the catches taken in the waters adjacent to Western Sahara. On the contrary, whereas 91.5% of the catches are taken solely in fishing zone No 6 (which covers only the waters adjacent to Western Sahara), only 35% of the financial contribution…come within the monitoring mechanism established by Article 6 of the 2013 Protocol."[96]

"To my mind, it follows from those factors that neither the Fisheries Agreement nor the 2013 Protocol contains the necessary legal safeguards for the fisheries exploitation to satisfy the requirements of the criterion which requires that that exploitation is for the benefit of the people of Western Sahara."[97]

"It follows from the foregoing that the contested acts, which are applicable to the territory of Western Sahara and the waters adjacent thereto in that they come within the sovereignty or jurisdiction of the Kingdom of Morocco, breach the European Union's obligation to respect the right to self-determination of the people of that territory and its obligation not to recognise an illegal situation resulting from a breach of that right and not to render aid or assistance in maintaining that situation. Furthermore, as regards the exploitation of natural resources of Western Sahara, the contested acts do not put in place the necessary safeguards in order to ensure that the exploitation is carried out for the benefit of the people of that territory."[98]

---

[94] *Id.*, paras. 275, 276.

[95] *Id.*, para. 276.

[96] *Id.*, para. 280.

[97] *Id.*, para. 279.

[98] *Id.*, para. 293.

In a judgment dated February 27, 2018,[99] the Grand Chamber of the CJEU found that the territory of Western Sahara is not covered by the concept of 'territory of Morocco' within the meaning of Article 11 of the Agreement,[100] declaring "if the territory of Western Sahara were to be included within the scope of the Fisheries Agreement, that would be contrary to certain rules of general international law... [including] the principle of self-determination." It went on to say that, as Western Sahara does not form part of the territory of Morocco, the waters adjacent to Western Sahara "are not part of the Moroccan fishing zone referred to in the Fisheries Agreement." It also found that the waters over which a coastal state exercises 'jurisdiction' should be deemed limited exclusively to the waters adjacent to its territory or waters within its exclusive economic zone.[101]

On July 19, 2018, the General Court of the CJEU dismissed the action brought by the Polisario.[102]

On April 6, 2019, after referring to the February 27, 2018 ruling of the European Court of Justice, the English High Court (EWHC) issued a declaratory judgment in favor of the WSCUK.

(e) Proposed EU-Morocco Agreements after 2018

(i) Sustainable Fisheries Partnership Agreement and Association Partnership Agreement

The most recent Protocol to the Fisheries Partnership Agreement expired by its terms on July 14, 2018. The Court's decision on February 27, 2018 concerning the Agreement, however, did not dampen the enthusiasm of the European Council, the European Commission, and Morocco, to negotiate a new Agreement and Protocol that would apply to Western Sahara. Instead, all three groups immediately started looking for ways to circumvent those rulings. Within a few months of these decisions, the Commission presented its newly negotiated Sustainable Fisheries Partnership Agreement with Morocco, explicitly extending it to waters off the coast of Western Sahara. In October, 2018, several Member States requested the Council's Legal Service to provide them with a legal opinion that would assess whether the Agreement was in line with applicable case law.

On November 7, 2018, the Legal Service presented its Opinion, suggesting

---

[99] Case C-266/16, Western Sahara Campaign UK, EU:C:2018:11. This was subsequently confirmed in relation to the Protocol by the judgment of July 19, 2018 in Case T-180/14, Polisario v. Council EU:T:2018:496, which can be found at curia.europa.eu.

[100] Case C-266/16, Western Sahara Campaign UK, EU:C:2018:11, Court Opinion, para. 64.

[101] *Id.*, para. 68.

[102] Case T-180/14, decision can be found at EU:T:2018:496, curia.europa.eu.

that the new agreement would be legal. It based its conclusion on three factors. First, that unlike the previous agreements that referred to waters over which Morocco exercised "jurisdiction," the proposed new agreement merely stated the geographical boundaries it would cover—including waters off the coast of Western Sahara. Second, that it found that the negotiators had consulted with the people of Western Sahara and obtained their consent. Third, that there was no recognition of Morocco's sovereignty over Western Sahara in the text.

On March 4, 2019 the European Council decided to approve the new Agreement,[103] and on June 10, 2019 the Polisario brought an action against the Council because of that decision.[104] The new Agreement entered into force on July 18, 2019.

At the same time as the EU and Morocco were renegotiating the FPA and its protocols, they were also attempting to modify the terms of the EU-Morocco Association Agreement[105] so as to permit goods exported from Western Sahara to benefit from the tariffs granted by the EU to goods from Morocco. Following the Court's decision on December 21, 2016 that the Agricultural Accord could not be applied to Western Sahara, on May 29, 2017 the Council authorized new negotiations with Morocco to overcome this obstacle.

On January 28, 2019 the Council published a decision[106] in which it approved an Exchange of Letters that would modify Protocols 1 and 4 of the Euro-Mediterranean Agreement that established the Association Agreement between the EU and Morocco. First it acknowledged that "Since the Association Agreement came into force [March 1, 2000] products from Western Sahara certified to be of Moroccan origin have been imported to the Union, benefiting from the tariff preferences laid down in its relevant provisions."[107] Then, citing the "advantages for the economy of Western Sahara arising from the granting of the tariff preferences laid down in the Association Agreement,"[108] that will have an "overall positive effect" for the "people concerned," it proceeded to claim that its decision was in full conformity with the Court's decision and international law in that "the Commission, in liaison with the European External Action Service, has taken

---

[103] Council Decision (EU) 2019/441, available at http://www.legislation.gov/uk/eudn/2019/441/contents.

[104] Case T-344/19. On June 12, 2019 the Polisario filed a companion case, T-356/19, challenging Council decision EU 2019/440 of November 29, 2018 further refining its earlier decision. Both can be found at eur-lex.europa.eu.

[105] Protocols 1 and 4 to the Euro-Mediterranean Agreement establishing an association between the European Communities and their Member States, on the one hand, and Morocco on the other. (OJ 2019 L34, p.1)("Association Agreement").

[106] Council decision 2019/217 of January 28, 2019, which can be found at eur-lex.europa.eu.

[107] Para. 4.

[108] Para. 8

all reasonable and feasible steps in the current context to adequately involve the people concerned in order to ascertain their consent to the agreement. Wide-ranging consultations were conducted and the majority of the social, economic and political stakeholders who participated in the consultations stated that they were in favour of extending the tariff preferences in the Association Agreement to Western Sahara."[109]

The amendments to Protocols 1 and 4 entered into force on February 7, 2019. On April 27, 2019, the Polisario brought suit in the European General Court challenging the decision of the Council to approve these amendments as well as the inclusion of products from the territory in the Association Agreement.[110]

(ii) Analysis

The decision of the Council with respect to the Association Agreement is flawed in several respects. The Council apparently believes that it has comported with the requirements set out in the Corell Opinion by suggesting that the Agreement would benefit the "people" of Western Sahara and has been concluded with their consent.

However, it has glossed over the issue of whether or not Morocco has the right to negotiate a trade agreement that concerns Western Sahara at all, regardless of the alleged benefits that might be derived from such an agreement. It completely ignored the legal analysis of Advocate General Wathelet:

"If the application to Western Sahara of an international agreement concluded with the Kingdom of Morocco, the territorial scope of which does not expressly include that territory, would be incompatible with the right of the people of that territory to self-determination, than an international agreement which, like the Fisheries Agreement and the 2013 Protocol, is applicable to the territory of Western Sahara and the adjacent waters and authorises the exploitation by the European Union of the fishery resources of Western Sahara would a fortiori also be incompatible with that right."[111]

The Opinion of the Legal Service with respect to the Sustainable Fisheries Partnership Agreement can be criticized for the same reason. It appears to have placed great emphasis on the fact that the framers avoided the issue of whether or not Morocco had "sovereignty" or "jurisdiction" over the waters of Western Sahara. However, it is difficult to see how by merely delineating the boundaries of a treaty to include areas that are not within the legally recognized boundaries of a state

---

[109] Para. 10

[110] Case T-279/19, which can be found at eur-lex.europa.eu.

[111] Wathelet Opinion 2, paras. 144–145.

and which, indeed, are within the legally recognized boundaries of a third party, the EU can conform to the principles of law and treaty interpretation adopted by the Court and articulated by the Advocate General in the Agricultural Accords case,[112] or the principles that the Court and the Advocate General elucidated in the case concerning the FPA brought by WSCUK.[113]

Accordingly, the real issues with respect to both the decision of the Council concerning the Association Agreement and the Opinion of the Legal Service are those of *consent* and *benefits.* The Council and the Legal Service apparently believe that it would be consistent with the Corell Opinion and pass muster under international law if it can be established that the "people" of Western Sahara have consented to the new agreements, and derive some benefit from them.

Indeed, the various companies which have profited from the exploitation of the resources of Western Sahara—the oil companies, the importers of phosphates, the investors in wind farms—as well as the European Union Legal Service, the European Council, the European Commission, and various European Parliamentary officials, have uniformly accepted the premise that Morocco enjoys the rights of an "administering power" with respect to the use of the resources of the territory, and have attempted to justify their involvement in such exploitation on the basis of the criteria for the exercise of such authority outlined in the Corell Opinion. Morocco, likewise, has assumed the position that it is fully complying with the international law criteria set forth by Corell, by benefitting the population of Western Sahara with its investments and consulting with groups within the territory.

However, none of these entities has interpreted these criteria correctly.

Although the European Court of Justice in its decision on the Agricultural Accord clarified that the right to self-determination under international law belongs to the *indigenous* people of Western Sahara, as was noted earlier, this distinction is not reflected in the position papers of the European Commission and the European Council concerning both that Accord and the FPA. In their various early position papers concerning the Agricultural Accord, the European Commission and European Council completely ignored the requirement that Morocco obtain the approval of the people of Western Sahara to have products from the territory included. When they did mention this requirement, they glossed over the distinction between the *people* of Western Sahara—the Saharawis—and the *population* of Western Sahara, which would include Moroccan settlers in

---

[112] Referring to Article 34 of the Vienna Convention on Treaties, entitled 'General rule regarding third States,' which provides that "A treaty does not create either obligations or rights for a third State without its consent" and held that the agreement could not be applied to a "third party"—in this case the people of Western Sahara—without their consent.

[113] Opinion, para. 293.

the territory, suggesting that all that Morocco needed to demonstrate in order to comply with international legal principles set forth by Corell was that the *population* living in Western Sahara was benefitting from its use of the resources of the territory. Likewise, although the European Union Legal Service noted that activities under the various trade agreements would be prohibited under international law if "those activities are carried out in disregard of the interests and of the wishes of the people" of Western Sahara,[114] in certain paragraphs of both its 2006, 2009, and 2018 opinions it appears also to have ignored the distinction between the *people* of the territory and the territory's *population*.

This is a misinterpretation of the requirements of international law. As was correctly noted by the European Court of Justice, the right to self determination—including the use of the resources of the territory—inures to the benefit of the indigenous inhabitants of the territory, the Saharawis, not Moroccan settlers, Moroccan officials or other foreigners. Indeed, as has also been noted in a similar context, the Moroccan settlers in the territory may be there in violation of the Fourth Geneva Convention,[115] and their presence may constitute a war crime under Article 8(2)(b)(8) of the Rome Statute.[116] And in addition to benefitting the indigenous people of the territory, it is clear from the Corell Opinion that Morocco's use of the resources of the Western Sahara must be in accordance with the *wishes* of the indigenous people of the territory—that is, with their consent.

This misinterpretation of the criteria laid down by Corell in his Opinion persists to this day.

Both the negotiators of the agreements concluded in 2019 and the Legal Service, have seemed to blur the line between *consulting* people and obtaining the *consent* of people. Also, they have failed to correctly identify which "people" must give their consent. Although the Legal Service contended that "all reasonable and feasible steps were taken to ascertain the consent of the people of Western Sahara to the draft Agreement and Protocol through the consultation of that

---

[114] Western Sahara Resource Watch, May 3, 2020, para. 18.

[115] James Crawford, Professor of International Law at the University of Cambridge, when asked to comment on the legal status of the Israeli settlements declared: "As regards these settlements, the Court notes that Article 49, paragraph 6, of the Fourth Geneva Convention provides: 'The Occupying Power shall not deport or transfer parts of its own civilian population into the territory it occupies.' That provision prohibits not only deportations or forced transfers of population such as those carried out during the Second World War, but also any measures, taken by an Occupying Power in order to organize or encourage transfers of parts of its own population into the occupied territory." *See,* J. Crawford, "Opinion on Third Party Obligations with respect to Israeli Settlements in the Occupied Palestinian Territories," TUC Org. UK, January 24, 2012 ("Crawford"), at 25, para. 60, quoting *Legal Consequences of the Construction of a Wall in the Occupied Palestinian Territory, Advisory Opinion,* I.C.J. Reports 2004, at 136, 183 (para. 120).

[116] Rome Statute of the International Criminal Court (signed July 17, 1998; entry into force July 1, 2002) 2187 U.N.T.S. 3. Under Article 8 of the Statute the transfer of a population into an occupied land may be considered a war crime.

people's representative," apparently the only "people" whose consent was obtained were groups aligned with the Moroccan government. The Polisario, the group acknowledged as the representatives of the "people" of Western Sahara by the United Nations, did not take part in such "consultations," nor did they give their consent. And the pro-independence Saharawi groups in the territory who *were* consulted, apparently disapproved the proposed Agreement.[117] Likewise, the Council's argument that it has abided by the international law mandate to procure the consent of the people of the territory to the Association Agreement is anemic at best. Just who are the "people concerned" who were consulted and who approved this agreement? Surely not the Polisario, or pro-independence groups within the territory.

Morocco has tried to convince European Union officials and others that the people of Western Sahara have approved its various trade agreements by pointing to the approvals it has received from groups such as the Advisory Council for Saharan Affairs (CORCAS). However, there is no evidence that CORCAS, which Morocco claims represents the Saharawi populations of the region and which is comprised solely of pro-Moroccan Saharawis appointed by the government, or the other pro-Moroccan groups "consulted" by representatives of the European Union, actually reflect the will of the majority of the Saharawi public in the territory, not to mention in the Tindouf camps. Indeed, it is a matter of record that Saharawis who do not accept Moroccan sovereignty are prohibited from organizing into groups where their opinions on the use of the resources of the territory can be voiced.

Moreover, both the Council and the Legal Service failed to examine just who would benefit from these agreements, the native Saharawis, or the majority of the population—and the ones who own the majority of economic activities in the territory—who are transplanted Moroccans.

The misinterpretation of the requirements that he set out in his Opinion with respect to the initial Fisheries Partnership Agreement led the former United Nations Undersecretary for Legal Affairs to declare in 2008:

"It has been suggested to me that the legal opinion that I delivered in 2002 had been invoked by the European Commission in support of the Fisheries Partnership Agreement. I do not know if this is true. But if it is, I find it incomprehensible that the Commission could find any such support in the legal opinion, unless of

---

[117] After summarizing the Legal Opinion, the Western Sahara Resource Watch offered this critique: "It seems that the Council's Legal Service has not bothered to assess the differences in definition of 'consultation' and 'consent,' or whether the groups that have participated in the consultation were in fact representative of the people of Western Sahara. The Legal Service have misrepresented the [External Action Service] documents and drawn the conclusion that the Moroccan government bodies constitute a representative of the people of Western Sahara—to the contrary of the CJEU." Western Sahara Resource Watch, May 3, 2020.

course the Commission had ascertained that the people of Western Sahara had been consulted, had accepted the agreement and the manner in which the profits from the activity was to benefit them. However, an examination of the Agreement actually leads to a different conclusion."

He summarized:

"Under all circumstances I would have thought that it was obvious that an agreement of this kind that does not make a distinction between the waters adjacent to Western Sahara and the waters adjacent to the territory of Morocco would violate international law."[118]

In a speech delivered at the annual conference of the Belgian Society of International Law on November 14–15, 2019, Corell again criticized the European Union's trade agreements with Morocco. After reiterating his earlier critiques, he again called the proposed new fisheries agreement deficient:

"To be legal…the revenues generated by the licenses in the zone of Western Sahara would have to be delivered not to Morocco's public treasury or equivalent but to a separate account that can be audited independently by representatives of the people of Western Sahara so that they can ascertain that the revenues are used solely in accordance with the needs and interests of their people."

He added that "This system must apply also to other natural resources in Western Sahara, such as phosphates, oil or gas, or other resources, be they renewable or non-renewable."[119]

Throughout the years the various oil companies, importers of phosphates, investors in wind farms, and those who have facilitated them, have likewise misconstrued the requirements of the Corell Opinion.

Kosmos Energy, Glencore, and the other oil companies that have been in the market, all entered into contracts with the Moroccan government under the Moroccan "Hydrocarbon Law," under which the territory of Western Sahara is deemed part of Morocco. In response to adverse publicity, Kosmos and Glencore first attempted to justify their operations under the principles laid down by the Corell Opinion by claiming that their activities to date were merely 'exploratory.' However, their agreement with Morocco not only encompassed exploration activities, it also encompassed the extraction and exploitation of any hydrocarbon resources discovered through such exploration activities.[120]

---

[118] Conference on Multilateralism and International Law with Western Sahara as a Case Study, hosted by the South African Department of Foreign Affairs and the University of Pretoria, held in Pretoria, South Africa on December 8, 2008.

[119] Keynote Address on Western Sahara by Hans Corell, Belgian Society of International Law Annual Conference, November 14–15, 2019, at 9, which can be found at https://www.havc.se.

[120] See, for instance, Part III—Exploitation Concession, Art. 5.

They then tried to claim that their activities met the criteria for exploitation set forth in the Corell Opinion. However, there was no indication that any revenue accruing to Morocco under the terms of those agreements would have been traceable or deposited in a separate account to benefit the Saharawis. Indeed, there was no indication that the benefits of any of these agreements would inure principally to the benefit of the Saharawis. Like the European Commission, Kosmos and the other companies glossed over the legal requirement that their agreements must inure principally to the benefit of the Saharawis, not the Moroccan settlors in the territory. In its position statement on hydrocarbon exploration offshore Western Sahara on its website Kosmos stated: "…our activities have been, and will always be, conducted in a manner that is both fully inclusive and for the benefit of *all the local population, without exception.*"

In addition, none of these companies obtained the consent of the Polisario, or indeed, any legitimate Saharawi civil society organization, for their activities. The "CESE",[121] cited by Kosmos as representing the people in the territory and approving its activities, is an organ of the Moroccan government, not an independent organization. Accordingly, if the CESE had consulted with any Saharawis, they would not represent the majority. On October 15, 2014 a number of Sahrawi citizens sent Kosmos a joint letter in which they confirmed this fact. Kosmos avoided this issue in its response.[122] The group that has been considered the representatives of the Saharawis from Western Sahara by the United Nations for the past forty years has been the Polisario.[123] Kosmos and the other oil companies never consulted with or obtained the approval of the Polisario, the people in the refugee camps or the majority of the Saharawis living in Western Sahara for their activities, and the Polisario actively denounced them.

The claim of these oil companies that their activities have been in line with the Corell Opinion was denounced by the author of the Opinion, former United Nations Undersecretary'for Legal Affairs Hans Corell. "The latest development with respect to natural resources," he noted in an article published in The International Judicial Monitor on February 23, 2015, "is a contract between Morocco and two companies, Kosmos and Glencore, relating to oil exploration and exploitation in

---

[121] The so-called "independent" constitutional body the Economic, Social and Environmental Council (CESE).

[122] While Kosmos indicated in its response, dated November 12, 2014, that it conducted meetings with Saharawis, particularly in Dakhla, to ascertain their opinions, it failed to mention the names of these Saharawis, the organizations they represented, or whether they were authorized to represent the majority.

[123] In 1979 and 1980, the General Assembly acknowledged that the Frente Polisario was the group that was "the representative of the people of Western Sahara" (G.A. Res. 34/37 (1979) and G.A. Res. 35/19 (1980), and in both General Assembly and Security Council resolutions ever since the Polisario has been considered a "party" to the dispute. Likewise, the Settlement Plan that created a ceasefire between Morocco and the Polisario in 1989 was based on the premise that the Polisario represented the indigenous people of Western Sahara.

the Cap Boujdour area off the coast of Western Sahara. I can see from the web that the two companies maintain that this contract is in conformity with my 2002 legal opinion. Regrettably, it is not."

The same charges can be asserted against the companies which import phosphates from the Boucraa mine. While Potash was in the market it attempted to justify such imports, first on the basis of economic necessity—that it needed the specific type of phosphate that is produced at the Boucraa mine—then with a claim that such importation is in full compliance with international law. To buttress the second claim it asserted that its operations "have significantly contributed to the development of Western Sahara and continue to provide substantial and sustainable economic and social benefits to the Saharawi population..." As support for its legal position it cited opinions from three law firms which allegedly "concluded that OCP's operations in the region directly benefit the people of the region and are consistent with international legal obligations." It also cited a report on OCP's operations by KPMG. These "opinions" and "reports" have not been made public, so their contents cannot be verified or examined. However, glaringly absent from any summary of these opinions and reports was any indication that Potash or OCP had obtained the *consent* of the Saharawis to export the phosphates from Boucraa.

The current importers of phosphates from Western Sahara have not even attempted to justify their actions. In 2019 the major importers of such products were: Paradeep Phosphates (India), Ravensdown (New Zealand), and Balance Agri-Nutrients (New Zealand).

Western Sahara Resource Watch has attempted to contact Balance several times from 2015 to date to ascertain its position on legal issues, but never received an answer to its questions. In 2014 it did write to WSRW, without elaborating further, that "The United Nations does not prohibit trade in resources from Western Sahara. Nor does such trade contravene a United Nations legal opinion."[124]

Ravensdown wrote to Western Sahara Resource Watch in April, 2019, indicating its opinion that it was following the "United Nations framework" for activities conducted in territories such as Western Sahara, which it interpreted to be: "The operations should promote economic advancement and provide direct and indirect benefits to the inhabitants of the territory and to the territory itself. Working conditions should be non-discriminatory. The operations should be conducted rationally and sustainably to ensure long-term access to resources."[125] Once again, this conflates the *inhabitants* of the territory with the indigenous *people*

---

[124] Western Sahara Resource Watch report "P for Plunder (2020)," *supra*, at 24.

[125] *Id.*, at 25.

of the territory, and glaringly absent from this synopsis is any mention of acquiring the *consent* of the people of the territory for such activities.

Although the Minister of Foreign Affairs of New Zealand, in 2020, wrote a letter to Western Sahara Resource Watch indicating that he "made it clear" to Ravensdown and Balance Agri-Nutrients that "they must comply with international law, seek independent legal advice, and that they import at their own risk,"[126] the companies have neither attempted to justify their activities further, nor indicated that they will desist importing such products.

Paradeep Phosphates in India (a subsidiary of Zuari Maroc Phosphates, a company partially owned by OCP), is currently the largest importer of phosphates from Western Sahara, accounting for nearly 43% of exports in 2019.[127] Western Sahara Resource Watch contacted Paradeep in 2015, 2017, 2018 and 2019 to obtain its position on the legality of the trade. The company has never replied.

Coromandel, according to its website, is the second largest fertilizer company in India. Western Sahara Resource Watch sent letters to Coromandel in 2019 and 2020 asking whether it intended to continue importing phosphates from Western Sahara, and whether it had fulfilled the requirement of international law that it obtain the permission of the people of the territory. To date it has received no reply.[128]

The companies which have facilitated the trade in phosphates are no less disingenuous.

Siemens Gamesa Renewable Energy (SGRE), a subsidiary of Siemens, took over the renewable energy branch following a merger with the Spanish energy technology company Gamesa in April, 2017. In December of 2017, Western Sahara Resource Watch wrote to Siemens Gamesa, to ascertain its position on the legality of its actions, in particular whether it had ever obtained the consent of the people of Western Sahara for its operations. The company failed to respond. In response to previous correspondence the company demurred, responding that it "does not take a stance or make judgements on issues of international public law."[129] However, Siemens had no problem referring to the territory of Western Sahara on its website as "Southern Morocco." "Foum el Oued will be built in one of the windiest areas of Morocco in the municipality of Laayoune, 9 km south east of the port of Laayoune in Southern Morocco," a Siemens press release of January, 2012, stated. Siemens Gamesa refused to answer the question as to whether it believes Western Sahara

---

[126] Western Sahara Resource Watch, May 9, 2020.

[127] *Id.,* at 19.

[128] *Id.,* at 26.

[129] Western Sahara Resource Watch, February 7, 2020.

to be separate from Morocco, instead only stating "the region of Western Sahara is disputed with the United Nations."[130] Siemens' website still refers to the Foum El Oued park as being in Morocco.[131] In 2018, Siemens Gamesa confirmed to WSRW that it had extended the maintenance contract for the Foum el Oued park for a further 15 years. The company still refused to comment as to whether it had sought the consent of the people of Western Sahara to its projects.

When asked about their participation in the Morocco's renewable energy plans, several of the Western companies concerned, including Siemens, tried to make a distinction between renewable and non-renewable resources, claiming that renewable resources, such as wind power, cannot be "exploited" and accordingly, do not fall within the guidelines set forth by the Corell Opinion for the use of natural resources by an administering power of a non-self-governing territory. According to a letter sent by Siemens to Western Sahara Resource Watch on October 11, 2016: "Wind farms are fundamentally different from, say, mines which extract finite resources in an irreversible way. The wind in Western Sahara, in contrast, is a renewable source of energy, and the operation of wind farms in no way diminishes it."[132]

However, Corell disagrees with this conclusion. As he noted in comments published in the Danish newspaper *Information*:

"If one uses the territory of Western Sahara for the benefit of Morocco and for foreign enterprises, without properly consulting the people of Western Sahara or ensuring that they are the ones profiting from the wind energy, it will be in violation of international law and UN principles for responsible businesses."[133] He stated that the principles he elucidated in his Advisory Opinion "apply to renewable as well as non-renewable resources and energy sources."

The activities of Siemens and other companies conducting business in Western Sahara have also elicited criticism from shareholders in such companies. The German shareholders' association has declared: "Wind power from Siemens enables illegal looting of raw materials. Wind turbines from Siemens Gamesa are installed in the part of Western Sahara that is occupied by Morocco. International courts have time and time again stated that this occupation is unlawful. All projects concerning the Western Sahara region need prior consent from the recognized representatives of the Sahrawi people. To date, Siemens Gamesa has not obtained this consent." It further noted that "As opposed to Siemens' assumptions, electricity

---

[130] *Id.*

[131] *Id.*

[132] Western Sahara Resource Watch report, "Powering the Plunder," November, 2016, at 21.

[133] Hans Corell, *Information*, at 1, cited in Western Sahara Resource Watch on November 2, 2016.

generation will have no long-term benefits for the Sahrawi," and after referring to the fact that 95 percent of the required energy for the Boucraa mine comes from the Siemens Gamesa wind turbines, it declared "With its wind turbines, Siemens Gamesa contributes directly to this looting and the continuing occupation."[134]

Neither Siemens nor any of the other companies investing in renewable energy projects in Western Sahara have made any attempt to ascertain the wishes of the Saharawis or to ensure that the benefits of their activities will inure principally to them. Rather, evidence suggests that they will inure principally to the benefit of the owners of the Boucraa mine—OCP.

Indeed, it is clear from the available evidence that Morocco has not used the proceeds from the exploitation of any of the resources of Western Sahara to improve conditions for the Saharawis in the territory. Rather, evidence suggests that the majority of such funds are used to augment the coffers of the Moroccan government and its officials and settlers.

As noted previously, Moroccan settlers are offered generous "perks" to relocate in the territory and occupy most of the upper level positions in the government and state controlled businesses, and the infrastructure investments made by Morocco primarily aid the Moroccan controlled businesses in the territory.

And most of the businesses that operate in the territory are controlled by the state, wealthy Moroccan individuals, or foreign interests, not Saharawis. For instance, a large plantation in the region of Dakhla is owned by "Les Domaines," a company owned by the King of Morocco. The arable land near Dakhla is divided into sectors with the largest one belonging to the King. The remainder is divided among companies that are mainly French-Moroccan conglomerates, and large settlements have been built to house the migrant workers from Morocco. No Saharawis own any of the land.[135]

With respect to the phosphate industry—the major commercial employer in the territory—the assertion of Potash that its activities principally benefitted the people of the territory directly conflicts with the testimony of Saharawis in the territory, thousands of whom gathered in a camp on the outskirts of Laayoune in 2010 to protest the conditions at Boucraa and the other conditions under which they were living. The French NGO France Libertes carried out a mission to Western Sahara in 2002 to assess the situation.[136] In one of its reports it concluded that since the Moroccan occupation of the territory the economic conditions of the

---

[134] Western Sahara Resource Watch, February 7, 2020.

[135] Western Sahara Resource Watch, December 13, 2015.

[136] *See*, for instance, the Report of the French NGO France Libertes (AFASPA): International Mission of Investigation in Western Sahara, January, 2003, www.france-libertes.fr., *supra*.

Saharawi workers at the Boucraa mines had deteriorated and that the Saharawis "are to a large degree marginalized entirely from this industry."[137] Indeed, the dire economic conditions faced by the Saharawis in the territory, in addition to their political repression, were the causes of the 2010 uprisings in Laayoune.

And the fact that Morocco may have invested in improving the infrastructure of the territory does not change matters. As was noted by one observer: "Most of the infrastructure development in the occupied territory has not been designed to enhance the standard of living of the Western Saharan people, but has instead involved the elaborate internal security system of military bases, police facilities, prisons, surveillance, and related repressive apparatuses; housing construction, subsidies, and other support for Moroccan settlors; and airport, seaport, and other transportation facilities designed to accelerate resource extraction. More fundamentally, the decision on how to use the proceeds from the mines and fisheries are being made by the Moroccan government in the capital of Rabat, not by the subjugated population."[138]

Despite the fact that neither Morocco nor the European Union officials responsible for negotiating trade agreements ever consulted with the legitimate representatives of the Saharawis before negotiating the trade agreements between them, and that there is no reason to believe that the revenue from such trade agreements principally benefits the Saharawis,[139] the European Union, on the basis of a quixotic—and self serving—interpretation of the Corell Opinion, has permitted EU fishing vessels for years to exploit the fishing reserves of Western Sahara without obstruction. And despite the blatant violations of the requirements of the Corell Opinion by companies partnering with Morocco to exploit the oil, phosphates and wind power resources of Western Sahara, these companies have continued to engage in these activities without restraint.

Accordingly, both the Council's decision with respect to the amendments to the Protocols of the Association Agreement negotiated in 2019, and the Opinion of

---

[137] *Id., see also,* E. Hagen, *International Participation in the Phosphate Industry in Occupied Western Sahara: The Local Content and Global Participation,* in INTERNATIONAL LAW AND THE QUESTION OF WESTERN SAHARA, *supra,* at 268.

[138] Stephen Zunes, in the *National Catholic Reporter,* May 12, 2015.

[139] Indeed, just the opposite. In 2005, according to references cited by Stephen Zunes and Jacob Mundy, it was revealed that some Moroccan generals responsible for policing the coast and regulating fishing were also large stakeholders in fisheries businesses that they had failed to regulate, leading to the near total collapse of the Moroccan and Western Saharan coastal ecosystems from overfishing. *See,* S. Zunes & J. Mundy, WESTERN SAHARA: WAR, NATIONALISM, AND CONFLICT IRRESOLUTION, *supra,* at 53. The authors further noted that "[o]ne of Hassan's legacies was to leave his heir a country in which fifty of the one hundred richest Moroccans were either military or police officers—their fortunes amassed through legal, parallel, and black-market activities...These men included the four officers who held the most influence over Western Sahara." Also, they noted that such high-level officers "have been given control over many aspects of the Western Saharan economy, especially in fisheries." at 251.

the Legal Service with respect to the Sustainable Fisheries Partnership Agreement, are not in compliance with the criteria set forth in the Corell Opinion.

Moreover, these decisions, while purporting to avoid the issue of Morocco's sovereignty over the territory, fail to recognize that there are a number of ways in which a state can implicitly recognize or lend support to another state's claims of sovereignty over territory besides explicitly stating so in a treaty. Advocate General Wathelet, in his Opinion concerning the case brought by the WSCUK, recognized the fact that by participating in a trade agreement that permits an "occupying power"[140] to exploit the natural resources of a territory, a state would implicitly be acquiescing in that state's claim of sovereignty over that territory.

In the words of the Advocate General:

> "As the Commission acknowledges, fishing in an EEZ [Exclusive Economic Zone] is a *sovereign* right of the coastal State. [citation omitted] Consequently, in concluding the Fisheries Agreement covering the waters constituting the EEZ of Western Sahara, the European Union recognises *de jure* that the Kingdom of Morocco exercises a sovereign right in those waters..."[141]

> "That recognition will be even clearer upon the entry into force of draft Law No 38–17, whereby the Kingdom of Morocco will establish an EEZ on the waters adjacent to Western Sahara."[142]

Moreover, the Council and Legal Service glossed over the central issue enunciated by both the Court and the Advocate General in the two cases concerning the previous Agricultural Accord and FPA: the fact that regardless of how it is crafted, any agreement between the EU and Morocco that would permit the natural resources of Western Sahara to be exploited by Morocco would violate the right to self-determination of the people of Western Sahara under international law and, thus, violate the laws applicable to the European Union.

As the Advocate General stated:

> "...by the contested acts, the Union rendered aid and assistance in maintaining the illegal situation resulting from the breach of

---

[140] It should be noted that the Advocate General adopted the characterization of Morocco as an "occupying power," rather than an "administering power," and rejected the notion that it could be considered the "de facto administering power" over Western Sahara. *See,* Paras. 221–259 of the Advocate General's Opinion.

[141] Para. 208.

[142] Para. 210.

the right of the people of Western Sahara to self-determination. That aid takes the form of economic advantages (in particular the financial contribution) which the Fisheries Agreement and the 2013 Protocol confer on the Kingdom of Morocco.[143]

Since the assertion of Moroccan sovereignty over Western Sahara is the result of a breach of the right of the people of that territory to self-determination, for the reasons which I have stated in points 147 to 186 of this Opinion, the European Union has failed to fulfil its obligation not to recognise the illegal situation resulting from the breach of the right of the people of Western Sahara to self-determination by the Kingdom of Morocco and also not to render aid or assistance in maintaining that situation."[144]

(2) Rights of an Occupying Power

The debate over the exploitation of the resources of Western Sahara discussed above assumed that the criteria announced by the Corell Opinion should be applied to Morocco's use of these resources. But should these be the criteria that are deemed applicable? Is it in keeping with the norms of international law to assume that Morocco should enjoy the rights of an "administering power," or should Morocco more properly be considered to have only the rights of an "occupying power"?

In rendering his decision, Corell glossed over the distinction between the rights of an "administering power" and those of an "occupying power" under international law. However, as has been noted previously, an argument can be made that Morocco should be considered an "occupying power" and that as an occupying power, it would enjoy even fewer rights under international law to dispose of the mineral wealth and other resources of Western Sahara than was suggested in the Corell Opinion.

The rights of an "occupying power" were by and large developed to delineate the rights and obligations of conquering powers during military conflicts. It has been held that an occupier does not acquire the rights of a sovereign in occupied territory, but only those limited military rights allowed to him under the international law of belligerent occupation.[145] Those rights with respect to

---

[143] Para. 211.

[144] Para. 212.

[145] See, E.H. Feilchenfeld, THE INTERNATIONAL ECONOMIC LAW OF OCCUPATION (1942), at 817. As was noted by Christopher Greenwood, a judge at the International Court of Justice: "It has already been seen that one of the cardinal principles on which the law of belligerent occupation is based is that the occupant does not acquire sovereignty over the occupied territory and is forbidden to annex it during the armed conflict. It follows from this

property in occupied territory are spelled out in the Hague Regulations of 1907, which are still universally accepted as the codification of existing international law on the subject.[146] Under Article 55 of these Regulations the occupying state must administer the immovable public property of occupied territories "in accordance with the rules of usufruct" and under commonly applied rules of usufruct in civil law, the usufructuary may not open new mines or other means of mineral extraction and exploit them, even at a reasonable rate.[147] This principle finds its analogue in common law in the prohibition of "waste" under a life tenancy, which prevents a life tenant from extracting oil, gas or other minerals from the land since that depletes the corpus and constitutes waste.[148]

Even if *arguendo* an occupying power had the right to open new mines and oil wells and to extract minerals and other resources from occupied lands, it would not enjoy the right to use the proceeds of such resources to enrich the home treasury of the occupant. Articles 52 and 53 of the 1907 Hague Regulations Respecting the Laws and Customs of War on Land, an occupying power is only allowed to seize or appropriate property to fulfill the needs of the occupying army or to defray the costs of administering the occupation of the local population. This principle was affirmed by the interpretation of the Hague Regulations set out in the resolution of the London International Law Conference in 1943 and the decisions in the trials of German war criminals. In a resolution adopted by the Conference the authors specified:

> "The rights of the occupant do not include any right to dispose of
> property, rights or interests for purposes other than the maintenance

---

prohibition of annexation and the essentially temporary nature of the occupant's authority that the occupying power may not extend its own administration to the occupied territory, for to administer the occupied territory as part of the occupant's own State is annexation in all but name." C. Greenwood, *The Administration of Occupied Territory in International Law*, INTERNATIONAL LAW AND THE ADMINISTRATION OF OCCUPIED TERRITORIES: TWO DECADES OF ISRAELI OCCUPATION OF THE WEST BANK AND GAZA STRIP, (Emma Playfair Ed, Clarendon Press Oxford (1992) at 260 ("Greenwood") (citing McNair and Watts, The Legal Effects of War, at 369).

[146] See, Judgment of the International Military Tribunal, Nuremberg, 1 Trial of the Major War Criminals 253–54 (1947); U.S. v. Von Leeb, 11 Trials of War Criminals Before the Nuremberg Military Tribunals Under Control Council Law No. 1, at 533. As Christopher Greenwood noted: "Both the Hague Regulations and the Fourth Geneva Convention also forbid the exploitation of the economy of the occupied territory for the benefit of the occupant's own economy." Greenwood, *supra*, at 250 (Referring to the Teachers' Housing Cooperative case, HC 393/82, noted in IYHR 14 (1984) at 301).

[147] The French Civil Code, Article 598, for example, provides: "He also has the use, in the same manner as the owner, of mines and quarries which are being exploited at the beginning of the usufruct; and, nevertheless, if the exploitation is one which requires a concession, the usufructuary can only enjoy it after having obtained the permission of the King (President of the Republic)." It should be noted that under some civil law regimes—including those of most Middle East countries—the usufructuary does not enjoy even this limited use of the resources.

[148] E. Kuntz, A TREATISE ON THE LAW OF OIL AND GAS, (W. H. Anderson, 1962) at 168.

of public order and safety in the occupied territory. In particular, the occupant is not, in international law, vested with any power to transfer a title which will be valid outside that territory to any property, rights or interests which he purports to acquire or create or dispose of; this applies whether such property, rights or interests are those of the State or of private persons or bodies."

On the basis of the above principle the Japanese exploitation of Sumatran oil fields during the Second World War in order to supply its general military and civilian needs was deemed in violation of the laws and customs of war and the transfer of stock in the oil fields to the Japanese was deemed illegal.[149]

The above principles have been reaffirmed by a number of scholars in a variety of contexts. It has been held that in no instance does the occupying power possess the right to take property for exploitation for commercial purposes, to fulfill the occupying power's domestic needs, or to benefit its economy.[150] It has also been held that it is forbidden to remove from occupied territory private or even public property and to merge that property into the proper economic life of the occupant.[151] It has further been held that if the occupation constitutes a wrongful act, the responsible state must make full reparations for any material or moral damage caused by the wrongful act.[152] Finally, it has been held that it is possible to exploit the natural resources of occupied territory only for the benefit of the local population, as that benefit is defined by international humanitarian law.[153]

In 1976, Monroe Leigh, the US State Department Legal Advisor, found that Israel should be considered an "occupying power" with respect to land belonging to Egypt in Sinai and the Gulf of Suez occupied by Israel after the 7 days war. He noted that an "Occupying Power" has only limited rights to enter into contracts that concern the occupied territory.[154] He further noted that "An occupant's rights under international law do not include the right to develop a new oil field, to use

149 See Whyatt, C.J. *The Singapore Oil Stocks Case*, 51 AJIL 808 (1957).

150 Edward Cummings, *Oil Resources in Occupied Arab Territories under the Law of Belligerent Occupation*, 9 Journal of International Law and Economics, 1974, at 574–578.

151 E. Cummings, *supra*, at 575, fn. 155.

152 Article 31 of the International Law Commission (ILC) articles on state responsibility.

153 *Case concerning Armed Activities on the Territory of the Congo (Democratic Republic of the Congo v. Uganda)*, Judgment, 19 December 2005, ICJ Reports 2005, para. 249.

154 Cassese later quoted with approval a passage from the Monroe Leigh opinion in which Leigh argued that there must be limitations on the rights of occupying powers to utilize the natural resources of occupied territory, because a rule holding out the prospect of acquiring unrestricted access to the use of resources would constitute an incentive to territorial occupation by a country needing raw materials and a disincentive to withdrawal. "It is submitted that this view is illustrative of the right way to interpret the Hague Regulations in the light of the general legal principles currently prevailing in the world community." Cassese, *supra*, at 425.

the oil resources of occupied territory for the general benefit of the home economy or to grant oil concessions" and on that basis he declared in a memorandum dated October 1, 1976, that Israel's oil development plans in Sinai and the Gulf of Suez were contrary to international law.[155]

And the rights of an occupying power do not permit the transfer of the belligerent state's population into occupied land, as was elucidated a year later by his successor, Herbert Hansell, in a letter concerning the establishments of Israeli settlements in occupied land.[156] He wrote:

"[T]he Israeli armed forces entered Gaza, the West Bank, Sinai and the Golan Heights in June 1967, in the course of an armed conflict. Those areas had not previously been part of Israel's sovereign territory nor otherwise under its administration. By reason of such entry of its armed forces, Israel established control and began to exercise authority over these territories; and under international law, Israel became a belligerent occupant of these territories.

Territory coming under the control of a belligerent occupant does not thereby become its sovereign territory. International law confers upon the occupying State authority to undertake interim military administration over the territory and its inhabitants; that authority is not unlimited. The governing rules are designed to permit pursuit of its military needs by the occupying power, to protect the security of the occupying forces, to provide for orderly government, to protect the rights and interests of the inhabitants, and to reserve questions of territorial change and sovereignty to a later stage when the war is ended…He is not entitled to treat the country as his own territory or its inhabitants as his own subjects…."

He concluded:

"On the basis of the available information, the civilian settlements in the territories occupied by Israel do not appear to be consistent with these limits on Israel's authority as belligerent occupant in that they do not seem intended to be of limited duration or established to provide orderly government of the territories and, though some may serve incidental security purposes, they do not appear to be required to meet military needs during the occupation."

Then, after noting that by permitting its civilian population to establish permanent settlements in occupied land, Israel had thereby breached Article 49, paragraph 6, of the Fourth Geneva Convention, he summarized by stating:

"While Israel may undertake, in the occupied territories, actions necessary

---

[155] United States: Department of State Memorandum of Law on Israel's Right to Develop new Oil Fields in Sinai and the Gulf of Suez, 16 Int'l Legal Materials (1977)

[156] Letter of the State Department Legal Advisor, Mr. Herbert J. Hansell, Concerning the Legality of Israeli Settlements in the Occupied Territories of 21 April, 1978.

to meet its military needs and to provide for orderly government during the occupation, for reasons indicated above the establishment of the civilian settlements in those territories is inconsistent with international law."

Other eminent scholars have endorsed these principles. As Christopher Greenwood once noted: "The basic principles of the law governing occupation are found in the Fourth Geneva Convention and the 1907 Hague Regulations, both of which codify "intransgressible principles of international customary law" which are to be observed by all States and which include provisions regarding the permissible uses of property during an occupation."[157] According to Professor Crawford, "It is…generally accepted that the occupier may not use the resources of the occupied territory for its own domestic purposes, but rather must use them 'to the extent necessary for the current administration of the territory and to meet the essential needs of the population.' (cite omitted) For example, this restriction was acknowledged by the occupants of Iraq in 2003 who informed the President of the UN Security Council that they would act to ensure that Iraq's oil is protected and used for the benefit of the Iraqi people, resulting in a binding Chapter VII resolution to enforce that principle."[158]

As was noted by Antonio Cassese: "In my view it follows from the provisions of the Hague Regulations…that the occupant can interfere in the economic activity of the territory under its control…only for the following purposes (a) to meet its own military or security needs…(b) to defray the expenses involved in the belligerent occupation; (c) to protect the interest and the well being of the inhabitants…It is strictly forbidden for the occupant to resort to one of the aforementioned measures for other purposes, e.g. with a view to drawing economic benefits for himself…."[159] He goes on to cite the example of the position of the United Kingdom to the projected building by Israel of a canal between the Mediterranean and the Dead Sea, in which it declared the project "contrary to international law" in that it would involve an alteration of property belonging to Jordan that would "exceed Israel's right as an occupying power."[160]

The fact that a state "administers" a territory *de facto* does not change it from an occupying power to an "administering power." Indeed, occupying powers normally "administer" the lands they occupy. Israel has "administered" the West

---

[157] Greenwood, *supra*, at 244–245.

[158] Crawford, *supra*, at 25, para. 60.

[159] A. Cassese. *Powers and Duties of an Occupant in Relation to Land and Natural Resources*, INTERNATIONAL LAW AND THE ADMINISTRATION OF OCCUPIED TERRITORIES: TWO DECADES OF ISRAELI OCCUPATION OF THE WEST BANK AND GAZA STRIP, (Emma Playfair Ed, Clarendon Press Oxford (1992) ("Cassese"), at 422.

[160] *Id.* at 422–423 (citing BYIL (1981), at 515).

Bank and the Gaza strip for years and is still considered an occupying power over these lands. South Africa "administered" Namibia for a number of years, yet was still considered an occupying power. Israel "administered" the Sinai Peninsula after the 7 days war and yet was considered an occupying power by the Legal Advisor to the United States State Department, Monroe Leigh.

The legal principles concerning the rights of occupying powers to utilize the resources of occupied territory are applied even during occupations of long durations. The International Court of Justice did not hesitate to apply them to Israel's occupation of the West Bank and Gaza or South Africa's occupation of Namibia. As Christopher Greenwood has noted: "Although it is obviously difficult to apply the law of belligerent occupation in a prolonged occupation, that law is not thereby rendered inapplicable."[161] He has also noted that any purported "annexation" of an occupied territory is not recognized under international law. "[A] purported annexation of occupied territory by the occupying power is ineffective to alter the status of the territory or its inhabitants, who remain subject to the law of belligerent occupation."[162]

States that have become occupying powers have recognized the limitations of their powers in a number of recent situations. For instance, when the United States occupied Iraq after the 2003 war it set up an administering authority that, among other things, entered into contracts with third parties to utilize the resources of Iraq. However, the United States was careful to include representatives of the Iraqi people in such decision making. The United States, moreover, did not attempt to enter into international treaties on behalf of Iraq. Nor did the United States attempt to enter into international treaties on behalf of Germany or Japan at the end of World War II, although it was the *de facto* administrator of these states for a number of years.

And it should be noted that the rules of occupation set forth in the Geneva Conventions were designed to address occupations that were considered *legal* by the international community either under the theory of self defense or because they were in accordance with an aim of the United Nations.

When an occupation is considered *illegal,* not only may occupying powers not legally enter into treaties or contracts, but all states are required under international law to refrain from entering into such agreements or fostering them in any way. This was clearly enunciated in the *Namibia* opinion. "The Court set out the scope of the doctrine of non-recognition at paragraphs 122–124 of the Namibia Opinion. In the first place, States may not enter into treaty relations with an unlawful regime

---

[161] Greenwood, *supra*, at 263.

[162] *Id.,* at 245.

with regard to the territory in dispute...and must 'abstain from entering into economic and other forms of relationship or dealings with South Africa on behalf of or concerning Namibia which may entrench its authority over the Territory.'"[163] The only "exception" to this obligation of non-recognition is with respect to acts that are necessary to maintain public order, such as the registration of marriages, the granting of licenses, and other routine administrative acts that benefit the local population.

The *Namibia* principle has been broadly accepted by a line of UK authority. In Carl Zeiss Stiftung v. Rayner & Keeler Ltd. (No. 2),[164] Lord Wilberforce entered a reservation that 'where private rights, or acts of everyday occurrence, or perfunctory acts of administration are concerned...the courts may, in the interests of justice and common sense, where no consideration of public policy to the contrary has to prevail, give recognition to the actual facts or realities found to exist in the territory in question.'[165] In Hesperides Hotels Ltd v. Aegean Holidays Ltd,[166] a case which arose out of the expropriation of property in northern Cyprus, Lord Denning MR said that he could if necessary 'hold that the courts of this country can recognize the laws or acts of a body which is in effective control of a territory even though it has not been recognized by the United Kingdom government de jure or de facto... in regard to the laws which regulate the day to day affairs of the people, such as their marriages, their divorces, their leases, their occupations, and so forth.'[167] In Gur Corporation v. Trust Bank of Africa Ltd.,[168] Lord Donaldson MR said that he saw great force in the reservation of Lord Wilberforce. In Caglar v. Billingham (Inspector of Taxes),[169] the Special Commissioners formulated the principle that 'the courts may acknowledge the existence of an unrecognized foreign government in the context of the enforcement of laws relating to commercial obligations or matters of private law between individuals or matters of routine administration such as the registration of birth, marriages or deaths,' but that the courts will not acknowledge the existence of an unrecognized State if to do so would involve them in acting inconsistently with the foreign polity or diplomatic stance of the UK.

In R (on the application of Kibris Turk Hava Yollari and another) v. Secretary of State for Transport [2012] All ER (D) 111 Oct. paras. 78–80, the Court of Appeals considered the application by a Turkish airline for permission to carry

---

[163] *Id.* p. 20, para. 48, quoting the Court at para. 124.

[164] [1967] 1 AC 853.

[165] *Id.* at 954.

[166] [1978] 1 QB 205.

[167] *Id.* at 218G.

[168] [1987] 1 QB 599.

[169] [1996] STC (SDC) 150.

passengers on scheduled service between the United Kingdom and northern Cyprus, a territory then under the *de facto* control and administration of the Turkish government. While the Court decided the case on the basis of the 1944 Chicago Convention, the Court also addressed the UK position on recognition, and in particular the scope of the Namibia exception. The Court said:

"Mr. Haddon-Cave submitted that the Namibia exception is a flexible principle and that the present case is a paradigm case for its application, given the importance of air travel and the adverse impact on ordinary people in northern Cyprus who are deprived of the advantages of international cooperation in the field.

"I cannot accept that submission. In my judgment, the issue in the present case falls well outside the ambit of the Namibia exception...This case is not concerned with private rights, acts of every day occurrence, routine acts of administration, day to day activities having legal consequences, or matters of that kind...The issues in the case are issues of public law, concerning the question whether it is lawful to grant a permit for international flights to and from northern Cyprus contrary to the wishes...of the recognized state of which that territory forms part...This is not the kind of subject matter at which the Namibia exception is directed."[170]

Accordingly, the weight of authority supports the position that states are under an obligation to refrain from any act that would constitute recognition of the purported international agreements or other acts of a state that concern a territory that it is illegally occupying. No recognition refers not only to formal recognition but also to acts that would imply such recognition.[171]

The attempted annexation of territory by force and against the will of its inhabitants is considered an illegal occupation under international law. As was noted by Professor Crawford: "As territory cannot be acquired by the unlawful use of force nor where that purported territorial acquisition violates the right to self-determination, States are obliged to not give legal credence—recognition of authority over the territory—to the unlawful acquisition...It is, at a minimum, intended to prevent insofar as possible 'the validation of an unlawful situation by seeking to ensure that a fait accompli resulting from serious illegalities do not consolidate and crystallize over time into situations recognized by the international legal order.'"[172]

As was noted previously, in 2012 Professor Crawford was asked for his opinion

---

[170] R (on the application of Kibris Turk Hava Yollari and another) v. Secretary of State for Transport (Republic of Cyprus, Interested Party) [2010] All ER (D) 111 (Oct), paras. 78–80.

[171] I.L.C. Draft Articles, Article 41, comment 5.

[172] Crawford, *supra*, at 18–19, para. 46; quoting Martin Dawidowicz, *The Obligation of Non-Recognition of an Unlawful Situation* in THE LAW OF INTERNATIONAL RESPONSIBILITY (J. Crawford, A. Pellet & S. Olleson, eds.) (OUP: Oxford, 2010) at 678.

about the legality of Israel's use of the agricultural products produced by the Israeli settlements on the West Bank. Some of his comments are pertinent to the arguments of the European Commission before the EU Courts concerning the agricultural Accord between the EU and Morocco.

Crawford noted that the International Court of Justice declared in the *Wall* opinion that by constructing the wall Israel had violated certain *erga omnes* obligations, namely "the obligation to respect the right of the Palestinian people to self-determination, and certain of its obligations under international humanitarian law"[173] and that states are under an obligation "not to render aid or assistance in maintaining the situation created by such construction."[174] He then noted that the Court further declared that all states parties to the Fourth Geneva Convention are under an obligation to 'ensure compliance by Israel with international humanitarian law.'[175]

He then explained: "The right of self-determination is one of the essential tenets of international law. Since the adoption of the Declaration on the Granting of Independence to Colonial Countries and Peoples, followed by the International Covenant on Economic, Social and Cultural Rights and the International Covenant on Civil and Political Rights, the concept of self determination as a whole has obtained the characteristic of a fundamental human right, both individual and collective. Some authors classify it as a peremptory norm (jus cogens),[176] and the Court in its Advisory Opinion [Wall] affirmed the *erga omnes* character of that right."[177]

His conclusion was that "To the extent that Israel maintains...its de facto annexation of West Bank territory, that annexation has prevented the Palestinian people from exercising their right to self-determination pursuant to General Assembly Resolution 1514 (XV),"[178] and that "States are under an obligation of non-recognition and must not aid or assist Israel in its perpetuation of the settlement program."[179]

He then discussed the legal consequences for states resulting from this obligation, stating: "The legal consequences for third States of this unlawful conduct on the part of Israel could arise in two ways: from the obligation of

---

[173] *Wall Opinion*, paras. 155–156

[174] *Id.* para. 159

[175] *Id.*

[176] Citing Ian Brownlie, *supra*, at 511–512; Antonio Cassese, INTERNATIONAL LAW (2nd Ed., OUP: Oxford, 2005) at 65; Malcolm N. Shaw, INTERNATIONAL LAW (6th Ed. CUP: Cambridge, 2008), at 808.

[177] Crawford, *supra*, at 11, para. 26.

[178] *Id*, p. 12, para. 28.

[179] *Id.*, p. 18 para. 45

non-recognition or the obligation 'not to render aid or assistance' in maintaining the unlawful situation."[180]

"The obligation not to assist the responsible State is 'limited to acts that would assist in preserving the situation created by the breach.' That is, it is limited to acts that would assist in preserving either (a) Israel's de facto annexation of the West Bank and other occupied territories in breach of the right to self-determination, (b) Israel's breach of Article 49(6) of Geneva Convention IV prohibiting the transfer of populations or (c) Israel's potential breach of Article 55 of the 1907 Hague Regulations."[181]

He then discussed specific acts that could constitute a violation of this obligation. He pointed out that Article 1(e) of the Agreement for Air Services Between And Beyond Their Respective Territories Between the Government of Israel and the Government of the United Kingdom of Great Britain and Northern Ireland (24 September 1975) defines "territory" as "the land areas and territorial waters adjacent thereto under the sovereignty, suzerainty, protection or trusteeship of that State," and noted that "Whether or not the Convention applies to the Occupied Palestinian Territories is uncertain, but if so, in the present state of affairs, the UK is under an obligation to regard this clause as ineffective."[182] He further noted that the UK/Israel convention on double taxation applies to income tax and company tax levied in "Israel" defined as "the territory in which the Government of Israel levies taxation,' and stated that "If the government of Israel levies taxes in any part of the West Bank...the UK is under an obligation not to take account of those taxes in relation to the other provisions of the convention."[183]

He concluded by discussing other forms of economic dealings: "Economic and commercial dealings between Israel and a third State may be considered as either a breach of the obligation of non-recognition (if such dealings do not fall within the Namibia exception) or they might be considered to amount to aid or assistance in the commission of an internationally wrongful act, contrary to Articles 16 and 41(2) of the ILC Draft Articles," noting that "Some pertinent examples of commercial dealings could be the purchase of agricultural produce from settlements..."[184]

States which have occupied territories illegally by force and for the purpose of territorial acquisition have historically been granted no legal right to enter into

---

[180] *Id*. p. 30, para. 72.

[181] *Id*, p. 32, para. 76.

[182] *Id*. p. 34, para. 82.

[183] *Id*. p. 35, para. 83.

[184] *Id*. p. 35, para. 84–85.

treaties on behalf of the territories so occupied. Moreover, other states are required under international law to refrain from entering into international agreements with such occupiers and to abstain from any activities which would facilitate or prolong their illegal occupation.

The rules that apply to Israel's exploitation of the resources of the West Bank and Gaza strip, as declared by the International Court of Justice and a number of learned commentators, should be deemed equally applicable to Morocco's exploitation of the resources of Western Sahara. According to those rules, Morocco would not enjoy the legal capacity to enter into international agreements that concern Western Sahara. It follows, then, that the EU as well as all states, would not, in their agreements with Morocco, be entitled to include provisions which would recognize such a capacity or facilitate Morocco's continued occupation.

Indeed, the legal principles cited by many scholars support the position that Morocco should be considered an "occupying power."[185] Likewise, the English

---

[185] The Advocate General of the EU cited the following sources in support of his conclusion in his Opinion on the legality of the 2013 FPA that Morocco should be considered an "occupying power" rather than a "de-facto administering power" over Western Sahara: "Roberts, A., 'What is military occupation?', British Yearbook of International Law, 1985, Vol. 55, pp. 249 to 305, especially pp. 280 and 281; Gasser, H.P., 'The Conflict in Western Sahara — An Unresolved Issue from the Decolonisation Period', Yearbook of International Humanitarian Law, 2002, Vol. 5, pp. 375 to 380, especially p. 379; Arai-Takahashi, Y., The Law of Occupation:Continuity and Change of International Humanitarian Law, and its Interaction with International Human Rights Law, Martinus Nijhoff, The Hague, 2009, p. 140; Chinkin, C., 'Laws of occupation', published in Botha, N., Olivier, M., and van Tonder, D. (eds), Multilateralism and International Law with Western Sahara as a Case Study, VerLoren van Themaat Centre, Pretoria, 2010, pp. 197 to 221, especially pp. 197 to 200; Benvenisti, E., The International Law of Occupation, 2nd ed., Oxford University Press, Oxford, 2012, p. 171; Fastenrath, U., 'Chapter XI Declaration Regarding Non-self-governing Territories', published in Simma, B., Khan, D.-E., Nolte, G., and Paulus, A. (eds), The Charter of the United Nations:A Commentary, 3e ed., Oxford University Press, Oxford, 2012, Vol. II, pp. 1829 to 1839, especially p. 1837; Koutroulis, V., 'The application of international humanitarian law and international human rights law in prolonged occupation: only a matter of time?', International Review of the Red Cross, 2012, Vol. 94, pp. 165 to 205, especially p. 171; David, É., Principes de droit des conflits armés, 5th ed., Bruylant, Brussels, 2012, p. 192; Ruiz Miguel, C., 'La responsabilité internationale et les droits de l'homme: le cas du Sahara occidental', Cahiers de la recherche sur les droits fondamentaux, 2013, Vol. 11, pp. 105 to 130, especially p. 107; Dawidowicz, M., 'Trading Fish or Human Rights in Western Sahara? Self-Determination, Non-Recognition and the EC-Morocco Fisheries Agreement', published in French, D. (ed.), Statehood, Self-Determination and Minorities: Reconciling Tradition and Modernity in International Law, Cambridge University Press, Cambridge, 2013, pp. 250 to 276; Bothe, M., 'The Administration of Occupied Territory' published in Clapham, A., Gaeta, P., and Sassòli, M. (eds), The 1949 Geneva Conventions: A commentary, Oxford University Press, Oxford, 2015, pp. 1455 to 1484, especially p. 1459; Kontorovich, E., 'Economic Dealings with Occupied Territories', Columbia Journal of Transnational Law, 2015, Vol. 53, pp. 584 to 637, especially pp. 611 and 612; Saul, B., 'The Status of Western Sahara as Occupied Territory under International Humanitarian Law and the Exploitation of Natural Resources', Sydney Law School Legal Studies Research Paper, No 15/81 (September 2015). See also judgment of 15 June 2017 of the High Court of South Africa in Case No 1487/17, The Saharawi Arab Democratic Republic and Front Polisario v The Owner and charterers of the MV 'NM Cherry Blossom', paragraph 29." Opinion, fn. 223. These are only a few of the many statements of legal experts and organizations which have come to this conclusion, the most recent being included in the recent letter to the European Parliament of NGO Human Rights Waatch arguing that international humanitarian law must apply: ("[T]he relationship between Morocco and Western Sahara is also one of occupation...In practice, in order for Morocco, as an occupying power, to lawfully exploit Western Sahara's resources, it would have to establish a fund with transparent bookkeeping that shows the resources utilized or exported, the revenue derived, and the channeling of those resources to be sole benefit of the people of Western Sahara." See, Western Sahara Resource Watch, November 2, 2019.

High Court, in its ruling on the suit brought by the WSCUK concerning the 2013 EU-Morocco FPA, did not hesitate in rejecting Morocco's status as an "administering power" and in referring to Morocco's unlawful occupation.[186]

This would also appear also to be the position of the European Union's Advocate General Wathelet, who stated in his Opinion on the FPA:[187]

"In my view, the theory put forward by the French Government, the Council and the Commission that the Kingdom of Morocco is the 'de facto administering power' of Western Sahara must be rejected...the Council and the Commission have been unable to give a single other example in which that expression has been used to describe the relationship between a State and a non-self-governing territory. It should be pointed out in that regard that in the contemporary and very similar case of the annexation of East Timor by the Republic of Indonesia, the expression 'de facto administering power' was not used to describe the status of the Republic of Indonesia in its relationship with East Timor. On the contrary, the International Court of Justice described the military intervention of the Republic of Indonesia in East Timor as an occupation."[188]

He then reiterated the rules governing the use of resources of a territory under occupation, citing Article 55 of the 1907 Hague Regulations in which it was stated that the occupier should be regarded only as administrator and usufructuary of property belonging to the territory, and must safeguard the capitol of such properties and administer them in accordance with the rules of usufruct.[189] He considered that Article 55 is applicable to the exploitation of the fisheries stocks of maritime zones situated alongside the coasts of the occupied territory.[190]

These conclusions were also those of the research branch of the German Bundestag, in its status report on the international law aspects of the conflict of Western Sahara, wherein it concluded that Morocco is not to be considered the administering power of Western Sahara, nor a 'de-facto administering power', since this term is not meaningful in context of international law [citing the opinion of the Advocate General in the preliminary ruling at the CJEU on the EU-Morocco Fisheries Agreement (C-266/16 2018)]. Moreover, the report comes to the conclusion that "good reasons support the assumption that Morocco has annexed

---

[186] After noting that Morocco cannot be considered the "administering power" of Western Sahara, the Court, in examining Morocco's sovereignty claim, expressed the view that "unauthorized military occupation cannot found the basis for legitimate territorial claims." *Western Sahara v. HMRC & SSEFRA,* [2015] EWHC 2898 (Admin.) October 19, 2015, Para. 40.

[187] Wathelet Opinion 2, in case C-266/16, delivered on January 10, 2018.

[188] Paras. 221, 224.

[189] Para. 258.

[190] Para. 259.

the part of Western Sahara under its control and that it continues to occupy it." Further on, it states that Western Sahara is under occupation and that "Morocco is to be considered the occupying power."[191]

This is likewise the position that has been advanced by the African Union. On October 15, 2015 the AU published on its website a Legal Opinion concerning Morocco's use of the resources of Western Sahara.[192] After first noting its opinion that the territory is under "colonial occupation" by Morocco,[193] it stated that "Morocco has no legal right under the UN Charter or international law to occupy or govern the Territory of Western Sahara."[194] It argued that the people of Western Sahara and their legitimate representatives, the Polisario and the Saharawi Republic,[195] "must not only be consulted but they must consent and effectively participate in reaching any agreement that involves the exploitation of natural resources" in the territory.[196] It argued that the companies which invest in, explore for, or exploit the resources of the territory are helping the "perpetuation or legitimization of the colonial situation." It concluded by stating that "any exploration and exploitation of renewable or non-renewable natural resources by Morocco, any other State, group of States or foreign companies in Western Sahara are.... aiding and abetting an illegal situation,"[197] and urged the United Nations "to protect the Sahrawi's renewable and non-renewable natural resources as it did in East Timor and Namibia...."[198]

International human rights advocacy groups have also advanced this position. In a letter Human Rights Watch sent to the members of the European Parliament in February, 2020, concerning the new draft fisheries agreement, urging that international human rights standards be applied, it stated:

"It remains the case, factually, that Morocco is in occupation of the territory and therefore the relevant international humanitarian law applies...."

It went on to argue that the proposed agreement "fails to meet the requirements of international law, and in particular of international humanitarian law (IHL)," and called upon the members of Parliament to seek an opinion from the European

191 See, https://www.wsrw.org/files/dated/2020-05-04/bundestag-statusreport-ws2019.pdf.

192 "Legal opinion on the legality in the context of international law of actions allegedly taken in the exploration and/or exploitation of renewable and non-renewable natural resources or any other economic activity in Western Sahara," The Office of the Legal Counsel and Directorate for Legal Affairs of the African Union Commission, African Union, October 15, 2015.

193 Id., at para. 21.

194 Id., at para. 57.

195 The Saharawi Arabic Democratic Republic ("SADR") now prefers to be referred to as the "Saharawi Republic."

196 Id., at para. 64.

197 Id., at para. 60.

198 Id., at para. 76.

Court of Justice on the compatibility with European Treaties, and specifically with international humanitarian law governing occupied territories, of the proposed agreement.

Again it reiterated that "the relationship between Morocco and Western Sahara is…one of occupation…" and, referring to the 2003 Development Fund of Iraq as an example, added, "In practice, in order for Morocco, as an occupying power, to lawfully exploit Western Sahara's resources, it would have to establish a fund with transparent bookkeeping that shows the resources utilized or exported, the revenue derived, and the channeling of those resources to the sole benefit of the people of Western Sahara."[199]

Accordingly, in the final analysis it may very well be that the principles laid down by the Corell Opinion will be disregarded by courts and international tribunals in favor of those applicable to an "occupying power" under international law, in which case the use of the resources of Western Sahara by Morocco would be even more restricted.

---

[199] *See,* Western Sahara Resource Watch, "Human Rights Watch Calls for Court Referral of EU-Morocco Fish Deal," February 2, 2019.

PART IV

Enforcement of Legal Rights

(1) United Nations

IT IS ONE thing to decide that as a matter of international law the Saharawis have a right to self-determination, a right to see the Settlement Plan and *Houston Accords* agreed with Morocco implemented, and a right to restrict the utilization of the resources of Western Sahara by Morocco during its period of occupation, but it quite another thing to determine a method to enforce such rights. Throughout history international legal scholars have been quick to find the existence of rights which cannot be enforced by existing legal or political instrumentalities, and rights without the means to enforce them are arguably no rights at all.

Indeed, one of the arguments belatedly raised by the Secretary General as justification for the abandonment of the Settlement Plan was that it provided no means of enforcement.

Yet, according to Baker, the United Nations has under Chapter 7 of its Charter adequate means to enforce the Saharawis rights—if it is willing to employ them.

Chapter 7 of the United Nations Charter concerns actions by the Organization to counter "threats to the peace, breaches of the peace, and acts of aggression." In accordance with Article 39 of that Chapter, the Security Council "shall determine the existence of any threat to the peace, breach of the peace, or act of aggression and shall make recommendations, or decide what measures shall be taken in accordance with Articles 41 and 42, to maintain or restore international peace and security."

Article 41 lists the means, short of armed force, that may be employed to give effect to the decisions of the Security Council, and includes "complete or partial interruption of economic relations and of rail, sea, air, postal, telegraphic, radio, and other means of communication, and the severance of diplomatic relations." If the Security Council considers that the measures provided for in Article 41 are inadequate to accomplish its objectives, under Article 42 it may "take such action by air, sea, or land forces as may be necessary to maintain or restore international peace and security. Such action may include demonstrations, blockade and other operations by air, sea, or land forces of Members of the United Nations."

United Nations resolutions passed under Chapter 7 have supported all the measures taken by the international community against Iraq since its invasion of Kuwait in 1990, including the Gulf War, the inspection of Iraq for weapons of mass destruction, the embargo against Iraq and the "oil for food program", and were subsequently invoked by the United States to support the military measures it took against Iraq in 2003. Security Council Resolution 1373, adopted after the September 11, 2001 attacks against the United States, also came under the rubric of Chapter 7.

However, the Security Council has rarely invoked its powers under Chapter 7. By far the majority of resolutions passed by the Security Council are implicitly or explicitly under the rubric of its powers under Chapter 6 of the United Nations Charter.

Chapter 6 has often been referred to as the "neglected step brother" of Chapter 7. Intended to set forth the modalities for facilitating the peaceful settlement of disputes, Article 34 empowers the Security Council to "investigate" any dispute or situation which might lead to international friction. In addition, Article 35 provides that any member state may bring such a dispute to the attention of the Security Council. Once apprised of such a dispute or situation, Article 36 empowers the Security Council to "recommend appropriate procedures or methods of adjustment," and Article 38 grants the Security Council similar advisory power at the request of one of the parties. What is glaringly absent from mention in Chapter 6 is any suggestion that the "recommendations" of the Security Council have the force of law and any provision for the enforcement of such "recommendations" if they are legally binding.

Because it lacks "teeth" resolutions under Chapter 6 have been easily passed— and just as easily ignored by parties to a dispute. As an example, since 1948 the Security Council has adopted at least 87 resolutions under Chapter 6—but not one under Chapter 7—"recommending" that Israel take certain actions concerning Palestine, not one of which has been implemented by Israel. Israel considers such resolutions advisory opinions not carrying the force of law, and Israel is not alone. As one writer put it, "The United States and other member States have often regarded Chapter VI not as a process with its own dynamics, but as a mere weigh station on the road to enforcement measures, with the gatekeeping function of Article 39 often moribund."[1]

Unfortunately for the Saharawis, to date all the Security Council resolutions concerning the Western Sahara issue have been adopted under Chapter 6 of the Charter. In an interview with PBS Wideangle on August 19, 2004, following his resignation, Baker cited this fact as the major impediment to a resolution of the issue, noting that "The Security Council has never been willing to impose a solution, that is, to move to Chapter 7 of the U.N. Charter from Chapter 6, which requires consensus of both parties."

As Baker further noted:

> "If you're going to say that you have to resolve the conflict by consensus agreement between the parties then the parties have got to want to resolve it...If, on the other hand, you can persuade let's say, the Security Council as we did in the lead up to the Gulf War to use Chapter 7 powers to impose upon one party or the other or ask one party or the other to do something they would not otherwise voluntarily agree to do, that's a little different. And it's easier to resolve a conflict when you have that power and that ability behind you."

If Baker is right the United Nations has the means at its disposal to enforce the Saharawis legal rights, the problem is that it lacks the political will to use them. This lack of will would be understandable, and perhaps laudable, if by invoking Chapter 7 the Security Council would be required to urge its members to provide military aid to enforce its resolutions. However, Article 41 of Chapter 7 gives the Security Council a wide variety of enforcement mechanisms short of military force, and there is no reason to believe that only the threat of military force would persuade Morocco to abide by the norms of international law.[2] Accordingly, without excluding any other available means of enforcing the Saharawis' rights, it would seem that there is one enforcement mechanism that is clearly available.

However, as noted previously, resort to Chapter 7 may not be necessary: the terms of the Settlement Plan as outlined by the Secretary General and agreed by the parties appear to have conferred substantial authority upon the United Nations to

---

[1] Steven R. Ratner, Assistant Professor of Law, University of Texas School of Law, in *Image and Reality in the UN's Peaceful Settlement of Disputes*, European Journal of International Law, Vol. 6, No. 3

[2] Indeed, economic and political sanctions have worked quite effectively in the arena of international arbitration and enforcement of the decisions of the ICJ and there is no reason to believe they would be less effective in support of the legal rights of the Saharawis.

render decisions that would be legally binding on the parties—and thereby capable of being enforced through the courts of member states in much the same fashion as an international arbitration award. If the United Nations has failed to exercise that authority it is arguably from lack of political will, not legal impediments.

Also, it may be time for the international legal community to re-examine its position on the scope of powers conferred upon the United Nations under Chapter 6. If nothing else, the dismal failure of attempts under Chapter 6 to resolve the conflict over Western Sahara should demonstrate the shortcomings of its present interpretation. Today, international arbitration treaties and judicial decisions have given the international commercial community copious mechanisms for addressing and enforcing disputes of a commercial nature. Likewise, the International Court of Justice at The Hague has been created to give states a means to settle issues of a legal nature.[3] However, no mechanism currently exists—other than resort to arbitration on an *ad hoc* basis with few rules and even fewer precedents or resort to the United Nations under Chapter 6—whereby states can voluntarily submit the type of dispute raised by Western Sahara to a mutually agreed third party for resolution. The United Nations could perform a vitally needed function in this area, but only if jurists are willing to adopt a broader interpretation of the powers of the United Nations under Chapter 6. Recent decisions of the International Court of Justice suggest that such an interpretation is possible.[4] If international jurists continue to maintain that decisions by the Security Council under Chapter 6 require the step by step consensus of all interested parties without any enforcement mechanism, utilizing Chapter 6 to settle disputes will be a waste of time.

(2) Court Actions

Until such a time as the powers of the United Nations under Chapter 6 are re-interpreted, or the United Nations Security Council decides to invoke its powers

---

[3] Article 94(2) of the UN Charter requires each member of the United Nations to comply with the decision of the ICJ in any case to which it is a party and further empowers parties to such cases to petition the Security Council to pursue measures to give effect to a judgment of the Court where parties fail to implement the Court's decision. In addition, courts of member countries are able to recognize and enforce the judgments of the ICJ under their domestic laws. Although resort to Article 94(2) has been rare, it has been invoked by the UK in 1951 with respect to the *Anglo-Iranian Oil Company* case; by Nicaragua in 1986 in the case against the United States; and by Bosnia-Herzegovina in 1993 in the case against the Federal Republic of Yugoslavia. *See*, Tanzi, A., *Problems of Enforcement of Decisions of the International Court of Justice and the Law of the United Nations*, 6 Eur.J.Int'l Law 539 (1995) at 540.

[4] There are indications that the legal community may be poised to recognize increased powers of the United Nations under Chapter 6. In the *Namibia* Advisory Opinion the International Court of Justice found that the relevant Security Council decisions under Chapter 6 were binding. *See*, *Legal Consequences for States of the Continued Presence of South Africa in Namibia (South West Africa) Notwithstanding Security Council Resolution 276* (1970), ICJ Reports (1971) 53, at para. 115. Unfortunately, this opinion has been interpreted narrowly and has had little impact on the development of the law in this area.

under Chapter 7, perhaps the most potent weapon at the disposal of the Saharawis to enforce their rights are the courts. The cases before the courts of the European Union to annul the agricultural and fisheries trade agreements with Morocco were only the first step in an effort by the Saharawis, and their followers, to enforce their legal rights through this avenue.

On April 1, 2018, a month after the appellate court's decision declaring the fisheries agreement to be inapplicable to the territory of Western Sahara, the Polisario brought suit in the European courts to annul the EU-Morocco Aviation Agreement insofar as it applied to the territory of Western Sahara. Reiterating principles announced in the decisions concerning the agricultural and fisheries agreements, the court on November 30, 2018 once again declared the Agreement inapplicable to the territory of Western Sahara, thereby delivering a blow to an avenue of commerce and tourism utilized by the Moroccan government as well as posing a substantial obstacle to commerce between the Canary Islands and the territory.

In 2017 the Polisario, through its state entity the Saharawi Arab Democratic Republic (SADR), launched a series of court actions to have ships carrying phosphate cargo from Western Sahara seized. While a court in Panama denied the SADR's attempts to seize the cargo of a ship in Panama's jurisdiction, a court in South Africa ruled that a ship with cargo bound for New Zealand had to remain in port until a legal challenge raised by the SADR could be heard or until a bond was posted. The central issue in the case was ownership of the cargo. The phosphates were sold and shipped by OCP, the state owned phosphate mining conglomerate of Morocco. The SADR, which is recognized as an independent state representing the people of Western Sahara by South Africa, claimed that the cargo was the property of the people of Western Sahara obtained by Morocco in a manner contrary to South Africa's Constitution and international law. In response, OCP claimed that Morocco exercises sovereignty over the territory of Western Sahara and mined and shipped the cargo in accordance with Moroccan and international law. On June 15, 2017 the Court maintained the preliminary injunction issued by a lower court, pending a final determination of ownership, finding that under the principles of international law applicable to the use of the resources of a non-self-governing territory, which it held applicable under South African law, the Polisario/SADR had established a *prima facie* case and a balance of convenience in their favor. On February 23, 2018 the High Court found that under these principles the cargo belonged to the people of Western Sahara, and not to OCP, and that OCP had no legal right to sell the cargo to the New Zealand importer. It also found that Morocco did not exercise sovereignty over the territory, relying upon the decision of the English court in *R (on application of Western Sahara Campaign UK) v. Revenue and Customs Commissioner and others*, and the Court of Justice of the European Union in *Council of the European Union v. Polisario Front*. This case was only the first in a series of similar actions filed by the Polisario/SADR in other jurisdictions.[5]

In addition to lawsuits challenging the ownership of cargo from Western Sahara, the Polisario and their supporters have taken action to curb investment in the companies that deal in products from Western Sahara. For the past twenty years Western Sahara Resource Watch has lobbied government wealth funds to encourage them to discontinue their investments in companies which partake in the illegal trade in goods from Western Sahara, resulting in a number of firms leaving the market. In 2020 the Polisario filed a lawsuit against the New Zealand Pension Fund demanding that it discontinues investing in the two companies importing phosphates from the territory.

These efforts are part of a new strategy to use court proceedings and economic pressure as a way to enforce the rights of the Saharawis under international law. And others may follow.

Also, it should be noted that the fact that the European Union allowed trade in such products to exist under its rubric has legal consequences that cannot be ignored. If the Court's position is correct that the parties did not have the legal right to trade in products emanating from Western Sahara, it supports the Polisario contention that for a long time an unacceptable and illegal trade in such products has been conducted by the parties with the full acquiescence of the EU—a practice which to the extent it harms the interests of the people of Western Sahara is rightfully one which can and should be challenged in the courts by the people who represent them. Likewise, if the Court's position is correct, it necessarily means that in the future the EU must be estopped from importing products from Western Sahara without the prior approval of the Saharawis. In either case the EU has been engaged for a number of years in the importation of products from Western Sahara contrary to principles of international law, and the people of the territory should be entitled to claim damages in the form of restitution for the value of such imports.

And the principles laid down by the European Court decisions may have implications for the exploitation of resources by others. For instance, Kosmos, Glencore, and other oil companies, entered into contracts with the Moroccan government under the Moroccan "Hydrocarbon Law" which, according to the

---

[5] The Polisario unsuccessfully attempted to seize the cargo of a ship in Panama. The Panamanian court classified the issue as "political" and held that national courts are not the appropriate venue for such issues. However, this decision has not deterred the Polisario from filing similar actions in other jurisdictions.

Preamble, concerns the "exploitation of hydrocarbons in Morocco." The territory of Western Sahara is designated its "southern provinces."[6] Indeed, the blueprint for the future development of hydrocarbon resources in the territory prepared by CESE[7] is entitled "New Development Model for the Kingdom's Southern Provinces."

Accordingly, there may be grounds for holding oil companies who engage in business in Western Sahara responsible in court proceedings for violating international law under the principles announced by the European Court. In addition, there may be grounds for holding such companies in violation of the international guidelines on corporate responsibility. As was noted by Hans Corell,[8] "Signing an agreement in which Morocco refers to Western Sahara as "the southern provinces of the Kingdom of Morocco" is at variance with Corporate Social Responsibility and the principles Protect, Respect and Remedy."

Likewise, if the principles applied by the European Court to the Agricultural Accord and Fisheries Agreement are applied to the Joint Declaration on Renewable Energy, it is clear that the Declaration will not be able to be applied to renewable energy projects in Western Sahara. If these principles are applied to the activities of Siemens and the other companies investing in such projects, it is clear that they will be found to have violated international law.

(3) United Nations Convention on the Law of the Sea (UNCLOS)

It is an unfortunate truth that the present international legal system offers individuals in the position of the Saharawis few avenues of redress before international tribunals for the injustices they suffer. As mentioned previously, when Morocco and Mauritania prosecuted their claims to the territory before the International Court of Justice, the Saharawis lacked standing to intervene even though they were the people who would be most directly affected by the Court's decision. This is because only states, or in some circumstances international organizations, may be parties to proceedings before the ICJ. Likewise, because it is not recognized by the United Nations as a "state" the SADR cannot participate directly in the activities of the United Nations or its agencies. Nor can it request an advisory opinion from the United Nations—the Corell Opinion was issued at the request of the President of the UN Security Council, not the Saharawis.

---

[6] See Article 21.

[7] *See* the position statement "Kosmos Energy: On Hydrocarbon Exploration Offshore Western Sahara" ("position statement") on Kosmos Energy's website.

[8] See, H. Corell, *The Responsibility of the UN Security Council in the Case of Western Sahara*, International Judicial Monitor, Winter 2015.

However, it may be possible for the Saharawis to see their rights adjudicated in at last two international *fora*, although even in these tribunals their claims might have to be brought by another entity. One of them is the dispute resolution mechanism established to enforce the United Nations Convention on the Law of the Sea (UNCLOS).[9]

The UNCLOS treaty, which Morocco has ratified, contains a number of provisions that concern a state's rights with regard to the exploration and exploitation of its adjacent waters.

According to the UNCLOS all "coastal states" have sovereign rights to the natural resources on the continental shelf outside their territory.[10] Article 77(1) of UNCLOS specifies that: "The coastal State exercises over the continental shelf sovereign rights for the purpose of *exploring it* and exploiting its natural resources." (italics added). This right to explore and exploit natural resources, however, may not extend to waters outside the internationally recognized boundaries of the state. Resolution III, which is annexed to the Convention, says that: "In the case of a territory whose people have not attained full independence or other self governing status recognized by the United Nations, or a territory under colonial domination, provisions concerning rights and interests under the Convention shall be implemented for the benefit of the people of the territory with a view to promoting their well-being and development." Western Sahara as a non-self-governing territory clearly falls within the scope of this provision. According to UNCLOS, therefore, the use of the waters adjacent to Western Sahara must be for the benefit of the people of Western Sahara, and would encompass both exploring *and* exploiting.[11] A claim could be raised that Morocco is not a "coastal state" with respect to the waters off the coast of Western Sahara, and that it therefore enjoys none of the privileges of a "coastal state"—including the right to permit exploratory and/or exploitation activities in these waters. Moreover, a claim can be raised that the agreements Morocco has entered into under which foreign oil companies are exploring and/or exploiting the oil reserves off the coast of Western Sahara, or exploiting its fishery resources, are not being conducted for the benefit of the people of Western Sahara, and thus Morocco is violating its obligations under UNCLOS.

---

[9] United Nations Convention on the Law of the Sea, 1982 (UNCLOS).

[10] Articles 76 and 77.

[11] According to the Norwegian Petroleum Fund's Council on Ethics, "Recommendation on exclusion from the Government Petroleum Fund's investment universe of the company Kerr-McGee Corporation," Oslo, April 11, 2005, there seems to be a "possible point of discrepancy" between the legal framework concerning the law of the sea, and the Corell Opinion, which held certain exploratory activities legal. "[I]n a situation of contradictory interpretations of international law, treaty law would prevail over a legal opinion. One might therefore suggest that there are sound legal arguments for arguing that not only exploitation of natural resources, but also exploration, could be deemed unlawful in the present case." at 3–4

UNCLOS contains extensive provisions governing how disputes brought under the treaty can be settled.[12] Any state party to the Convention, as well as others in certain circumstances, may submit a dispute related to the interpretation or application of the Convention to an international tribunal to obtain a legally binding decision. Ratification of the Convention by a state constitutes acceptance of these provisions. Although states still have the option of using informal consultations or mediations to resolve their disputes,[13] when such means fail to settle a dispute, a party may oblige the other party to resolve the dispute through one of the mechanisms provided by the Convention. Article 287 provides four *fora* for the settlement of disputes the parties may choose when signing, ratifying or acceding to the Convention: the International Court of Justice, arbitration in accordance with Annex VII, specialized arbitration for certain disputes concerning fisheries, environmental protection, scientific research or navigation and pollution in accordance with Annex VIII, or the International Tribunal for the Law of the Sea (ITLOS).[14]

The International Tribunal for the Law of the Sea (ITLOS) is a specialized tribunal the UNCLOS Convention established as part of its compulsory third party dispute settlement provisions. Although it was primarily intended to settle disputes between states, the definition of "state parties" in the Convention is not limited to states,[15] but includes territories with full internal self governance and international organizations with treaty making competence.[16]

Although parties have a choice of *fora* in which to settle a dispute, the settlement of a dispute by one of them is obligatory. Moreover, unlike some other Conventions, UNCLOS does not permit states to make "reservations" to its rules unless specifically authorized by the statute.[17] The only "reservations" allowed by the statute are described in Article 298. That article provides that a state may declare in writing at any time that it will not accept the compulsory dispute mechanism provisions with regard to certain categories of disputes. These include

---

[12] *See,* Arts. 74(2), 83(2), 151(8), 159(10), 162(2)(u-v), 165(2)(i-j), 186–91, 264, 279–99, 302; Annex III, arts. 18(1)(b), 21(2); Annexes V-VIII; Annex IX art. 7.

[13] *See,* Section 1 of Part XV.

[14] Article 282 also provides that the parties also have the option of choosing another third party tribunal of their choice.

[15] *See,* art. 1 (2)(2).

[16] *See,* arts. 305–06. ITLOS also has jurisdiction over corporations and individuals as well as state entities, so it can handle a wider variety of disputes than the International Court of Justice. Such entities include natural and juridical persons. However, the tribunal's third party settlement provisions are open to these parties only as specifically provided for in the Convention, *see* art. 291 (2), and individuals and corporations are given access to the tribunal—or can be brought before the tribunal—in extremely limited situations.

[17] Article 309 states: "No reservations or exceptions may be made to this Convention unless expressly permitted by other articles of this Convention."

(1) sea boundary delimitations or those involving historic bays or titles in which case they must first be submitted to conciliation under Annex V section 2 of the treaty,[18] (2) disputes concerning military activities, or (3) "disputes in respect of which the Security Council of the United Nations is exercising the functions assigned to it by the Charter of the United Nations unless the Security Council decides to remove the matter from its agenda or calls upon the parties to settle it by the means provided for in this Convention." In circumstances in which the parties disagree on the choice of a forum, they must settle their dispute through arbitration.[19] The binding nature of the decisions of these *fora* is made explicit in several articles of the Convention.[20]

When ratifying UNCLOS, Morocco did not express any preference as to a dispute resolution tribunal. Accordingly, unless it agrees otherwise, or the dispute is considered to involve the issue of "fisheries" as that term is defined in Annex VIII,[21] any dispute brought against it will be determined by arbitration under Annex VII.[22]

The most likely avenue of redress for the Saharawis is through an action brought before an Annex VII tribunal by one of the member states of UNCLOS aggrieved by the actions of Morocco in the territory. The SADR has already granted a concession to an Australian oil firm to conduct exploratory activities in the territory, and its adjacent waters, upon its independence. On behalf of this firm Australia may be able to request an interpretation of Morocco's rights vis a vis the territory under UNCLOS, particularly if the terms of the concession were to be changed to provide for immediate access. Likewise, should the SADR enter into a fisheries agreement with a state friendly to its interests, that state might have standing to request such an interpretation.[23]

Also, it is possible that the Polisario/SADR might be granted standing to file a dispute under UNCLOS as a liberation movement or "quasi-state" able to

---

[18] It provides further that any dispute which "necessarily" involves the concurrent consideration of any unsettled dispute concerning sovereignty or "other rights" over continental or insular land territory shall be excluded from such submission.

[19] *See*, Art. 287(3) and (5).

[20] *See*, Arts. 188(2), 292(4), 296; Annex VI, arts. 15(5), 33, 39; Annex VII, art. 11; Annex VIII, art. 4.

[21] If the dispute is deemed to involve "fisheries" as that term is defined in Annex VIII, a special tribunal will be convened under the rubric of Annex VIII.

[22] Morocco could, of course, argue that one of the exceptions of Article 298 applies, in particular the exclusion of matters subject to action on the part of the Security Council. However, to date, the Security Council has not addressed the issue of Morocco's use of the resources of Western Sahara and it can be argued that the issue has not been made a part of the ongoing negotiations on the subject of Western Sahara currently before the Security Council.

[23] Although disputes concerning the regulations of fisheries within a coastal state's exclusive economic zone are not required to be settled through the UNCLOS dispute resolution mechanisms set forth in Article 287, under international law the waters off Western Sahara are not within Morocco's exclusive economic zone, so that exception does not apply.

enter into treaty obligations or a territory with full internal self-governance. As previously noted, the definition of "state parties" in the Convention is not limited to states, but includes territories with full internal self governance and international organizations with treaty making competence.

There is precedent for entities similar to the Polisario or SADR being considered by the international community as having the ability to negotiate treaties with states. For instance, France and the Algerian Front de Liberation Nationale concluded the Evian agreements which ended the conflict between them. The Oslo agreements between Israel and the Palestinian Liberation Organization ("PLO") are another example. On April 29, 1994 Israel and the PLO ("representing the Palestinian people") even concluded a protocol on economic relations. Later on the PLO signed an Association agreement with the European Union. All of these agreements have been duly recognized and accepted as valid by the international community and the United Nations.

There is no reason why the Polisario/SADR should not be considered to have the same powers. Indeed, the Polisario/SADR has already entered into "treaties" or agreements with both Mauritania[24] and Morocco,[25] the latter fully endorsed by the United Nations, and has been accorded by the United Nations the status of representative of the people of Western Sahara for the ongoing negotiations over sovereignty for the territory conducted by the organization. In addition, the SADR has entered into an agreement for membership in the AU, as well as agreements with states whereby a number of them have granted it recognition.

Moreover, it could be argued that the SADR has all the attributes of statehood or a "territory with full internal self governance": it has a functioning government, is a full-fledged member of an international organization, has been recognized by a number of states, and although it does not physically control all of the territory of Western Sahara, it does control a certain portion of it. Although the purpose of the broad definition of "state parties" in the UNCLOS convention was undoubtedly to grant access to entities such as the European Union, there is no reason why it could not be applied as well to entities such as the Polisario/SADR.

Finally, although the jurisdiction to issue advisory opinions is not expressly provided for in UNCLOS, ITLOS ruled that it had the authority to issue such opinions in accordance with Article 21 of the Statute.[26] ITLOS has, in addition,

---

[24] The Polisario/SADR and Mauritania entered into the Algiers Accord of 1979 ending the conflict between the two countries.

[25] Among other things, the Polisario and Morocco concluded on August 29, 1997 the Lisbon Compromise Agreement on Troop Confinement, as well as the agreement in 1991 that formed the basis of the ceasefire and creation of MINURSO.

[26] It held that the term "all matters" referred not only to "disputes" but to "advisory opinions" provided for in any other agreement which confers jurisdiction on the Tribunal. *Advisory Opinion on Request for an Advisory Opinion Submitted by the Sub-Regional Fisheries Commission* (April 2, 2015) ITLOS [53]—[60].

opened the door with respect to the participation of NGOs. In *Responsibilities and Obligations of States sponsoring persons and entities with respect to activities in the Area (Request for Advisory Opinion submitted to the Seabed Dispute Chamber)* the Tribunal's Registry informed two NGOs that although their *amicus* briefs would not be added to the file, they would be posted on the Tribunal's website and transmitted to the states and international organizations participating in the proceedings. Accordingly, should the dispute be settled by ITLOS, one could envisage a number of regional organizations—such as the AU—and NGOs—such as Western Sahara Resource Watch or a number of Saharawi organizations—participating in procedures to obtain an advisory opinion from ITLOS concerning Morocco's use of the off-shore resources of Western Sahara.

In short, there are a number of possible ways in which either the Polisario Front or the SADR might be able to acquire the status to file a claim before UNCLOS, only a few of them mentioned here.

(4) International Criminal Court (ICC)

The second tribunal through which the Saharawis may be able to see the violation of its rights under international law addressed is the International Criminal Court ("ICC").

The ICC was created in 2002 by the Rome Statute as a means to address "the most serious crimes of concern to the international community as a whole:" war crimes and crimes against humanity.[27] Unlike ITLOS, the ICC addresses the actions of individuals.[28] This means that the Court cannot prosecute claims against corporations, international organizations, or states. But an individual need not personally commit an act in order to be held liable; he can be held liable for acting jointly with someone else who commits a crime or for aiding and abetting the commission of a crime. This means that members of the board of directors of companies who aid and abet the commission of a war crime or crime against humanity may theoretically be prosecuted.

And the activities that can be considered either "war crimes"[29] or "crimes

---

[27] Part 2, Article 5 of the Rome Statute sets forth the jurisdiction of the ICC as follows: "The jurisdiction of the Court shall be limited to the most serious crimes of concern to the international community as a whole." These include (a) crimes against humanity, and (b) war crimes.

[28] Article 25 of the Rome Statute stipulates in section 1: "The Court shall have jurisdiction over natural persons pursuant to this Statute."

[29] Article 8 (a) defines "war crimes" as "grave breaches of the Geneva Conventions of 12 August 1949," including, but not limited to, "torture or inhuman treatment," "willfully causing great suffering or serious injury to body or health," "extensive destruction and appropriation of property, not justified by military necessity and carried out unlawfully and wantonly," and "unlawful...confinement."

against humanity"[30] are broad. Besides imprisonment, or other severe deprivations of physical liberty in violation of fundamental rules of international law and torture, crimes against humanity include "persecution against any identifiable group" on "political, racial, ethnic, cultural, religious, gender…or other grounds that are universally recognized as impermissible under international law, in connection with…any crime within the jurisdiction of the Court." "War crimes" are defined as "grave breaches of the Geneva Conventions of 12 August 1949", including, but not limited to, "torture or inhuman treatment," "willfully causing great suffering or serious injury to body or health," "extensive destruction and appropriation of property, not justified by military necessity and carried out unlawfully and wantonly," and "unlawful…confinement." The transfer of the population of an occupying power into occupied territory in contravention of the prohibitions contained in Article 49, Paragraph 6 of the Fourth Geneva Convention of 12 August 1949,[31] is specifically recognized as a ground for recourse.[32]

The fact that such a transfer of population may lead to criminal responsibility has been noted in the past. In his final report submitted to the UN Sub-Commission on Human Rights in 1997, the UN Special Rapporteur on the Human Rights Dimension of Population Transfer stated: "The settlement, by transfer or inducement, by the Occupying Power of parts of its own civilian population into the territory it occupies or by the Power exercising de facto control over a disputed territory is unlawful." (Article 5) "The above practices of population transfer constitute internationally wrongful acts giving rise to State responsibility and to individual criminal liability." (Article 9) Hans Corell noted in the article he published in 2015 in the *International Judicial Monitor*, cited previously, that Morocco's attempt to persuade its civilian population to enter the territory in 1975 constituted a violation of international law. Morocco's continued attempts to persuade its population to settle in the territory since that time is no less a violation.

---

[30] Article 7 describes a number of actions that can be considered "crimes against humanity", including, but not limited to, "imprisonment or other severe deprivation of physical liberty in violation of fundamental rules of international law," "torture," and "persecution against any identifiable group or collectivity on political, racial, ethnic, cultural, religious, gender…or other grounds that are universally recognized as impermissible under international law, in connection with any act referred to in this paragraph or any crime within the jurisdiction of the Court."

[31] Article 49, Paragraph 6 of the 1949 Fourth Geneva Convention provides: "The Occupying Power shall not deport or transfer parts of its own civilian population into the territory it occupies." Article 85(4)(a) of the 1977 Additional Protocol I provides that "the transfer by the Occupying Power of parts of its own civilian population into the territory it occupies" is a "grave breach of the Protocol."

[32] Article 8(b) includes "other serious violations of the laws and customs applicable in international armed conflict." Under Article 8(2)(b)(viii): "[t]he transfer, directly or indirectly, by the Occupying Power of parts of its own civilian population into the territory it occupies constitutes a war crime in international armed conflicts." Article 8 also includes "committing outrages against personal dignity, in particular humiliating and degrading treatment."

Of course, there would be certain constraints on the ability of the Saharawis to prosecute an action before the ICC.

First, as noted above, the Court's jurisdiction is limited to situations that are considered "the most serious crimes of concern to the international community as a whole" and the prosecutor has wide discretion to reject claims that, while perhaps valid, are not serious enough or involve a sufficient enough number of people to reach this threshold—even if requested to do so by a member State. In the past the prosecutor has rejected a number of claims on this ground. In addition, the crimes must be committed after the date the Rome Convention came into force, July 1, 2002.

The claims that the Saharawis can bring fall into three categories, human rights violations, violations of the Fourth Geneva Convention, and violations of economic rights. Although Morocco's violation of the human rights of the Saharawis in the early years of its occupation would clearly constitute serious violations, it is unclear how the prosecutor would evaluate the claims of recent violations. The previous claims prosecuted by the Court were based upon tens of thousands of people being killed, tortured or raped. Likewise, there has never been a case so far in which the prosecutor has accepted a claim based upon a violation of economic rights and it is unclear how the prosecutor would evaluate the seriousness of such a claim. Moreover, although it is specifically included as a basis for jurisdiction, there has never been a case so far in which the prosecutor has accepted a claim based upon the transfer of population by an occupying power. So, the Saharawis would be breaking new ground at the ICC with claims based upon these arguments. However, it can be argued that the ICC *should* break new ground—that the types of crimes committed by Morocco and those with whom it does business constitute just as serious a threat to international peace as the killing of thousands of civilians, and will probably be the way future aggressors will consolidate their power over a subjugated people.

Of course, the Saharawis could not seek the prosecution of the state of Morocco or any of the corporations which do business with Morocco; they can only seek the prosecution of individuals. Moreover, since neither the United States nor Morocco have ratified the Rome Statute the Saharawis would not be able to seek the prosecution of any of their citizens. However, most of the nations of Europe have ratified the Rome Convention, and many of the officers and directors of companies doing business with Morocco are citizens of these countries. These individuals cannot be charged with committing war crimes themselves. However, they could be charged with aiding and abetting the commission of war crimes or engaging in a conspiracy to commit war crimes through the activities of the corporations they control. According to Article 25, section 3, a person shall be criminally responsible if she or he commits the crime "whether as an individual, jointly with another or through another person, regardless of whether that other person is criminally responsible," "orders, solicits or induces the commission of such a crime," "for the purpose of facilitating the commission of such a crime, aids, abets, or otherwise assists in its commission or its attempted commission, including providing the means for its commission," or in any other way "contributes to the commission or attempted commission of such a crime by a group of persons acting with a common purpose." This is arguably broad enough to include both the activities of the companies which are actually engaging in commerce in the territory as well as the financial institutions which are enabling them to do so.

Prior to filing a complaint the Saharawis would have to determine that the states whose citizens are abetting the commission of these crimes are unwilling or unable to prosecute effectively these individuals. As a preliminary matter, the Saharawis may need to obtain a court dismissal of criminal proceedings in a state court, or a letter by a prosecutor refusing to file charges, in order to proceed with a complaint before the ICC. This may actually benefit the Saharawis, since it might force the concerned countries to take action rather than see the case turned over to the ICC.

Moreover, the Saharawis would have to argue that they are currently in a "state of war" or "armed conflict" with Morocco. The jurisdiction of the ICC extends only to acts committed during a state of war or armed conflict. Today the ceasefire that had been in effect between Morocco and the SADR/Polisario has been terminated by the Polisario, and hostilities have re-commenced. This constitutes a state of war. In addition, the ceasefire was only a temporary cessation of hostilities for the purpose of permitting the United Nations to conduct a referendum, not an agreement to end the state of war between the parties permanently, and the fact that it could have been lifted at any moment suggests that a state of war between the parties never really ended.[33]

As noted previously, the Saharawis would be breaking new ground at the ICC by instituting—or having a member state institute—a petition to have the prosecutor investigate claims against individuals who are aiding and abetting Morocco's unlawful practices. However, the international community may benefit

---

[33] The Court has not yet determined whether it has jurisdiction over acts committed during a ceasefire. Some legal scholars have suggested that a "ceasefire" has the same legal effect as a peace treaty and therefore terminates the applicability of the "law of war" and replaces it with the "law of peace." Under this interpretation the Court would lack jurisdiction to rule on activities conducted during a ceasefire. Other scholars suggest that whether or not a "state of war" exists depends upon the terms of the ceasefire and, in particular, whether it was intended to end a conflict or merely suspend it for a period. Whether or not the SADR can prosecute claims before the ICC that occurred during the ceasefire may depend upon how the ceasefire between the Polisario and Morocco in 1991 is interpreted.

from "pushing the envelope" at the ICC and demanding that it investigate crimes that are clearly within its jurisdiction but which have so far been ignored.

There would be strong economic interests at stake in an action before any of these courts or tribunals. The European Union has a strong economic interest in the continuation of its trade agreements with Morocco in fisheries and agricultural products. It is estimated that more than two thirds of the fisheries products exploited under the previous EU-Moroccan treaty originated in the waters off Western Sahara, much of them harvested by vessels from the EU and destined for EU consumers. The economic stake for Morocco in these agreements is important as well. Under the terms of the present fisheries agreement the European Union would grant an annual payment to Morocco of 30 million Euros (14 million of which would go to the support of the Moroccan fishing sector) and Morocco would receive approximately 10 million Euros in fees from ship owners. And Morocco has a strong economic interest in maintaining its control over the Boucraa mines: the fact that OCP controls the output of phosphates from Boucraa places it in a position to dominate the international phosphate market[34]—a position it will lose if Boucraa becomes controlled by an independent Western Sahara. Likewise, there are important economic interests at stake for the King of Morocco in the agricultural agreement. The holding "Les Domaines" will be the most affected by any decision to eliminate trade in agricultural products originating in Western Sahara. Also, since many of the wind farms Morocco plans to construct as part of its renewable energy plans will lie in Western Sahara, a decision precluding this investment will eviscerate its current program and greatly hamper its efforts to expand mining at Boucraa. And a ban on the exploitation of resources from Western Sahara by the courts in Europe will have a ripple effect not only in Europe, but in other markets as well.

As a result, if the European High Court's analysis of international law principles in the context of the agricultural agreement is applied to the exploitation of other resources, such as phosphates, or influences decisions of courts in other jurisdictions, or is applied to the activities of companies and individuals as well as states, Morocco may find itself severely constrained in its future exploitation of the majority of resources of the territory. This, more than anything else, might finally enable the Saharawis to realize their right to self-determination at the United Nations.

The European Union courts have opened the door. Only the future will tell how wide.

---

[34] OCP is the world's largest producer of phosphates; Western Sahara is the second largest. According to the United States Geological Survey together they produce over 72% of the world's phosphates, an important ingredient in the production of fertilizer. The next largest producer—China—accounts for a mere 6%. The phosphate production of other countries is marginal.

PART V

Resolving the Conflict— Autonomy vs. Independence

REGARDLESS OF WHETHER or not the Saharawis can successfully enforce their right to control the use of the natural resources of the territory and stem the human rights abuses that occur there, the question of how to resolve the question of sovereignty over the territory will still remain. So, ultimately, one must examine the two possible outcomes presently on the table: autonomy and independence.

Exactly what is the autonomy proposal made by Morocco, and how realistic would it be as a solution to this conflict? Allegedly based on the Spanish approach to regional autonomy in such areas as the Canary Islands and the Basque region, it would allow the populations of the "Sahara Autonomous Region" control over the local administration and police, the economic development of the region, the region's budget and taxation, the local infrastructure, the housing, education, health, employment, sports, social welfare and social security of the local population, the region's cultural affairs, and its environment.[1] It would also permit the local population to establish lower level courts which would have jurisdiction over local affairs.

The Moroccan government would retain exclusive jurisdiction over:

1. The attributes of sovereignty such as the flag, the national anthem and the currency
2. The constitutional and religious prerogatives of the King
3. National security, external defense and defense of territorial integrity

---

[1] The Moroccan Autonomy Proposal of 2007, para. 12.

4. External relations
5. The Kingdom's juridical order (the Kingdom's Supreme Court and Constitutional Council would be the highest judicial bodies)[2]

After negotiation, the proposal would be submitted to the "populations concerned" in a free referendum "in keeping with the principle of self-determination and with the provisions of the UN Charter."[3]

At first blush it would seem to provide a reasonable compromise to the conflict, granting the Saharawis extensive control over local affairs with involvement by Rabat only with regards to international relations. But as always, the devil is in the details.

The Saharawis would be subject to the Moroccan Constitution. The King would retain the powers he is granted under the Moroccan Constitution, under which he may override or suspend any act of Parliament, governmental body or court decision, and a representative appointed by the King would exercise ultimate power over the locally elected institutions of the region. Although there would be a local police force, the King would retain command of the army and its various installations in the territory. As for the courts, although locally appointed courts would have jurisdiction over local matters, the Moroccan Supreme Court would have the final say in any legal matter. In the opinion of several observers, the plan presented by Morocco in 2007 lacked any actual "autonomy." "Western Sahara would remain firmly subordinated to the powers of the central Moroccan state."[4]

But there is even a greater reason why autonomy may not prove to be a viable solution. Moroccan supporters rightly point to a number of situations in which autonomous regions have been carved out of states with beneficial results. The autonomous region of the Aaland Islands is one such example. However, these success stories have always involved essentially democratic governments. The record of autonomous regions created by authoritarian states is not as propitious. History has shown that it is extremely difficult—if not impossible—for an autonomous region to survive within an autocratic state. In 1952 the British protectorate of Eritrea was accorded autonomous status within Ethiopia by the United Nations. In 1961, however, the Ethiopian emperor unilaterally revoked this status, annexing Eritrea, resulting in thirty years of conflict between the two countries. Likewise, when Serbian leader Slobodan Milosevic's decided to revoke the autonomous

---

[2] *Id.*, paras. 6, 14.

[3] *Id.*, paras. 8, 27.

[4] *See*, S. Zunes & J. Mundy, WESTERN SAHARA: WAR, NATIONALISM AND CONFLICT IRRESOLUTION, *supra*, at 244.

status of Kosovo in 1989 he precipitated a conflict that was only ended two years later after NATO's intervention. And we should not forget the current problems of Hong Kong, trying to maintain democratic institutions within the People's Republic of China.

And the King of Morocco remains one of the last of the absolute monarchs. Despite its recent marginal gains in the areas of human rights and the equality of women, Morocco continues to be ruled by a government in which the King and a few of his advisers wield almost absolute power. As was noted by two observers,[5]

> "To date, there is no indication that Morocco is becoming a democratic country in which power resides in institutions accountable to the electorate. Instead, the king remains the dominant religious and political authority in the country...All new measures have been introduced from the top, as the result of decisions taken by the king and on the basis of studies carried out by commissions he appointed. Moreover, none of the measures impose limits on his power....
>
> [U]nless the power of the king is curtailed and counterbalanced by that of institutions over which he has no control, talk of democratization in Morocco is moot. Today the king has the power to appoint a prime minister and government without taking election results into account, to terminate the government and parliament at will, and to exercise legislative power in the absence of parliament. A veritable shadow government of royal advisers keeps an eye on the operations of all ministries and government departments. Not only are important decisions taken by the palace, but their execution is also managed—some argue micromanaged—by the royal encourage. The question thus is not whether Morocco will continue its democratic transformation, because, contrary to the views of some, such a transformation has not even started."

The United States government is fully aware of the lack of true democracy within the Kingdom. In its 2015 Country Report on Human Rights the State Department declared:

5   *See,* M. Ottaway and M. Riley, "Morocco From Top-down Reform to Democratic Transition?" Carnegie Papers, Middle East Series, Carnegie Endowment for International Peace, No. 71 (September 2006)("Carnegie Papers") at 3.

"The most significant human rights problems were the lack of citizens' ability to change the constitutional provisions establishing the country's monarchical form of government, corruption, and widespread disregard for the rule of law by security forces."[6]

The situation reported by the State Department in 2015 has not changed in subsequent years.

Is it realistic to believe that the Moroccan King would permit a truly independent and democratic regime to exist within his Kingdom, with its implications for unrest among other population groups? Is it realistic to believe that despite its record of breaking every past promise to the Saharawis and the international community, Morocco would actually keep the promises contained in its autonomy proposal? Is it realistic to believe that after refusing to hold Morocco to its past promises, the United Nations would enforce its promises in the autonomy proposal? Zunes and Mundy cautioned that "Based on Rabat's pattern of breaking promises during the UN and OAU peace processes and on the Security Council's willingness to tolerate such behavior, the autonomy statute should thus have inspired widespread concern as to its durability."[7]

Of course, now that President Trump has unilaterally declared Morocco's sovereignty over Western Sahara, and has entirely bypassed the United Nations in doing so, it is not even clear whether this autonomy proposal, with all its flaws, will continue to be offered. Much will depend on the approach to the problem taken by his successor.

If there is reason to be skeptical about Morocco's autonomy proposal, is there a valid reason to reject the idea of an independent state in the Sahara? Certain commentators have argued that an independent Saharawi state would be doomed to failure because it would lack self-sustaining resources. However, this argument appears specious in light of Morocco's desperate struggle to retain control of the rich deposits of phosphates (second largest in the world), fisheries, agricultural produce, sources of renewable energy and perhaps petroleum deposits in the region.

As Christopher Ross, the former Personal Envoy of the Secretary-General to Western Sahara from 2007 to 2017 declared:[8]

"The argument that some in Washington have been making for decades to the effect that an independent state in Western Sahara would be another failed mini-state is false. Western Sahara is as large as Great Britain and has ample resources

---

6   2015 U.S. Country Report on Human Right Practices in Morocco, p. 2.

7   Carnegie Papers, *supra*, p. 245.

8   Facebook, December 13, 2020.

of phosphates, fisheries, precious metals, and tourism based on wind surfing and desert excursions. It is much better off than many mini-states whose establishment the US has supported. The Polisario Liberation Front of Western Sahara has demonstrated in setting up a government-in-exile in the Western Sahara refugee camps in southwestern Algeria that it is capable of running a government in an organized and semi-democratic way."

Others have tried to portray the Polisario as terrorists, or anti-western radicals, or inept and corrupt leaders, unable or unwilling to form a progressive, democratic government and institutions. However, contrary to allegations by Morocco, there is no reason to believe that a government established by the Polisario would be unable to govern the territory effectively or discourage terrorist activities. Indeed, the fact that despite almost insurmountable obstacles and a dearth of funds the Saharawis in exile have been able to organize themselves into efficiently run refugee camps and a sophisticated government that has been accorded the status of statehood by a number of other states, has been an active member of the AU for a number of years, and has been able to counterbalance Morocco's influence on the international stage for the past forty years suggests, if anything, that they have the political acumen to create a model state in the region.

Insofar as terrorism is concerned, once again, apart from the self-serving contentions of Morocco there is absolutely no evidence that the Polisario are "terrorists" or condone terrorism. The essentially moderate form of Islam they practice make them an unlikely partner of radical Islamacists. Moreover, the Saharawis background in desert and guerilla warfare make them better suited as a partner to the United State in counter-terrorism activities than the Moroccans. In short, there are no valid security reasons for opposing the creation of an independent Western Sahara governed by the Polisario or other leaders chosen by the Saharawis.

Indeed, in an interview with the Spanish newspaper "El Pais" on March 2, 2002, former Secretary of State James Baker said that he believed in an independent Saharawi republic. He said that he had told the Security Council that he believed that a "Sahrawi state within the old Spanish colony would be viable and would contribute to the stability of the Maghreb."[9]

Likewise, in an article that appeared in the Winter 2015 edition of the International Judicial Monitor, Hans Corell suggested that one option that could be adopted by the UN Security Council and that would be consistent with the legal right of the people of Western Sahara to self-determination, would be for the Security Council to simply declare the territory an independent state.

In his words:

---

[9]   http://www.afrol.com/News2002/wsa007_baker.htm.

"In view of the fact that the issue of Western Sahara has been on the agenda of the United Nations for four decades, the solution may be…that the Security Council recognises Western Sahara as a sovereign state. Also this option should be acceptable from a legal point of view. It would not deprive the people of Western Sahara from seeking a different solution to their self-determination in the future, if they so wish."[10]

In conclusion, there is no logical reason for the international community to reject the idea of an independent state in the Sahara. The reason why it has not been supported is, and always has been, political.

---

[10] Hans Corell, "The Responsibility of the UN Security Council in the Case of Western Sahara," International Judicial Monitor, Winter 2015, that can be found at *https://www.havc.se*. He later suggested that if there was a question over whether the people of the territory would be able to establish a viable state, MINURSO could be tasked with the responsibility of assuming control over the territory for a five year period before independence. However, as was noted previously, there would appear to be no reason to doubt that the Saharawis would be able to rule effectively an independent Western Sahara.

PART VI

Political Issues

AS NOTED IN the discussion of the legal issues involved in the Western Sahara dispute, the real impediment to the enforcement of the Saharawis' rights and the real reason for the current impasse are political concerns, or more precisely, the foreign policy of the United States and other major powers.

Indeed, the recent callous decision of President Trump to trade the rights of the indigenous people of Western Sahara, and the wealth of their territory, for the questionable benefit of having Morocco extend diplomatic relations to Israel, is but the latest example of the United States' disingenuous policy towards the issue.

Since it first arose on the international scene the United States has been a major player in the saga of Western Sahara. Unfortunately, in order to obtain some perceived immediate tactical political advantage, United States policymakers have engaged in a history of diplomacy that has forfeited on the issue of Western Sahara the principles of human rights and adherence to international law for which the United States has historically stood.[1]

From its decision in the mid 1970s to extend massive aid and provide sophisticated weapons to King Hassan II to help bolster his regime, to the present day diplomatic battles at the United Nations, and President Trump's abandonment of the people of the territory, records indicate that the United States has followed a two pronged policy: declaring in public that it supports the right to self-determination of the

---

[1] Many commentators have deplored the United States' involvement in this issue. *See,* for instance, Y. Zoubir, *Geoplolitics and Realpolitik as Impediments to the Resolution of Conflict and Violations of International Law: The Case of Western Sahara,* INTERNATIONAL LAW AND THE QUESTION OF WESTERN SAHARA, *supra,* at 276 ("[T]he United States was instrumental in allowing Morocco to seize the Western Sahara."); T. Franck, *The Stealing of the Sahara, supra;* J. Mundy, *Neutrality or Complicity? The United States and the 1975 Moroccan Takeover of the Spanish Sahara,* The Journal of North African Studies, No. 3, September 2006, at 275–306 ("Mundy")

Saharawis, while behind the scenes doing everything possible to ensure that the dispute is settled only on terms that are acceptable to Morocco.[2]

Recently published archives[3] demonstrate what can only be characterized as a less than forthright approach to this issue. There are indications that in 1975 the CIA warned then Secretary of State Henry Kissinger of the likelihood of a Moroccan incursion into Western Sahara—with potentially dire political consequences for the Rabat regime—weeks before the Green March was announced.[4] On October 17, 1975, one day after the King announced his intention to assemble the Green March and only hours after the International Court of Justice had published its Opinion rejecting Morocco's claims to the territory, Kissinger misrepresented the ICJ finding in an Oval Office meeting with President Ford, declaring: "Morocco is threatening a massive march on Spanish Sahara. The ICJ gave an opinion which said sovereignty had been decided between Morocco and Mauritania. That basically is what Hassan wanted."[5] It is unclear what course of action was agreed at that meeting. However, events which followed suggest the heavy hand of the United States in negotiations between Morocco and Spain which commenced at that time. The *New York Times* published an article in 1981 indicating that one of former Deputy Director of the CIA Vernon Walter's last missions in the CIA "was a trip in late 1975 to Spain, where in meetings with King Hassan II of Morocco and Spanish officials he convinced Spain to give up control of Western Sahara."[6] On November 2, Kissinger called on King Hassan to pursue such "bilateral and multilateral diplomatic efforts" to end the crisis. However, by that time it was too late—Moroccan forces had secretly crossed into Western Saharan territory on October 31, sparking the first shots in what was to become a long, intractable war.

---

[2] Indeed, eminent scholars have accused the United States with demonstrating a pro-Moroccan bias from the very start of the dispute, ensuring that the United Nations resolutions condemning the King's proposed "Green March" in 1975 were weak, and stopped short of ordering Morocco to "cease and desist." They note, for example, S.C. Res. 379 (1975), adopted by the Security Council at its 1852nd Mtg. on Nov. 2, 1975 and S.C. Res. 380 (1975), adopted by the Security Council at its 1854th Mtg. on Nov. 6, 1975. *See* Franck, T., *The Stealing of the Sahara, supra,* at 714. When the General Assembly in 1976 passed two conflicting resolutions, the first calling for self-determination for the territory and the second recognizing the Madrid Accords, the United States abstained from voting on the first and voted in favor of the second, thereby firmly aligning itself with Morocco and against the principle of self-determination. G.A. Res. 3458(A), U.N. Doc. GA/5438, at 254–55; G.A. Res. 3358(B), U.N. Doc. GA/5438, at 256 (1975).

[3] The archives cited below were released pursuant to a Freedom of Information Act request and published or referenced by Jacob Mundy, in *Neutrality or Complicity? The United States and the 1975 Moroccan Takeover of the Spanish Sahara,* The Journal of North African Studies, Vol. II, No. 3, September 2006, ("Mundy") *supra.*

[4] *See,* S. Zunes & J. Mundy, WESTERN SAHARA: WAR, NATIONALISM & CONFLICT IRRESOLUTION, *supra,* at 60–61. The authors also refer to a statement of then U.S. Ambassador to Algeria, claiming that the "official" record will never reveal the full truth, "but Secretary Kissinger, intentionally or otherwise, may have given Hassan what the latter took to be a green light during a conversation in the summer of 1975."

[5] Mundy, *supra,* at 294.

[6] *Id.,* at 277.

What followed was an attempt by all parties to divert attention away from these secret "bilateral and multilateral diplomatic efforts" under the façade of the "Green March." Kissinger's deputy Atherton summed up the policy in a briefing with Kissinger on November 5: "Let the marchers go into it ten kilometers, and let a token number go all the way to [Laayoune], and having done this turn around and go back. And to do all they can to see that the UN self-determination procedure comes out in favor of Morocco. This has been carried back to Hassan." Any referendum that would be held would be designed so as to achieve the political ends of the major powers. Arthur Hartman, head of European Affairs, noted that the Spanish government was "very explicit" about "what they would do in influencing" the referendum for Morocco.[7]

When the UN Security Council convened to draft a resolution condemning the Green March it was the United States and France who successfully resisted more forceful action.[8] This tepid response of the Security Council had Washington's desired effect—Spain found it prudent to pursue direct talks with Morocco on November 8, and the next day Hassan called off the Green March.

Within a week, the Madrid Accords were announced.

Following the Madrid Accords, when Morocco was lobbying for its acceptance by the UN despite the armed resistance of the Saharawis and the opinion of the International Court of Justice that the Saharawis had the right to choose their political status, the United States government did nothing to stand in its way. On the contrary, turning a blind eye both to questions of legality, the fighting that had enveloped the territory following the arrival of Moroccan troops, and the mass exodus of Saharawi civilians that such a move had provoked, on December 10, 1975 the United States abstained in the UN General Assembly on an Algerian-backed resolution (3458A) which reaffirmed the UN's traditional calls for a referendum, and instead voted in favor of a rival resolution (3458B) backed by Morocco, because as a State Department official later explained, "[this resolution] took note of the Madrid Agreement, which we believed at the time offered the best basis for an eventual peaceful settlement."[9] As a noted law professor commented at the time: "Thus, the United States firmly aligned itself against self-determination,

---

[7]   S. Zunes & J. Mundy, WESTERN SAHARA: WAR, NATIONALISM& CONFLICT IRRESOLUTION, *supra*, at 63.

[8]   *Id.* According to the authors in "all these 'toothless' resolutions, it was reportedly the United States and France that successfully resisted more forceful actions by the Security Council."

[9]   Statement of Nicholas A. Veliotes, Deputy Assistant Secretary, Bureau of Near Eastern and South Asian Affairs, Department of State, October 12, 1977, in "The Question of Self-Determination in Western Sahara,"Hearings before the Subcommittees on International Organizations and on Africa of the Committee on International Relations, House of Representatives, 95th Congress, October 12, 1977 (U.S. Government Printing Office, Washington, D.C. 1977) p. 39.

against the majority of African states, and in favor of an arbitrarily instituted, antidemocratic solution at dramatic variance with the rules of the games as hitherto observed."[10]

Throughout this period it was clear that despite its avowed support for the right to self-determination, United States policy makers were intent on manipulating the United Nations' process to achieve their political goals. In conversations with President Ford in the Oval Office on the morning of November 3, 1975, Kissinger suggested that the United States let the United Nations handle the thorny problem of providing for self-determination in Western Sahara "like West Irian, where they fuzz the 'consulting the wishes of the people' and get out of it."[11] On November 11, 1975 he again suggested that the United States "Just turn it over to the UN with a guarantee it will go to Morocco."[12] And again, on November 11, 1975 he declared "[King] Hassan has pulled back in the Sahara. But if he doesn't get it, he is finished. We should now work to ensure he gets it. We would work it through the UN [to] ensure a favorable vote." The following day he added: "It has quieted down, but I am afraid Hassan may be overthrown if he doesn't get a success. The hope is for a rigged UN vote…."[13]

If the UN proved ineffectual during this period to deal with the problem of Western Sahara, it should come as no surprise to U.S. officials. Daniel P. Moynihan, the United States Ambassador to the UN during the late 1970's wrote in his memoirs about Western Sahara that "The Department of State desired that the United Nations prove utterly ineffective in whatever measures it undertook. This task was given to me, and I carried it forward with not inconsiderable success."[14] In a letter he wrote to Trent Lott on April 29, 1999 he was to cite his role in the Western Sahara affair as "thoroughly dishonorable."[15]

During the years of fighting between the Polisario and Morocco, despite its public avowals of neutrality, the United States government, in reality, did everything it could to enhance the Moroccan position. President Carter's arms agreements with Morocco in 1979 and 1980—when the Polisario were beginning to turn the tide of the war in their favor—were twenty times what they had been in

[10] Thomas M. Franck, *The Stealing of the Sahara, supra,* at 718.

[11] Folder 'November 10, 1975', Box 16, Collection NSA Memoranda, Ford Library, referred to in Mundy, *supra,* at pps. 297–298.

[12] Mundy, *supra* at 298.

[13] *Id.,* at 300.

[14] Moynihan, Daniel Patrick, A DANGEROUS PLACE, (Little Brown, 1978) at 247. The quote referred both to his actions with respect to East Timor and to those with respect to Western Sahara.

[15] Letter shown by a staff member at the time to John M. Miller, Media and Outreach Coordinator, East Timor & Indonesia Action Network (Interview with J.M. Miller, October 11, 2005).

1978.[16] Although Carter had tried to restrict the use of such weapons in Western Sahara, this restriction was removed by Ronald Reagan when he took office. Shortly after taking office in 1981 Reagan announced additional arms sales to Morocco worth $182 million, as well as the lifting of the restrictions placed by Carter on the delivery of some other goods.[17] In addition, following the debacle at Guelta Zemmour, when the Polisario downed several Moroccan aircraft, the United States flooded Morocco with "technical advisors" assigned the task of buttressing the armed forces, and sophisticated communications and radar equipment intended to facilitate the location of Polisario units.[18]

This less than even handed approach to the issue persisted after the declaration of a ceasefire and adoption of the Settlement Plan in 1991 and well into the period of voter registration. Frank Ruddy, the highest ranked American in MINURSO in 1995, charged that when he complained about what he viewed as attempts by Morocco to unfairly influence and create obstacles to the work of the Commission, his complaints were dismissed by high ranking government officials in the United States and the United Nations.[19] Ruddy's complaints do not appear in any reports of the Secretary General to members of the Security Council. However, Human Rights Watch later issued a paper, based on interviews with dozens of UN staff in Western Sahara, that confirmed many of his allegations and offered a scathing report of UN operations.[20]

The attempts by James Baker to fashion a plan that would put aside the voters list established by MINURSO and declare eligible to vote in a referendum (if one was ever held) the thousands of Moroccans who replaced the indigenous population in the territory following the Moroccan occupation—and UN attempts to persuade the Polisario to accept the idea of "autonomy" within Morocco rather than independence—raised this agenda of the United States government, and the complicity of UN officials in it, squarely to the surface for the first time.

In an interview with PBS Wideangle on August 19, 2004, Baker admitted that when he first took the job as Personal Envoy of the Secretary General he was "led to believe that the conflict was ripe for some sort of autonomy-based solution where the Moroccans would give self-government to the Sahrawi...." Indeed,

---

[16] In 1980 Carter proposed $250 million in new arms sales agreements, whereas the two previous years had seen a mere $10 million in such agreements. *See,* S. Zunes & J. Mundy, WESTERN SAHARA: WAR, NATIONALISM AND CONFLICT IRRESOLUTION, *supra,* at 65, citing statistics of the U.S. Department of Defense.

[17] Hodges at 358–9.

[18] *See,* S. Zunes & J. Mundy, WESTERN SAHARA: WAR, NATIONALISM AND CONFLICT IRRESOLUTION, *supra,* at 66.

[19] A speech he gave at Georgetown University, Washington, D.C. on February 16, 2000 entitled "The United States Mission for the Referendum in Sahara: Lofty Ideals and Gutter Realities," p. 6. Ruddy later resigned in protest.

[20] "Keeping it Secret: The United Nations Operation in Western Sahara," Human Rights Watch, September 30, 1995.

former UN Undersecretary-General Marrack Goulding in his recently published autobiography *Peacemonger*[21] revealed that Secretary General Kofi Annan had the idea of "autonomy" in mind when he appointed Baker. According to Goulding, his mission in 1997 was "to go to Houston to persuade James Baker III to accept an appointment as Special Representative and try to negotiate a deal based on enhanced autonomy for Western Sahara within the Kingdom of Morocco."[22] And there are indications that this secret policy of top UN officials went as far back as Perez de Cuellar. According to Goulding, he had suspicions at the time of the adoption of the Settlement Plan that then UN Secretary General Javier Perez de Cuellar "had an undeclared agenda with the Moroccans."[23]

There are indications that the Moroccans believed in such an "undeclared agenda." An interview with former Moroccan Minister of the Interior, Driss Basri, whose power was second only to the King himself and who was in charge of the Western Sahara dossier, reported in the Moroccan weekly *Al-Ayam* shortly after his dismissal from office following the death of King Hassan, is illuminating. In the interview Basri acknowledged that he "was for the referendum only in a tactical way" and that in conversations with King Hassan, wherein he expressed concerns over pursuing this direction, the King responded: "Do you think we are devoid of common sense? We would not embark in a referendum if we are not sure we would win it." When asked why he supported the Houston Accords, he remarked that the Accords were not intended to be a "solution" to the conflict, but merely "a starting point of an American plan" at the end of which "the Sahara will enjoy extensive autonomy" and "will preserve the American interests." He further remarked that "The objective was to withdraw the Sahara dossier from the UN and hand it to the Pentagon and the State Department. All things that preceded were just pretexts," and that Morocco did not have the UN as its "interlocutor" but rather "the United States."[24]

The option of a referendum of self-determination through which the Saharawis could choose the option of independence may never have been really on the table at all.

And comments by the former Ambassador to Morocco Marc Ginsberg show

[21] Goulding, M., PEACEMONGER (John Murray (Publishers) Ltd. (London, 2002).

[22] *Id.*, at 214–215.

[23] *Id.*, at 212. In Goulding's words: "Perez de Cuellar was by [early October, 1991]...asserting his views more vehemently than was his wont. I came increasingly to feel that he had an undeclared agenda with the Moroccans, to which Diallo [UN Secretary General's Special Advisor in charge of Western Sahara] and Rizvi [Deputy Special Representative for Western Sahara] and perhaps Manz [Second Special Representative for Western Sahara], were privy. Perhaps he was hoping that, before the end of his mandate, he could mediate a political solution based on enhanced autonomy for Western Sahara within the Kingdom of Morocco."

[24] http://www.wsahara.net/03/alayambasrieng.html.

the involvement of United States officials in efforts to scuttle the referendum plan. In a statement he made to the House Committee on Foreign Relations on April 20, 2016, he claimed that during the period 1994–1998 he "devoted considerable time…to reformulate U.S. policy in the region." This included two years of secret diplomacy to explore the feasibility of granting autonomy to the Saharawis under Moroccan sovereignty.[25]

Comments by other United States officials suggest that rather than confront Moroccan intransigence on the subject of a referendum, the United States continued its policy of appeasement throughout the past three administrations.

John Bolton, probably best known as an Ambassador of the United States to the United Nations under President Bush, also served as an advisor to James Baker during the period in which Baker was attempting to resolve the conflict as Special Representative of the UN Secretary General. He recounted his frustration over failed attempts to resolve this conflict during the Bush administration in his book *Surrender is Not An Option: Defending America at the United Nations and Abroad.* Noting that Van Walsum, who had taken over Baker's responsibilities when he resigned, "tried repeatedly in 2005 to see if any Council member, especially the United States, planned to pressure Morocco to adhere to its many commitments to hold a referendum," he reported that none, except Algeria, was willing. In his words, "The biggest obstacle…was, as usual, the State [Department] bureaucracy, joined unusually by the NSC's Elliot Abrams.[26] They accepted Morocco's line that independence for the Western Sahara—which nearly everyone thought the Sahrawis would choose in a genuinely free and fair referendum—would destabilize Morocco and risk a takeover by extreme Islamicists. This is why the administration had rejected the last "Baker Plan" in 2004, and why Baker finally resigned…I wondered what had happened to the Bush administration's support for "democracy" in the broader Middle East…I engaged in a number of frustrating and unsuccessful efforts to find support for the referendum elsewhere in the U.S. government…."

Indeed, after Bolton's departure as U.S. Ambassador to the United Nations, Abrams became the central character in the Bush administration's Western Sahara policy team. He unabashedly backed Morocco, largely on the ground that Moroccan cooperation in the war on terror (e.g. extraordinary renditions and proxy

---

[25] Levick.com/blog/public-affairs/statement-former-ambassador-marc-ginsberg.

[26] Elliot Abrams, the neo-conservative and staunchly pro-Israel advisor to a number of Republican presidents, most noted for his role in the Iran-Contra scandal, was the principal architect of a multi-million dollar pan-sahel counter-terrorism initiative in Chad, Niger, Mali, Mauritania, Morocco and Algeria "Trans Saharan Counter Terrorism Initiative." A staunch supporter of Morocco, he supported the argument of Morocco that an independent Western Sahara would be weak and open to terrorist and anti-U.S. influences.

torture) had become "indispensable" to the United States. By early 2007, Abrams had implemented what one U.S. analyst considered "a major U.S. policy shift... backing Morocco's unilateral imposition of its so-called Western Sahara Initiative, or autonomy plan."[27]

Despite their continued lip service to the idea of self-determination, United States officials have heaped lavish praise on Morocco for putting on the table a "concrete proposal" for autonomy and has signaled its support for Moroccan initiatives in the Manhasset negotiations—despite the fact that these initiatives have attempted to force this option upon the people of Western Sahara whether they want it or not, despite the fact that the proposals put forth by Rabat fell seriously short of offering real "autonomy," and despite the dismal record of autonomous regions created by other authoritarian states.

Even prior to the commencement of what were supposed to be talks without "preconditions" the U.S. made its preference clear. In remarks in hearings before the House Foreign Affairs Committee on June 6, 2007, Assistant Secretary of State for Near Eastern Affairs David Welch indicated that he was "pleased to report the first serious movement in the Western Sahara conflict" which he characterized as "an obstacle to increased regional integration" which "impedes U.S. policy interests" and leaves the territory "a potentially attractive safehaven for terrorist planning or activity." He indicated that the U.S. "welcomed Morocco's recent initiative to resolve this dispute," and "considered the Moroccan proposal to provide real autonomy for the Western Sahara serious and credible."

On the commencement of the first of these direct talks in June of 2007, B. Lynn Pascoe, the Undersecretary General for Political Affairs of the U.S. State Department, heralded the talks as opening a "new phase in the search for a solution to the conflict." On August 13, 2007, following the first of these talks and the first of the Moroccan initiatives, he again left no doubt as to the U.S. preference by issuing a press release stating that "We believe that meaningful autonomy is a promising and realistic way forward and that the Moroccan initiative could provide a realistic framework for negotiations." Again, on January 11, 2008, he proclaimed that "We believe the Moroccan proposal to provide real autonomy for the Western Sahara provides a serious and credible option, and we hope that the Polisario will engage in discussions on this proposal as a realistic starting point that could lead toward resolution of the dispute." President Bush, himself, made this pro-Moroccan policy explicit when he wrote to the King in 2007 that the United States "understand[s] the sensibility of the Moroccan people on the question of

---

[27]   *See*, S. Zunes & J. Mundy, WESTERN SAHARA: WAR, NATIONALISM AND CONFLICT IRRESOLUTION, *supra*, at 243.

Western Sahara and would not try to impose a solution to this conflict."[28] As if to back up his words, the U.S. arranged for Morocco to receive "special funds" in the name of the War on Terror.

This pro-Moroccan policy was carried over into the Obama administration. In 2012, while she was Secretary of State, Hillary Clinton supported a rider to the U.S. Foreign Aid Bill which enabled restrictions on foreign aid to Morocco to be relaxed so that funds "may be used in regions and territories administered by Morocco" rather than restricted to territory over which Morocco's sovereignty was recognized as had been the previous policy. And as part of the reward for extending diplomatic ties to Israel, it is reported that President Trump has agreed to extend even more military aid to the Moroccan regime. Such funds are more likely to be used to ward off any renewed military action on the part of the Polisario and further entrench Morocco's control over the territory then to benefit the people of Morocco or thwart Moroccan Islamic fundamentalists.

It is clear that Morocco considered Hillary Clinton to be among its greatest allies. According to an article appearing in *The Intercept* on April 22, 2015, a controversial cache of what appear to be Moroccan diplomatic documents, dubbed "Marocleaks" by the French and North African press, began appearing online on October 3, 2014[29] They include a December 2012 memo from the Moroccan Embassy in Washington, D.C. in which the author proclaimed that there had been "significant progress in defending the ultimate interests of Morocco." That was the last year of Hillary Clinton's tenure as Secretary of State. The following year, when John Kerry took over, according to *The Intercept* "the tone shifted."

Members of Congress clearly showed what side they were on. Chairman Lantos of the House Foreign Affairs Committee sent a letter to the President, signed by 173 members of the House of Representatives "urging him to back the Moroccan plan," and on April 30, 2008, a letter was released by a bipartisan group of "prominent foreign-policy thinkers" led by former Secretary of State Madeleine Albright praising the Moroccan initiative.[30] In April of 2009 and March of 2010 letters from a number of Congressmen and Senators advocating the Moroccan line were also sent to President Obama and then-Secretary of State Hillary Clinton. And in comments he made before the House Committee on Foreign Relations

[28] U.S. Department of State, Office of the Spokesman, Media Note, Western Sahara, 2006/274, April 11, 2007.

[29] *Inside Morocco's Campaign to Influence Hillary Clinton and Other U.S. Leaders*, The Intercept, April 22, 2015.

[30] Statement of Chairman Lantos at a hearing concerning "U.S. Policy Challenges in North Africa", April 30, 2008. This letter does not reflect the views of all members of Congress. We note, in this regard, that a contrary position on this issue was adopted by Senators Feingold, DeMint, Kennedy, Inhofe, Leahy and Kohl in a letter they sent to the Secretary of State on May 27, 2008, and that a bipartisan letter to the President sent by 27 Senators and Congressmen on August 3, 2007 also adopted a different position.

on April 20, 2016, former Ambassador to Morocco Marc Ginsberg declared that he considered independence for the Saharawis "the least justifiable option for American security," and argued that the Polisario "must be pressured to accept… that the Moroccan offer of limited sovereignty is…the only option before it."[31]

None of these officials or former officials expressed the slightest concern over the fact that the Moroccan proposal in the eyes of most observers was against the will of the people of the territory,[32] and contrary to principles of international law.

Indeed, it is striking that so many former and present United States officials publicly backed Morocco in its attempt to force the Saharawi people to accept autonomy as the only solution to the conflict over Western Sahara. These officials are free to suggest that the United States government depart from its historic support of the concept of self-determination and to suggest that a political solution instead be found to resolve the conflict. However, it is incorrect to suggest that restricting the options open to the peoples of Western Sahara to the one favored by Morocco would be consistent with the right of these peoples to self-determination under international law[33] or that Morocco's current take-it-or-leave-it proposals would permit the Saharawis to exercise this right. Also, these officials should recognize the fact that by backing such a political solution they will be attempting to force a Moslem population who wish to establish a government based on democratic principles to forego this wish in favor of incorporation into a country which is ruled by one of the last remaining absolute monarchs.

Of course, now that the Trump administration has blatantly abandoned any attempt to make United States' policy comport with international law, and has bypassed the attempts of the international community to address the conflict through the United Nations, there is no telling what position these officials will take. And there is no telling what position the incoming Biden administration will take. However, if history is any guide, it is unlikely that United States will have the courage to take a stand against Moroccan intransigence.

What accounts for this unabashedly pro-Moroccan stand by U.S. top officials in the face of its obvious illegal occupation of a territory against the will of its inhabitants and its refusal to abide by its agreement to permit a referendum determine the territory's future?

---

[31] *See,* levick.com/blog/public-affairs/statement-former-ambassador-marc-ginsberg.

[32] All of these officials stipulated that any autonomy proposal produced by Morocco would have to be accepted by the Saharawi people but failed to indicate what would happen should the Saharawis reject such a proposal, which many commentators feel would be a likely outcome in a fair referendum.

[33] In this regard we note the words of the UN Secretary General: "the United Nations cannot sponsor a plan that excluded a referendum with independence as an option while claiming to provide for the self-determination of the people of Western Sahara." S/2006/817, Oct. 16, 2006, para. 14.

Despite the opinions of some commentators, there appear to be no practical or technical reason why a referendum adhering to the terms of the Settlement Agreement could not be conducted.[34] All the conditions needed to carry out a referendum in accordance with the provisions of the Settlement Plan, whose provisions were agreed by both parties, have either been fulfilled or can be fulfilled by appropriate decisions of MINURSO, acting under the supervision of the United Nations Security Council and the African Union. The most difficult decision—deciding who should be eligible to vote in the referendum—was decided after much deliberation and a voters' list published in 1999. The eligibility decisions of MINURSO were in strict compliance with the criteria for eligibility agreed by the parties.

Rather, the reasons must lie within the foreign policy concerns of officials of the United States and some of its allies, most notably France.[35]

One factor early in the conflict may have been the fact that the leaders of the independence movement appeared to be the kind of "freedom fighters" who headed most of the pro-communist movements during the Cold War.[36] Despite the fact that the Soviets never supported the Saharawi nationalist movement,[37] some observers have suggested that the U.S. was worried about the potential emergence of a pro-Soviet state in Western Sahara, and that those fears intensified U.S. determination to support Morocco and to stem the military achievements of the

---

[34] It should be noted that Morocco's argument that there were disagreements over eligibility criteria that prevented the referendum from taking place in 2000 is not based on the facts. The criteria applied by MINURSO were those agreed by the parties in 1994, and by the time the provisional voters' list was published in 1999 all controversies over eligibility requirements had been settled. Indeed, after the publication of the provisional voters' list Morocco attempted to appeal the rejection of many of the applicants it had put forward. It was only when it determined that these appeals would probably not be successful that it decided to pull out of the process. Morocco never during the period of voter identification questioned the criteria that were applied. Indeed, these criteria were essentially proposed by Morocco itself.

[35] France had been an active player in this conflict since its inception, backing both Mauritania and Morocco when they invaded the territory in 1975, providing aircraft, sophisticated military equipment, and military advisors to both Mauritania and Morocco during the war, intervening in the war with air support for Mauritania, and supporting Morocco's positions on all issues within the Security Council after the war ended, including blocking attempts by other members of the Security Council to expand MINURSO's mandate so that it could monitor human rights abuses in the territory.

[36] As was noted by Stephen Zunes and Jacob Mundy in WESTERN SAHARA: WAR, NATIONALISM AND CONFLICT IRRESOLUTION, *supra*, at 115: "Early Polisario propaganda portrayed a secular-modernist movement along the lines of Algeria's early democratic-socialist nationalism, with touches of 1950s pan-Arabism not unlike the original PLO and hints of Libyan leader Mu'ammar Qadhdhafi's unique brand of socialism. Many observers initially identified Polisario with the early FRELIMO (Frente de Libertacao de Mocambique/Liberation Front of Mozambique), under Eduaardo Mondlane, or with Amilcar Cabral's PAIGC (Partido Africano da Independencia da Guine e Cabo Verde/African Party for the Independence of Guinea and Cape Verde) in Guinea-Bissau. And of course, Polisario's founder, El-Ouali Mustapha Sayed, was reportedly inspired by the writings of Frantz Fanon while studying in Morocco."

[37] The Polisario was the only liberation movement in Africa which neither requested nor received the support of the Soviet Union.

Polisario.[38] James Baker lent credence to this observation when he declared that U.S. support for Morocco was justified because "in the days of the Cold War…the Polisario Front was aligned with Cuba and Libya and some other enemies of the United States, and Morocco was very close to the United States."[39]

It is true that in its early years the Polisario identified closely with such nationalist guerrilla movements as those that had been fighting Portugal in Angola, Mozambique and Guinea-Bissau and that one of its earliest supporters was Libyan President Quaddafi. However, it should also be noted that the Polisario received the backing of most of the nations of the African continent,[40] and that one of its strongest supporters was another "freedom fighter", Nobel laureate Nelson Mandela. And it is interesting that the Polisario was the only independence movement in Africa that did *not* ask for or receive the support of the Soviet Union—or the backing of the Socialist Party of Spain, who didn't consider them "socialist" enough!

Indeed, the Polisario leadership even in its earliest days defied easy classification. Despite some "revolutionary" rhetoric in its speeches, the programs and policies it has created to administer the Saharawi exile camps in Algeria over the past forty years do not reflect the philosophy of radicals intent on establishing an anti-Western "communist" regime; rather they suggest admiration for the democracy of the United States and many of it programs. And the "socialist" label that was considered a political kiss of death during the period of the cold war seems decidedly less threatening in the age of antiterrorism, where the new enemy is not communism but rather religious fundamental extremists, where the democratic socialism practiced in such Western states as Sweden is often cited as a model, and where rogue "socialist" states such as Algeria have morphed into mainstream allies.[41]

---

38 Y. Zoubir, *Soviet Policy toward the Western Sahara Conflict,* 34 Africa Today, No. 3, 1987, at 17–32; *Geopolitics and Realpolitik as Impediments to the Resolution of Conflict and Violations of International Law: The Case of Western Sahara,* INTERNATIONAL LAW AND THE QUESTION OF WESTERN SAHARA, *supra,* at 290–291.

39 Interview with Mishal Husain, PBS TV, 19 August 2004, *http://www.pbs.org/wnet/wideangle/shows/sh=ahara/ transcript.html.* As Mundy put it: "Morocco, one of the United States' oldest allies, occupies a pivotal geostrategic location at the mouth of the Mediterranean. Rabat's policies since independence were pro-Western, and heavily aligned with French and US interests in Africa and the Middle East. The Moroccan regime under King Hassan II…served as a key backchannel in the Arab-Israeli dialogue leading to the first Camp David summit." As will be discussed later, Morocco has also engaged in extensive lobbying efforts to preserve its friendship with the United States—and United States officials—reportedly spending millions of dollars per year on Washington lobbyists.

40 In this regard it should be noted that the government in exile established by the Polisario, the SADR, has been admitted as a member of the African Union (AU) and has received recognition as the legitimate government of Western Sahara from most of its members.

41 Statistics indicate that far more commercial activities exist today between the United States and Algeria, with its vast oil wealth, than between the United States and Morocco, and Algeria is not on the list of nations supporting terrorism.

Rather than being religious fundamentalist and militant Islamists, the Polisario have demonstrated both in the "program of national action" they adopted in 1974, the government and programs[42] they have set up in exile since that time, and their recently published "Constitution",[43] that they practice, if anything, a progressive form of Islam, where religious freedom is tolerated,[44] and that if permitted to govern Western Sahara they would establish precisely the type of moderate essentially democratic government the United States seeks to encourage in the Middle East, based upon principles of democracy, private enterprise,[45] religious freedom, and laws which uphold the rights of women and minorities.[46]

This appears to be the view of James Baker. In an exchange with PBS interviewer Mishal Husain on Wideangle on August 19, 2004, Baker agreed with Husain's observations that the Saharawis had a "sophisticated society" with a 95 % literacy rate despite the fact that they were living in refugee camps, and a democratic form of government that offered women a "very prominent" role, something that was "extraordinary in the Arab and Muslim world." When Baker was asked whether that was not a society that should be championed, he replied that "from a strictly human-rights standpoint and from the standpoint of the right of all people to self-determination, the answer to your question is yes."

Excuses for the continuation of pro-Moroccan policies in the post-Cold War period, made in private by State Department officials, have ranged from the perceived need to bolster the government of Morocco to ensure that the King does

---

[42] The refugee camps administered by the Polisario have been acknowledged by relief organizations to be "superbly organized" with each camp electing its own "popular council" which coordinate food distribution, education, health care, crafts and justice. Clinics have been established in each camp, and a hospital to care for more serious cases. Students have been sent abroad for medical and other training. Several schools have been built which have provided primary education for several thousand children and an adult literacy campaign was established to educate adults, primarily women, very few of which had previously been educated. See Hodges, *supra*, at 234.

[43] The Constitution of the Sahrawi Arab Democratic Republic, Adopted by the 12th Congress of the Frente Polisario, 14–20 December 2007.

[44] Indeed, several Christian organizations have representatives living in the Polisario camps and have worked on educational and relief efforts with the Polisario for a number of years.

[45] As Ibrahim Hakim, the SADR's former Minister of Foreign Affairs remarked in 1977: "The Sahara will be a primary commodity producing country, it is necessary to develop these primary resources and it is obligatory to cooperate with the industrialized countries...If the western companies respect Saharan sovereignty, they will be welcome in the Sahara." Hodges, *supra*, at 343. Indeed, nowhere in the writings of the Polisario are indications that they intended to create a government run economy; which would run counter to the fiercely independent nature of the Saharawi culture which values private enterprise.

[46] Indeed, as early as in its "program of national action" adopted at its second congress, held in 1974, the Polisario listed its goals as the "creation of a republican, national regime, with the effective participation of the masses", the rejection of distinctions based upon tribal affiliation or caste status, the provision of adequate housing and health facilities, the provision of free, compulsory schooling, and the reestablishment of political and social rights for women. The Constitution adopted by the Polisario sets forth these principles once again. During its period of exile in refugee camps in Tindouf, the Polisario have established a system of democratically elected local officials, boasting a number of women members, and a system of universal education where Saharawi students are educated to the college level and often beyond.

not suffer the fate of the Shah of Iran,[47] the fear that an independent Western Sahara would be fertile ground for anti-U.S. terrorists, to the practical impossibility of ousting the Moroccans from the territory against their will.

The first argument: that the U.S. must ensure that nothing destabilizes the government of Morocco—even if such destabilization is the result of its own folly—has been relied upon by U.S. policy makers from the first days of the conflict. As Professor Thomas M. Franck noted shortly after the Moroccan invasion:

> "In Washington's eyes, the right of a mere 75,000 persons to self-determination is of far less consequence, the more so as they might in any event tend to be dominated by Algeria, than is the stability of King Hassan's shaky throne. Thus, in the name of practical politics, the United States has deserted its historic commitment to the principle of self-determination. Instead of asserting the paramountcy of an important world-order norm, the United States has allowed politics to dictate its international posture. In doing so, we have been brought face to face, once again, with the question whether the United States, as a leading global power, has a greater interest in preserving and re-enforcing the integrity of the rules by which the game is supposed to be played or in winning subgames regardless of how our actions affect the rules. Put another way, the Sahara case faces us with a classic conflict of legal and political values."[48]

Yet the folly of blindly supporting U.S. allies in the face of violations of human rights—and abandoning principles of international law in the process—has been amply demonstrated since Professor Franck uttered those words in 1976, and manifests itself today in the marginalization of United States influence in the region, and the fact that regardless of such support the United States has been powerless to prevent the toppling of authoritarian regimes when the citizens of a country have amassed the political will to confront them. Moreover, as we have noted above, the imperatives supposedly justifying such support—if they ever were valid—are decidedly less so today. An independent Western Sahara

---

[47] As noted by Stephen Zunes in *East Timor and Western Sahara: A Comparative Analysis on Prospects for Self-Determination*, supra, at 120, "Both American and French diplomats privately acknowledged that a major reason for not opposing Morocco's irredentist aims over Western Sahara was the fear that it would lead to the collapse of their ally King Hassan, a concern which continues for the monarchy as a whole. As a result, they have not been willing to be forceful, even when the Moroccans began delaying and sabotaging the 1991 agreement for a referendum."

[48] Franck, T., *The Stealing of the Sahara*, supra, at 696.

based on democratic principles and controlled by Saharawi nationalists would probably be better able to counter radical Islamacist terrorism in the region than the authoritarian government of Morocco. And as far as economic interests are concerned Algeria—not Morocco—is the most important economic partner of the United States in the region.

The shop-worn argument that it is imperative to support Morocco on the issue of Western Sahara to avert an overthrow of the monarchy is also questionable. There are indications that a number of issues are causing unrest in Morocco, not just the issue of Western Sahara. As Sidi Omar of the Moroccan Human Rights Association noted, "The Western Sahara is a political question that helps the Moroccan authorities resolve internal issues. It is on the dark side of politics."[49] Indeed, the issues that are fueling discontent in Morocco stem from the lack of real democracy and the concentration of power and wealth in the hands of the King, top military leaders, and appointed officials—issues that were not adequately addressed in the "new" Constitution.[50] Policy makers who are concerned about destabilizing the throne might do better to encourage the King to introduce greater democracy to the Kingdom rather than to concentrate on the issue of Western Sahara.[51]

Also, the importance of Morocco in achieving United States policy goals has greatly diminished over time. During the Carter and Reagan administrations Morocco played an important role in efforts to resolve the Israeli-Palestinian conflict. Indeed, Morocco under King Hassan II was considered one of Israel's most effective facilitators in the Arab world. Hassan acted as a go-between for talks

---

[49] Hubbard, M. *Forgotten Victims Languish in Tussle Over W. Sahara,* Christian Science Monitor, 10 May 1996.

[50] As was noted by Paul Silverstein in an article for the Middle East Research and Information Project published on July 5, 2011: "The king will continue to name the prime minister and approve the cabinet over which he presides (Articles 47and 48); command the military (Article 53); approve the nomination of judges (Article 57); pronounce all enacted laws (Article 50); and "at His initiative" dismiss ministers and dissolve the parliament (Articles 47 and 51). The derided Article 19 of the previous constitutions, which spelled out the king's spiritual and temporal authorities and derived the latter from the former, is now split into two separate articles (41 and 42). One recognizes the king as the "commander of the faithful" who "ensures respect for Islam" and guarantees "the free exercise of religion," while the other names him as Morocco's chief of state, supreme representative, symbol of the unity of the nation, guarantor of the durability and continuity of the state." The two types of authority are thus delinked, but the king's person remains inviolable (Article 46) and those who call his rule into question are thus subject to prosecution." http://ww.merip.org/mero/mero070511.

[51] Indeed, in an article in Middle East Report (No. 218) entitled *Political Authority in Crisis: Mohammed VI's Morocco,* the author, Abdeslam Maghraoui, a visiting fellow at the Center of International Studies, Princeton University, suggested that the new king has been unable to reform the authoritarian system he inherited , a system of rule by the fiat of an "enlightened despot" supported by a group of appointed "advisors" (the old *makhzen*), and that there has been little progress in achieving any real democracy in the Kingdom. This is turn has led to severe unrest among the population and the growth of Islamic movements creating a threat to the throne quite apart from the issue of Western Sahara. As has been noted previously, other observers have also challenged claims that Morocco is heading towards greater democracy. *See,* M. Ottaway and M. Riley, Carnegie Papers, *supra,* at 3. Despite a new constitution this situation has not appreciably changed.

between Moshe Dayan and representatives of Anwar Sadat before Sadat's 1977 trip to Jerusalem, and was a behind the scenes facilitator of the meetings that resulted in the Camp David accords. However, King Mohammed VI does not enjoy the same political effectiveness as his father, and with the death of Hassan in 1999 Morocco has found itself marginalized as a player in talks to resolve the conflict.

President Trump's decision to permit Morocco to annex Western Sahara in exchange for Morocco extending diplomatic recognition to Israel will not change that. Indeed, it might have the opposite effect: granting a blessing to Morocco's illegal annexation of Western Sahara might be interpreted as legitimizing the Israeli settlements in land that would have to be given to the Palestinians if a two-state solution to the Arab-Israeli conflict is to succeed. And while Morocco's political importance to the United States has diminished over the past ten years, the importance of Algeria—both in terms of economic interests and in combatting the "war on terror" has increased.

As noted by former Personal Envoy of the UN Secretary-General to Western Sahara Christopher Ross, "President Trump's decision to recognize Moroccan sovereignty...threatens U.S. relations with Algeria...and undercuts the growth of our existing ties in energy, trade and security and military cooperation. In sum, President Trump's decision ensures continued tension, instability, and disunion in North Africa."[52]

As noted previously, the second excuse—that an independent Western Sahara would succumb to terrorism—is devoid of any factual basis whatsoever.

The final excuse—and the one favored by the former UN Secretary General—that the international community would be unable to dislodge the Moroccans from the territory by force, although a legitimate concern, seems somewhat anemic in light of recent United States incursions into Afghanistan and Iraq and the relative diplomatic influence of the two nations. The recent example of East Timor shows that when the international community is united behind the principle of self-determination resort to force to implement it is rarely required.[53]

---

[52]   Facebook, December 13, 2020.

[53]   As with the case of Morocco, the U.S. initially supported its "ally" Suharto when he invaded East Timor in 1975, doubling Indonesia's military aid and blocking the United Nations from taking effective enforcement action to halt the invasion. Only after grassroots efforts in Congress in 1991—following a series of massacres that gained worldwide attention—did the State Department, under pressure from Congress, reverse its pro-Jakarta stance and co-sponsor a successful resolution in the UN Human Rights Commission criticizing Indonesian abuses in East Timor. This started the political snowball rolling. The U.S. in 1994 started limiting arms sales to Indonesia. In 1996, 15 U.S. Senators sent a letter to the President proposing efforts to have the UN conduct a referendum of self-determination for the inhabitants of East Timor. In May of 1998, Suharto, despite his backing from the United States, was forced from office and replaced by B.J. Habibie. Habibie, faced with growing pressure from the United States, in 1999 agreed to allow the East Timorese to decide whether they wanted to be an autonomous province within Indonesia or independent. On May 5, Indonesia and Portugal signed a UN brokered agreement, establishing the process for an August vote in East Timor. Despite a campaign of intimidation by the Indonesian military, the

Indeed, East Timor demonstrates quite clearly that when faced with a loss of military aid and economic sanctions and the political support of its major power allies, few third world governments can afford to maintain a course in defiance of international law. Most experts on the conflict in Western Sahara—including well-placed Moroccan officials—do not think military force on the part of the international community would be necessary in order to resolve the conflict; they believe that American political pressure would be sufficient.[54] As Driss Basri, the former Moroccan Minister of the Interior responsible for the Western Sahara dossier once noted, "Nowadays the solution to the issue of the Sahara will only be an American solution."[55]

It would appear that today there is simply no valid foreign policy or national security reason to support Morocco's refusal to abide by international law and fulfill its commitments to the Saharawis.

On the other hand, the risk to world order of permitting states like Morocco to violate the United Nations Charter, abandon with impunity their peacekeeping arrangements with the United Nations and the world community, and snub decisions of the International Court of Justice, cannot be exaggerated. As two observers put it: "The ongoing Moroccan occupation of Western Sahara is one of the most egregious yet most underchallenged affronts to the international system in existence today. The ramifications of the international community's failure to counter this basic violation of the prohibition against aggression are of far greater consequence than just the denial of self-determination."[56] And President Trump's acquiescence in this aggression will rebound against the interests of the United States for years to come. Indeed, Western Sahara provides a roadmap for states that wish to acquire by force territory that does not belong to them. Following the Western Sahara debacle what nation or group of people will willingly permit the United Nations to broker a settlement to a conflict? The very existence of a role for the United Nations in future peacekeeping missions is at stake. And without

---

East Timorese came out to vote for independence in record numbers (records indicate that 98.6% of those registered to vote went to the polls on August 30). On September 4, 1999 the UN announced that 78.5% of those voting had voted for independence. The Indonesian military then escalated its violent campaign; however, it was checked when on September 9, President Clinton suspended all military transfers and training and announced the coordinated suspension of pending World Bank and IMF funds to Indonesia. Faced with a near total cut off of military aid and international financing, the government of Indonesia finally ratified the August 30 vote and renounced any claim to the territory.

[54] Indeed, former Interior Minister Driss Basri has suggested that the objective of the Houston Accords was to "withdraw the Sahara dossier from the UN...and hand it to the Pentagon and State Department," and that all the meetings and negotiations that preceded it were just "masquerade." According to Basri the "indirect" interlocutor for the Moroccan's was the United States. Interview with *Al-Ayam*, 29 May—4 June 3.

[55] *Id.*

[56] S. Zunes & J. Mundy, WESTERN SAHARA: WAR, NATIONALISM AND CONFLICT IRRESOLUTION, *supra*, at 260.

the United Nations as a mediator in international conflicts the United States will either need to fulfill this role unilaterally or let the world devolve into increased armed conflict and terrorism.

Last but not least, policy makers should reflect upon the impact of the United States' role in the Western Sahara conflict on the remnants of United States' credibility and image in third world countries, most notably those in the Middle East and Africa. All the rhetoric the United States can muster cannot disguise the fact that for more than forty years now the poorer countries of the Middle East, the former communist countries and most of Africa have been united in opposing the United States on this issue. They, not the United States, have been championing the cause of self-determination, democracy and human rights.

For a long time Morocco has spent considerable sums of money in Washington to see to it that the U.S. government maintains its current pro-Moroccan position.[57] According to the Sunlight Foundation and other sources, in 2009 Morocco spent 3 million dollars on lobbyists in the United States, and in 2010 these lobbyists held more meeting with officials of the United States government than the lobbyists of any other country in the Middle East/North Africa region.[58] And those expenditures have continued. In both 2018 and 2019, according to the Center for Responsive Politics,[59] Morocco spent nearly 2 million dollars on lobbying activities in the United States. This represents more than half the total expenditures of all foreign governments in those years. And in 2016, out of total expenditures of foreign governments of $3,711,335, Morocco accounted for $3,075,540—more than 80%.

And through Moroccan-financed NGOs the government spends even more money trying to shape public opinion in its favor.[60] Indeed, after the demonstrations in Morocco proper in early 2010 and when U.S. policymakers were debating whether to increase MINURSO's mandate to include the monitoring of human rights abuses, the Moroccan American Policy Center, a Moroccan lobbying

---

[57] As an example, the Clinton Foundation reportedly received $28 million in donations from the King of Morocco or the Moroccan government during the tenure of Hillary Clinton as Secretary of State, $15 million through its state owned phosphate company OCP.

[58] Sunlight Foundation Report, February 1, 2011.

[59] See, OpenSecrets.org., a project of the Center for Responsive Politics.

[60] Such organizations as the Moroccan American Cultural Center, Moroccan American Trade and Investment Council, and the Moroccan American Center for Policy, which are offshoots of the Moroccan American Center, spend considerable sums yearly on propaganda efforts aimed at painting a rosy picture of conditions in Morocco and convincing officials, the media and the public at large to accept the Moroccan position on Western Sahara. All of these organizations are funded by the Moroccan government. According to the Department of Justice's Foreign Agents Registration Act (FARA) site, the Moroccan American Center for Policy had been actively lobbying U.S. policymakers during the time NGOs were petitioning to have MINURSO's mandate expanded to include monitoring human rights abuses, spending $648,590 on consultants and another $183,279 on advertising and public relations from May to October 2012.

group,[61] according to the Sunlight Foundation, went on a 'lobbying frenzy,' meeting with 130 congressional offices. And there are indications that, if anything, these activities will be increased in the future. In October of 2020, the United States' subsidiary of Morocco's largest corporation, OCP, which is the exporter of phosphates from Western Sahara, and no fewer than four lobbying firms, registered with the United States government as foreign agents for the corporation. The stated aim of these groups was to "re-establish" close ties with the old guard and to establish new ties with the new-wave of legislators in Washington, D.C. and the White House, to pursue its policies.[62]

But perhaps the most insidious avenue Morocco has used to influence public opinion is through reputable think tanks, professional associations and other reputable organizations whose boards feature former government officials and academics with known ties to Morocco, or a vested interest in the acceptance of the Moroccan autonomy proposal, or who can be swayed by Moroccan pressure, and who have filled academic conferences and the internet with one-sided views on the issue.

Indeed, according to an article appearing in *The Intercept* on April 22, 2015, the "Marocleaks" documents "show how the Moroccan government…orchestrated the use of consultants, think tanks and other 'third party validators' to advance the North African nation's goals within elite U.S. political circles."[63]

Such groups, one cable said, "have considerable influence" on government officials. Mentioning the State Department as one agency that could be swayed through think tank advocacy, the memo goes on to state "our work focuses on the most influential think tanks…across the political spectrum." The memo lists several think tanks such as the Atlantic Council, the Heritage Foundation and the Hudson Institute.[64]

And the efforts of Moroccan officials to sway public opinion in the United States are aided by a number of individuals with close ties to Morocco who hold positions of influence in such think tanks. An example is William Zartman, the former Director of the Conflict Management Program at SAIS, who recently stepped down after a quarter century of presiding over the board of the Tangier American Legation Institute for Moroccan Studies. A self avowed friend of Morocco, Professor Zartman was granted the honor of being designated Commander of the

---

[61]   According to Sunlight this group was paid $2.3 million in 2010 for its lobbying efforts. See Sunlight Report, May 26, 2011.

[62]   ForeignLobby.com: "Mining Giant Leads Moroccan Lobbying Blitz," October 14, 2020.

[63]   *Inside Morocco's Campaign to Influence Hillary Clinton and Other U.S. Leaders,* The Intercept, April 22, 2015.

[64]   *Id.*

Order of Ouissam Alaouite, by King Mohammed VI in 2000. Under his influence, the Potomac Institute and SAIS published in 2009 a report entitled "Why the Maghreb Matters," which urged policymakers to endorse the Moroccan plan. No attempt was made to present different opinions. The supposedly "independent task force," who prepared the report, besides including Zartman, also included a member of the law firm Covington & Burling, a law firm whose clients included OCP and Kosmos, and members of the board of the Potomac Institute include a number of former officials who have publicly declared their support for the Moroccan proposal. And this is only one of several publications of Professor Zartman, and several reports issued by United States think tanks, that show a bias towards the Moroccan position.

Undoubtedly, the individuals who author these reports possess a good faith belief in the policies they advance. However, it is somewhat disturbing to those who believe that reputable think tanks should endeavor to present an unbiased and balanced review of issues to observe the totally one sided approach to the conflict taken by policy centers which purport to be "independent."

And the efforts by Morocco to control the dialogue on the issue does not stop with think tanks—it extends to the media and professional organizations. It is all part of a self-declared Moroccan campaign "to take the offensive to counter the enemies of our national cause" by "isolating" supporters of self-determination for Western Sahara.[65] The campaign—and the money behind it—has been effective: inaccurate and biased facts about the conflict fill the airwaves and learned treatises. This has ranged from distorted descriptions of life in the Polisario camps, to unflattering portraits of Polisario leaders, to false accounts of the conditions under which Saharawis live in the Moroccan controlled territory.

In 2014 Nadir Bouhmouch, a Moroccan film maker and human rights advocate, after visiting the Tindouf camps, wrote an article in *Pambazuka News* braving the displeasure of the Moroccan government[66] by debunking some of these distortions.[67]

The disinformation he cited included the allegation that the refugees are "trapped" in the Tindouf camps, unable to leave. He called this allegation "false," noting that "Freedom to leave is not limited whatsoever by the SADR government but is in fact encouraged…It is very easy to contradict the claim based on the fact

[65] *Inside Morocco's Campaign to Influence Hillary Clinton and Other U.S. Leaders,"* The Intercept, April 22, 2015, *supra.*

[66] He noted attempts by Moroccan officials to stifle any reports that contradicted the official misinformation they were publishing, citing the editor Ali Anzoula's arrest on trumped up charges of "terrorism" for publishing articles critical of the government's Saharan policies and journalist Ali Lmbrabet's fines for exposing information about the refugee camps.

[67] Nadir Bouhmouch, *The Tindouf Refugee Camps: A Moroccan's Reflections*, Pambazuka News, February 5, 2014.

that many Sahrawis from the Western Saharan territories under Moroccan control have visited the camps and have returned to Morocco with no constraints by the SADR. In fact, the only constraints on Sahrawi freedom of travel are the ones imposed by the Moroccan government that obstructs refugees from visiting their families in the Western Sahara."

Another allegation he debunked is that the SADR prohibits "freedom of expression." He admitted that the one television station in the camps was state owned, but cited the number of other outlets for expression, such as an independent radio station which "talks rather freely," and a film school which operates "with little constraint." He also noted groups of younger camp residents who freely criticized the SADR's pacifist policies. Unlike the situation in Western Sahara, he remarked, foreign journalists "enjoy an ample amount of freedom in the refugee camps."

He went on to criticize the information given to Moroccan citizens about Morocco's role in Western Sahara, claiming that "Moroccan history has also been rewritten in history textbooks and other sources in order to justify the Moroccan occupation of Western Sahara."

"It is very common to find that Moroccans believe the 1975 annexation of the Western Sahara to have been a peaceful event accomplished through largely civilian efforts…," he noted. "This narrative, however, is a false one…Morocco's takeover of the Western Sahara was far from being a peaceful event."

Among other things he cited the "violence" that was perpetrated by Moroccan forces, including the use of napalm and white phosphorous in attacks on civilians and the mass graves recently discovered.

Another "myth" promulgated by Moroccan authorities he cited is the allegation that the camps are controlled by Algeria. "Moroccans are taught to think of Algeria as an enemy state. Some believe that the Polisario was the creation of the Algerian government. Hence, there is a widespread belief that Algeria governs the Tindouf refugee camps…This belief is also unfounded."

He concluded with the following thoughts:

"My experiences growing up with Moroccan propaganda, my visit to the occupied Western Sahara territories, and my visit to the refugee camps have made evident for me that the great majority of the claims made by the Moroccan press are baseless. This is a natural result of a decades-long history of imprisonment, repression, censorship and high fines against journalists. In order to bring to light more accurate information in the face of such limited press freedom, Moroccan civil society should begin visiting the refugee camps regularly and forming dialogue groups with Sahrawis."

"Average Moroccans should refrain from relying on the press which tends to be controlled by the state...."

The dissemination of false "facts" about the history of the dispute and the Polisario are bad enough, but perhaps the most flagrant and pernicious lie spread by Morocco is that disagreements over the criteria for voter eligibility led to Morocco's withdrawal from the referendum process in 2002. As the record clearly shows, there was no disagreement over the criteria that MINURSO used to vet potential voters. Morocco simply disliked the fact that MINURSO declared most of its proposed applicants ineligible under these criteria.[68] Morocco pulled out of the process for the simple reason that it saw that if the voters' list produced by MINURSO—or any list of legitimate Saharawis—was used in a referendum, it would probably lose. As Christopher Ross, the former Personal Envoy of the Secretary-General to Western Sahara recently wrote: "In the end [the attempt to conduct a referendum] failed because Morocco decided that a referendum was contrary to its claims of sovereignty and, in doing so, got no push back from the Security Council."[69] And since that time Morocco has resisted any plan that would possibly grant the people of the territory the option of independence—even one that would permit the applicants put forth by Morocco who were deemed ineligible to vote by MINURSO the ability to vote![70]

With the need to combat Islamic terrorists throughout the world the need for a Moslem Arab nation built on principles of democracy and respect for human rights may be more important than ever. It may be time for the United States to stop letting Morocco set the agenda on this issue and to re-evaluate its policy towards an independent Western Sahara. President Trump's decision to sacrifice the people of Western Sahara on the altar of political expediency should not be left to stand. As Christopher Ross argued, "This foolish and ill-considered decision flies in the face of the US commitment to the principles of the non-acquisition of territory

---

[68] As discussed previously, the Settlement Plan agreed by the parties in 1988 stipulated that the people who would be eligible to vote would be the people included on a census of the population conducted by Spain in 1974; roughly 74,000 individuals. Later, after Moroccan lobbying, the criteria were expanded to include five bases of eligibility. Morocco expressed no problem with the application of these criteria until the voters' list was published in 1999 and it saw that a majority of the applicants it had proposed were deemed ineligible. MINURSO had ample reason for excluding these applicants. During the interview sessions there were numerous occasions in which the Saharawi elders chosen by Morocco to interview the applicants approached MINURSO personnel after the sessions claiming that they had been coerced by Morocco into approving candidates who were not Saharawis. There was also evidence that Morocco had been coaching Moroccan applicants on how to appear to be Saharawis in order to "pad" the voters' list. There were a number of incidents in which alleged Saharawis could not identify members of their tribes or the location in the territory where they claimed to live. In any event, demographic experts suggested that it would have been impossible for the more than 180,000 applicants put forth by Morocco to have had the ties to the territory they claimed.

[69] Facebook, December 13, 2020.

[70] This was the last plan proposed by James Baker before he resigned.

by force and the right of peoples to self-determination, both enshrined in the UN Charter." Simply appointing public relations experts to reshape the image of the United States in the Middle East, throwing money at the problem, and sending our troops into harm's way, will not eliminate the disrespect the inhabitants of the region have for United States policy makers and counter the appeal of Islamic radicals; only standing up in practice for the principles the United States purports to support will.

It is time the Emperor got some clothes.

INDEX

www.ingramcontent.com/pod-product-compliance
Lightning Source LLC
Chambersburg PA
CBHW080621030426
42336CB00018B/3038